Civil Procedure in Norway

Civil Procedure in Norway

Second Edition

Anna Nylund

This book was originally published as a monograph in the International Encyclopaedia of Laws/Civil Procedure.

Founding Editor: Roger Blanpain
General Editor: Frank Hendrickx
Volume Editor: Wannes Vandenbussche

Wolters Kluwer

Published by:
Kluwer Law International B.V.
PO Box 316
2400 AH Alphen aan den Rijn
The Netherlands
E-mail: lrs-sales@wolterskluwer.com
Website: www.wolterskluwer.com/en/solutions/kluwerlawinternational

Sold and distributed by:
Wolters Kluwer Legal & Regulatory U.S.
7201 McKinney Circle
Frederick, MD 21704
United States of America
E-mail: customer.service@wolterskluwer.com

ISBN 978-94-035-0186-4

e-Book: ISBN 978-94-035-0356-1
web-PDF: ISBN 978-94-035-0366-0

The Author

Anna Nylund is Professor of Procedural Law at the University of Bergen. She received her Doctorate in Law from University of Helsinki in 2006. Nylund teaches Civil Procedure, Comparative Law, and Alternative Dispute Resolution. Her main research topics are comparative and European aspects of civil procedure law, alternative dispute resolution, dispute system design and child participation rights. She has co-directed several research projects including *Scandinavian Mediation Research* 2016–2018, *Procedural Autonomy Across Europe* 2018–2019 and *Rethinking Nordic Courts* 2018–2020. She regularly presents at international conferences and is a member of several national and international scholarly associations, including the Norwegian Academy of Science and Letters, the board of the Nordic Association of Procedural Law, the board of the Centre for Advanced Study at the Norwegian Academy of Science and Letters, and the Council of the International Association of Procedural Law. She was the co-editor of several books and serves on the editorial board of the *Arctic Review of Law and Politics* and *Teise – Law Journal.*

The Author

Table of Contents

List of Abbreviations

ArbA	Arbitration Act
ADR	Alternative Dispute Resolution
CCTV	Closed-circuit TV
CJA	Courts of Justice Act
CJEU	Court of Justice of the European Union
DA	Dispute Act
EA	Enforcement Act
EC	European Communities
ECHR	European Convention on Human Rights
ECtHR	European Court of Human Rights
EEA	European Economic Area
EFTA	European Free Trade Association
ESA	EFTA Surveillance Authority
EUR	Euro
HR	Høyesterett (Supreme Court of Norway)
LA	Agder Lagmannsrett (Agder Court of Appeal)
LB	Borgarting Lagmannsrett (Borgarting Court of Appeal)
LH	Hålogaland Lagmannsrett (Hålogaland Court of Appeal)
MNA	Medlem av den norske advokatforeningen (Member of the Norwegian Bar Association)
NCA	Norwegian Courts Administration
NOK	Norwegian Kronor
Rt.	Norsk Retstidende
s.	Section
USD	United States Dollars

List of Abbreviations

General Introduction

§1. General Background

I. Background Information on Norway

1. The modern Norwegian state emerged in 1814, when Denmark ceded Norway to Sweden. Norway had been a province of Denmark since 1536. Norwegians used the opportunity to declare Norway independent and adopted a Constitution. The Swedish king then declared war on Norway; thereafter, Norway entered into a union with Sweden, in which the Swedish monarch was considered the king of Norway. However, Norway kept its Constitution and many of its institutions developed under the Danish rule. Norway's ties to Denmark also remained close despite Swedish rule. In 1905, Norway gained independence from Sweden.

2. Norway covers an area of approximately 385,000 km^2, making it the sixth largest country in Europe, though it is the third least densely populated. The Norwegian coastline is rugged with fjords, and a significant part of the mainland is mountainous. Only 3.5% of the land area is used for agriculture. The geography and the topography of the country result in large distances and long travel times for road and rail transportation.

3. The kingdom of Norway is a multiparty, mature democracy. Governments are often formed as coalitions of two or more parties, and minority governments are common. The unicameral Stortinget consists of 169 representatives elected in proportionate elections every four years. The Monarch has only ceremonial powers, while the Prime Minister exercises executive powers. The Supreme Court exercises the highest judicial power.

4. Norway consists of eleven counties (*fylke*), each of which is governed by a directly elected local government. The counties are divided into 356 self-governing municipalities, each of which is administered by a directly elected council. The largest urban areas are Oslo, Bergen, Stavanger, Trondheim and Drammen, where the urban area sprawls across municipal borders. Due to reforms, the number of municipalities and counties has been decreasing.

5. The population of Norway is approximately 5,300,000 people, consisting primarily of ethnic Norwegians. The Sami people, an indigenous people living in Northwestern Europe, have a particular protection in the Constitution. Due to an earlier policy of Norwegianization, many Sami have lost their language, and some have lost their traditional reindeer-herding and fishing culture. The Kven people represent another national minority, but due to Norwegianization they have lost most of their ethnicity and language. In recent decades, Norway has faced immigration from a number of European and non-European countries. Today, about 15% of the population are first- or second-generation immigrants.

6. Norwegian is the official language of Norway. There are two forms of written Norwegian, *bokmål* (book language) and *nynorsk* (new Norwegian). *Bokmål* is based in Danish and was traditionally used by the upper social strata. Ivar Aasen created *nynorsk* in the mid-1800s by compiling west-Norwegian dialects. Today, the two versions are converging, but most Norwegians use *bokmål* as their preferred written language. There is no standard spoken Norwegian; speakers use their (regional) dialect even in major media. In the northern parts of Norway, different Sami languages are used to varying degrees.

7. About 70% of Norwegians are members of the Church of Norway, a Lutheran church. However, only a small percentage of the population attends church regularly.

8. Norway is one of the most prosperous countries in the world, with a gross domestic product of USD 67,390 per capita in 2020.[1] The Norwegian economy is a mixed economy, with a large welfare state combined with a capitalist free market economy with some state ownership. The petroleum sector is large: Income generated by the oil and gas sector is directed to the state sovereign oil fund (Government Pensions Fund – Global, popularly known as the Oil Fund), giving Norway the largest capital reserve per capita in the world. Fisheries, hydropower, military material and shipping are the other important industries.

9. Norway is a founding member of the European Free Trade Association (EFTA). In 1994, the European Economic Area (EEA) Agreement tied the EFTA countries more tightly to the European Communities (EC), now the European Union (EU), as a vehicle for transition into full EC membership. However, as Norwegians turned down full EU membership in 1994, EFTA/EEA has remained a parallel organization to the EU for more than two decades. It has its own institutions, including the EFTA Court in Luxembourg and the EFTA Surveillance Authority (ESA) in Brussels. Through the EEA Agreement, Norway is part of the single European market, and EU secondary legislation and case law related to the four freedoms – free movement of goods, capital, services and people – is binding in Norway.

1. World Bank, https://data.worldbank.org/indicator/NY.GDP.PCAP.CD?locations=NO. Visited 20 Jan. 2022.

II. Introduction to the Norwegian Legal System

10. The roots of the Norwegian legal system can be traced back to the tribal, oral legal system of the Viking Ages. The Viking Age roots are still visible, *inter alia*, through the tradition of an informal and pragmatic approach to law and a mixture of statutory law and case law as the primary sources of law. Roman law has never been directly applicable in Norway, but it has had a notable impact on legal thinking and terminology. Civil law thinking has had a significant impact on Norwegian law, yet Norway, like its Nordic peers, does not fit into the dichotomy of civil/common law.[2]

11. The demarcation between private law and public law has played an important role in Norwegian law. The subdivisions of law follow mainly the same pattern as in civil law countries. The classification of civil procedure law is, however, ambiguous. On the one hand, it is clearly connected to private law, and on the other hand, civil procedure law belongs to the Institute of Public Law at the Faculty of Law at the University of Oslo.[3]

12. The main source of law is statutory law. All statutory laws are relatively short and regulate a specific area of law; they are not codes, in contrast to continental European law. Hence, there is no coherent code of civil procedure, and civil procedure, arbitration and enforcement are regulated by different statutes. The consequence of the lack of codifications is the lack of a single systematic approach and stringent use of terminology.

13. Another important source of law is case law. The role of courts has been strong in the Norwegian legal system since the Middle Ages, as statutory law has never been comprehensive. Since its early days in the first half of the nineteenth century, the Supreme Court has performed judicial review of the constitutionality of statutory law.

14. Further sources of law include preparatory works for bills (*travaux preparatoires*), which present the general background for the statute, the goals of the statute and comments on each section of the law. Legal scholarship, government regulations other than law, customary law and real arguments are also recognized as sources of law.

---

2. For an overview of Norwegian law, *see, e.g.*, Jørn Øyrehagen Sunde, *Daughters of God and Counsellors of the Judges of Men: Changes in the Legal Culture of the Norwegian Realm in the High Middle Ages*, in *New Approaches to Early Law in Scandinavia* 131–183 (Stefan Brink and Lisa Collinson eds, Trounhout 2014); Jørn Øyrehagen Sunde, *Champagne at the Funeral – An Introduction to Legal Culture* 11–28 (Jørn Øyrehagen Sunde and Knut Einar Skodvin eds, Fagbokforlaget 2010) and Jørn Øyrehagen Sunde, *The Art of Being Artful – The Complex Reception of Law* 29–44 (Jørn Øyrehagen Sunde & Knut Einar Skodvin eds, Fagbokforlaget 2010).
3. The Faculty of Law at the University of Bergen and the Faculty of Law at University of Tromsø – The Arctic University of Law do not have institutes.

15. The legal method is based on deriving arguments from several different sources and then weighing them to find a reasonable solution. Although the wording of the law is important, other sources of law may lead to a solution different from what the wording suggests. Reasonable and pragmatic solutions are preferred over strictly formal justice.[4]

16. Pragmatism is a key value in Norwegian law. Laws should offer pragmatic, workable and flexible solutions rather than only formal justice. The rule of law is important, and the solutions should be foreseeable, as well as just and reasonable. The use of open norms allowing for flexible application and taking into account the particularities of the case at hand reflects the pragmatic stance. In order to achieve a pragmatic solution, norms are often open and flexible, allowing the decision-maker plenty of discretion to find the most appropriate, practicable and just solution.

§2. Delimitation of the Subject Matter

I. Definition of the Term 'Civil Procedure'

17. Civil procedure is not clearly defined in Norwegian law. Civil procedure is the general form of procedure; thus, the definition is a negative one. All procedures that are not defined as criminal or special procedures are civil. The rules of civil procedure apply to civil and commercial matters, including tort, consumer, family and real estate law. Administrative law cases are adjudicated under the rules of civil procedure as well. The rules of civil procedure also form the backbone of many types of special proceedings and are applied unless special rules have been enacted; in the latter case, the special rules state that the general rules apply where appropriate and with the limitations and additions in the special rules. Civil procedure also applies to litigation arising from arbitration and mediation.

18. Norwegian civil procedure does not recognize non-contentious cases (*jurisdiction voluntaria*). However, courts have tasks falling outside contentious litigation, such as appointing a receiver for the estate of a deceased person, administering bankruptcies and other insolvency proceedings, and judicial cancellation of negotiable instruments. The procedural rules for the non-contentious (administrative) tasks are regulated in statutory law on the subject matter for the issue, such as the Administration of Estates Act,[5] the Bankruptcy Act[6] and the Judicial Cancellation Act.[7]

---

4. Ingvild Helland & Søren Koch, *Introduction to Norwegian Legal Method*, in *Nordic and Germanic Legal Methods: Contributions to a Dialogue Between Different Legal Cultures, with a Main Focus on Norway and Germany* (Ingvild Helland & Søren Koch eds, Mohr Siebeck 2014).
5. *Skifteloven* 21 Feb. 1930.
6. Act on Debt Settlement and Bankruptcy (Bankruptcy Act), *Lov om gjeldsforhandling og konkurs (konkursloven)* 1984 no. 58.
7. *Lov om mortifikasjon av skuldebrev m.v.* 1959 no. 1.

19. Civil procedure covers both dispositive and indispositive cases. The default expectation is that a case is dispositive; that is, the parties may settle the case at any time, and the parties have the full power to decide on the proceedings, such as which arguments and evidence the parties bring forward. Admittance of facts is usually binding on the court. Indispositive cases are cases in which public policy considerations limit the right of the parties to make agreements and to settle the case. The court has a duty to ensure the factual and legal issues are sufficiently clarified, if necessary, by actively introducing new evidence and arguments. Claims relating to compulsory measures, child custody and contact and cases where environmental issues are significant are considered indispositive. The definition is not exhaustive, and an action may consist of both indispositive and dispositive issues.

20. The concept of indispositive cases is related to the concept of *ordre public* (public policy), but the concepts do not fully overlap. Mandatory rules should not be confused with indispositive cases. Many rules, such as consumer and employment law, are mandatory, but they do not make the case indispositive.

II. Distinction with Other Types of Procedure

21. Norwegian law recognizes only two different types of procedures: criminal procedure and civil procedure. Only proceedings on applying coercive measures to investigate, prevent or sanction deeds that are formally sanctioned as crimes are defined as criminal proceedings. All other types of proceedings are by definition classified as civil procedure.

22. Administrative cases are defined as civil cases, and court proceedings follow the same course as other civil cases. However, there are special rules for proceedings involving civil coercive measures, such as compulsory care of children and coercive care for mental health patients (Chapter 36 of the Dispute Act, *tvisteloven*, hereinafter, DA).[8]

23. Other types of special proceedings are either considered particular forms of civil procedure or not defined as part of procedural law at all. Cases related to parental responsibility belong to the former category, and bankruptcy and enforcement proceedings belong to the latter. However, the distinctions are not firm or settled. Some types of proceedings fall somewhere between civil and criminal proceedings; this is particularly true in the case of restraining orders and damages and other civil claims based on a crime. Since general courts adjudicate all cases, the delimitation between civil and criminal proceedings is not strict. Damages based on crime and restraining orders may be either adjudicated in criminal proceedings or separated into civil proceedings.

8. Act relating to mediation and procedure in civil disputes (The Dispute Act), *Lov om mekling og rettergang i sivile tvister, tvisteloven* 2005 no. 90. Unofficial translation available at https://lovdata.no/dokument/NLE/lov/2005-06-17-90. The terminology used in the unofficial translation sometimes differs from the terminology used in this edition.

III. Separate Court Systems and Rules of Procedure

24. Norway has only a single set of courts and no administrative courts. Moreover, the number of special courts is very limited, and practically none of these are formally considered courts, despite the fact that they are de facto courts with almost exclusively adjudicative functions. The most important are the Labour Court (*Arbeidsretten*), the Insurance Court (*Trygderetten*) and the Land Consolidation Courts (*jordskiftedomstol*), although only the latter are formally considered courts. These have a narrow, specialized jurisdiction. The Labour Court decides collective labour contracts and is the first and final court. General courts have jurisdiction over individual labour contracts. The Insurance Court decides cases on social benefits. The Land Consolidation Courts decide on the borders of real estate and rights related to real estate. Rulings of the Insurance Court and Land Consolidation Courts may be appealed to the regular court system.

25. The Court of Impeachment (*riksretten*) pronounces judgments against members of the Council of State, the Supreme Court and the Parliament for criminal or other unlawful conducts in which the members have breached their constitutional obligations. The Court of Impeachment comprises six members elected by the Parliament and the five longest-serving Supreme Court justices, including the Chief Justice of the Supreme Court. The Parliament elects the members for a six-year period. The court has heard eight cases since 1814, with the latest being in 1926–1927.

26. Further, a number of administrative agencies are quasi-courts that lack the formal status of courts. For purposes of EEA law and the European Convention on Human Rights (ECHR), these agencies are classified as tribunals. Among these are the County Social Welfare Boards (*Fylkesnemndene for barnevern og sosiale saker*), which decide issues on, *inter alia*, compulsory care of children and compulsory care of alcoholics and drug users, and the Norwegian Board of Appeal of Industrial Property Rights (*Klagenemnda for industrielle rettigheter*), which is an administrative body that decides matters on intellectual property rights. In practice, the local Consumer Authority(*forbrukertilsynet*), numerous sectoral consumer dispute boards and the Consumer Complaints Commission (*forbrukerklageutvalget*) provide consumers with accessible dispute resolution. The boards provide dispute resolution services to more than 20,000 consumers annually.[9]

27. Civil litigation is intended to be a last resort, and most disputes should ideally be solved outside the court system. The disputants are often required to exhaust other dispute resolution mechanisms, such as dispute resolution boards, and proceedings in the boards are more advantageous in terms of time and costs.

9. The three providers with the highest number of complaints are the Consumer Authority, the Norwegian Financial Services Complaints Board (*Finansklagenemnda)* and the Norwegian Parking Appeal Tribunal (*Parkeringsklagenemnda).* The three combined receive more than 20,000 complaints each year. In contrast, only a few hundred complaints per year are filed with the other boards.

28. Norway does not have a constitutional court. The Supreme Court acts as a constitutional court and holds power and duty to review whether laws and other government regulations are against the constitution (The Norwegian Constitution section 89, *Kongerike Norges Grunnlov,* 1814 no. 17).[10]

§3. Sources of Civil Procedure Law

I. A Brief History of Civil Procedure Law

29. The first norms of a procedural character in Norway appeared in the medieval legislation. The procedural norms were scattered and tied to substantive norms in the Codes of Magnus the Law-mender in the 1270s. During the high medieval period, the three-tier court system of Canonical law from the Catholic Church was introduced into the Norwegian system. In 1590, the three-tier hierarchy of the courts was reinforced by making the first instance compulsory for most cases.

30. The Norwegian Code of 1687, largely based on the Danish Code, contained a specific section (the first book) on the rules of procedure. It was in essence a codification of medieval case law and practical applications thereof. It was not the result of scholarly work or a conscious reception of foreign law. The rules did not differentiate between civil and criminal procedures. In 1795, Conciliation Boards were introduced as a method of solving smaller disputes at the local level by using lay judges. Even today, the Conciliation Boards maintain their role as a first step for smaller cases. The procedural rules in The Norwegian Code remained in force until the Civil Procedure Act of 1915 entered into force in 1927. The practical applications shifted over time, but the basis was still medieval. Criminal procedure was modernized much earlier through the Criminal Procedure Act (*straffeprosessloven*) of 1887.[11]

31. The Civil Procedure Act of 1915 (*tvistemålsloven*) represented a significant turn in the regulation of civil procedure. The Civil Procedure Act was inspired by the German Code of Civil Procedure of 1877 and the Austrian Civil Procedure Code of 1895. The ideas of Franz Klein and the concepts and terminology used in the Austrian Code of 1895 were particularly reflected in the Civil Procedure Act. However, the Norwegian Civil Procedure Act did not copy Austrian law; rather, the Austrian Code was adapted into the Norwegian civil procedure tradition. In contrast to many other European countries, the Norwegian tradition retained a significant element of hearings and other traits often associated with common law rather than civil

---

10. The Constitution was laid down on 17 May 1814 by the Constituent Assembly at Eidsvoll and subsequently amended, most recently in June 2018. The Constitution of the Kingdom of Norway 1814, *Kongerike Norges Grunnlov*. Unofficial English translation available at https://lovdata.no/dokument/NLE/lov/1814-05-17.
11. Maria Astrup Hjort, *Sources of Inspiration of Nordic Procedural Law: Choices and Objectives of the Legal Reforms* in *Rethinking Nordic Courts* (Laura Ervo, Pia Letto-Vanamo & Anna Nylund eds, Springer 2021).

law. The Civil Procedure Act was built on that tradition.[12] The Danish Administration of Justice Act (*retsplejeloven*) of 1916 includes many of the same elements as the Civil Procedure Act. The DA of 2005, which entered into force on 1 January 2008, repealed the Civil Procedure Act.

32. The Courts of Justice Act (hereinafter, CJA)[13] regulates, *inter alia*, the organization of courts, appointment of judges, the calculation of time limits, legal counsel and service of documents for both civil and criminal procedures.

II. The Constitution and International Law

33. Access to court and a fair trial were not regulated in the Norwegian Constitution before 2014. Today, section 95 regulates the right to a fair and public trial in an independent and impartial court within a reasonable period of time. The Constitution does not specify the content of the fair trial rights but relies on principles laid out in case law and legal doctrine.

34. Norway is a party to the ECHR (1951) and to the International Convention on Civil and Political Rights (1961). Both Conventions guarantee the right to a fair and public hearing within a reasonable time. The Conventions are implemented in Norwegian law through the Human Rights Act.[14] The Act gives the Conventions a semi-constitutional character, as it gives them precedence over any other legislative provision in conflict with them. Case law from the European Court of Human Rights (ECtHR) in particular has influenced civil procedure law: the principles of civil procedure have gained more weight as legal arguments, and the interpretation or content of certain provisions has changed.

35. Through the EEA Agreement, many parts of EU law are applicable in Norway. Norway does not participate in judicial cooperation; hence, secondary law on cross-border cases is not applicable in Norway, unless the provisions are embedded in secondary law that has been incorporated into the EEA Agreement. However, Norway is a party to the Lugano Convention, [15] a treaty parallel to the Brussels I

12. Halvard Haukeland Fredriksen, *German Influence on the Development of Norwegian Civil Procedural Law* (Volker Lipp & Halvard Haukeland Fredriksen eds, Mohr Siebeck 2011); Jørn Øyrehagen Sunde, *'Der organische Zusammenhang des Rechts': How the Reception of Savigny Came to Influence Legal Reception in Norwegian Law in the 19th Century and the First Part of the 20th Century, in Reforms of Civil Procedure in Germany and Norway* (Volker Lipp & Halvard Haukeland Fredriksen eds, Mohr Siebeck, 2011).
13. Act relating to the courts of justice (The Courts of Justice Act), *Lov om domstolene* (*domstolloven*), 1915 No. 15. Unofficial English translation available at https://www.domstol.no/globalassets/upload/da/domstol.no/domstoladministrasjonen/internasjonalt/courts-of-justice-act-english-translation-uten-paragrafinnledning.pdf.
14. Act relating to the strengthening of the status of human rights in Norwegian law (The Human Rights Act), *Lov om syrking av menneskerettighetenes stilling i norsk rett*, 1999 no. 30. Unofficial English translation available at http://app.uio.no/ub/ujur/oversatte-lover/data/lov-19990521-030-eng.pdf.
15. Convention on jurisdiction and the recognition and enforcement of judgments in civil and commercial matters signed in Lugano 2007, OJ L 339/3, 21.12.2007.

bis Regulation,[16] and rules with a procedural component in secondary law and case law on the single market are applicable. Norway has also implemented some EU procedural law voluntarily. Although the EU Charter on Fundamental Rights is not part of the EEA Agreement, EEA law must conform with it to ensure equal application.[17]

III. The DA

36. The main source of law for civil proceedings is the DA, which entered into force on 1 January 2008. It regulates the main principles and conduct of general civil proceedings. The aim of the 2005 Reform was to make the civil procedure more efficient in meeting the challenges of the twenty-first-century disputants and to codify the development of law achieved through case law. The DA stresses expedient and cost-efficient proceedings, wherein the resources spent on the civil litigation are proportional to the issues at stake and the need to find a substantively correct solution. The name of the Act reflects the ideal of providing resolution of disputes through a variety of methods, where litigation ending in a court ruling is only one such option.

37. The committee drafting the law drew inspiration from the report of Lord Woolf on the reform of the English rules of civil procedure in particular. Elements derived from English law include an emphasis on judicial management and the preparatory stage and the introduction of a pre-filing stage consisting of the exchange of information and efforts to achieve settlement. Many of the elements introduced in 2008 reflect global trends, such as court-connected mediation, a stronger emphasis on the small claims track and class actions.

38. Despite the visible influence of elements from English civil procedure law, many of the typically Nordic traits are still present, as are the influences of Germanic civil procedure thinking. The Norwegian judge is still a generalist; the rules

16. Regulation (EU) No. 1215/2012 of the European Parliament and of the Council of 12 December 2012 on jurisdiction and the recognition and enforcement of judgments in civil and commercial matters, OJ L 351/1, 20.12.2012. ELI: http://data.europa.eu/eli/reg/2012/1215/oj.
17. For more detailed accounts of the relationship between Norwegian civil procedure and EEA law, *see* Anna Nylund, *Procedural Autonomy, the EEA Agreement and Norwegian Law: Bridging the Gap and Maintaining it Too*, in *Procedural Autonomy Across Europe* (Bart Krans & Anna Nylund eds, Intersentia 2020); Halvard Haukeland Fredriksen & Magne Strandberg, *Norwegian Civil Procedure under the Influence of EU Law, in Transformation of Civil Justice: Unity and Diversity* (Alan Uzelac & C.H. van Rhee eds, Springer 2018); Anna Nylund, *Norway: An Insider Outside – Or an Outsider Inside – European Civil Justice*, in *The European Union and National Civil Procedure* (Anna Nylund & Bart Krans eds, Intersentia 2016) and Halvard Haukeland Fredriksen, *Bridging the Widening Gap Between the EU Treaties and the Agreement on the European Economic Area*, 18(6) Eur. L. J. 868–886 (2012).

are general and flexible, leaving the judge plenty of discretion to tailor the proceedings to the case at hand. Although the committee was in favour of abolishing Conciliation Boards, the Parliament decided to retain them. The role of the Germanic terminology and thinking has been maintained, although the direct influences of Germanic law have diminished.

39. The DA contains nine parts with a total of thirty-eight chapters.

IV. Other Sources of Civil Procedure and Law

40. The DA is not a comprehensive civil procedure code. On the contrary, parts of civil procedure are regulated in other acts. The CJA contains common rules for civil and criminal proceedings, such as rules on the organization of courts, judges, legal counsel and service of documents. Questions related to enforcement proceedings are included in the Enforcement Act (hereinafter, EA),[18] and questions related to bankruptcy and debt restructuring are included in the Bankruptcy Act. Arbitration is regulated in the Arbitration Act (hereinafter, ArbA).[19] A number of acts governing substantive rights have procedural provisions, such as the provisions on court proceedings in cases on custody, residence and visitation of children in the Children Act.[20]

41. Principles of civil procedure have gained weight as a source of civil procedure. One central reason for this is the turn towards human rights in general and the requirement of a fair trial in particular, under the influence of, particularly, European human rights law. Another reason is an increased interest in principle-based argumentation and the fact that increased flexibility and discretion should be combined with legal principles that indicate which factors should guide decision-making. General principles of civil procedure are part of the syllabus in civil procedure courses and are frequently discussed in legal doctrine.

42. Case law from national courts, particularly the Supreme Court, is an important source of law in civil procedure. Many norms are open, leaving the discretion to the judge and leaving room for courts to develop guidelines for interpretation and application of the provisions. The legislature deliberately drafts open laws and occasionally even leaves lacunae, which it expects the courts to fill.

43. The preparatory works (*travaux preparatoires*) of the DA are still to some extent referred to, although their use has been declining in recent years with the growth of case law. The committee report drafting the rules is extensive and gives

18. *Lov om tvangsfullbyrdelse (tvangsfullbyrdelsesloven)* 1992 no. 86.
19. *Lov om voldgift* 2004 no. 25. Unofficial English translation available at https://lovdata.no/dokument/NLE/lov/2004-05-14-25.
20. Act relating to Children and Parents (The Children Act), *Lov om barn og foreldre (barneloven)* 1981 no. 7.

background information, arguments for interpretation and overviews of case law. For instance, the committee report lists case law delimiting the objective identity of the case.

44. The academic tradition of civil procedure law has remained thin, with few academic treatises apart from textbooks and handbooks. Since the turn of the millennium, academic literature and research have been increasing significantly, with several doctoral theses published as books and several active researchers in the field.

§4. General Features of the Administration of Justice in Civil Matters

I. Characteristics of the Procedure

45. Civil procedure in Norway is adversarial and party-driven. The parties decide on whether to initiate proceedings, the scope of the proceedings and whether the proceedings are continued. The most central principles of civil proceedings are the principle of party disposition (*disposisjonsprinsippet, ne ultra petita*) and the principle of party presentation (*forhandlingsprinsippet, da mihi factum dabo tibi ius*). The court is bound to the claims and the cause of action and legal grounds the parties present for their claims, as well as to the main features of the factual background of the case. The parties are responsible for presenting the necessary facts and evidence. The court may apply any legal provision it considers applicable according to the principle of *iura novit curia.* The parties are responsible for providing accurate claims, arguments and evidence supporting their claims.

46. Although the proceedings are party-driven, the judge is not a passive umpire. Judges often ask questions when the parties present their arguments. The judge must actively manage the case to provide swift and inexpensive resolution of conflicts. The principle of case management is recognized as a foundational principle of civil procedure.

47. Although the parties decide the scope of litigation and are responsible for providing evidence, the goal of civil proceedings is to provide for substantively correct results, i.e., uncover the truth. However, there are many exceptions and even other principles limiting the possibility of reaching the substantive truth. The principles of party disposition and party presentation may bar the court from uncovering the truth. There is also tension between the principle of proportionality, which requires the judge to limit excessively expensive evidence, and the principle of substantive truth.

48. Public proceeding is a central principle in Norwegian law. Court records and court hearings are accessible to the public unless a weighty reason requires otherwise. The principles of orality, immediacy and concentration are closely connected to public proceedings. These principles prescribe that the court makes the rulings on the merits based on the claims, evidence and arguments presented to it directly in a single, concentrated court hearing. The parties must orally present the claims and arguments put forward in written statements in the main hearing. Neither the parties nor their counsel nor witnesses may read statements. However, notes containing important data may be used as an aid. The court schedules the main hearing over a single day or over two or more consecutive days.

49. Rules on evidence reflect the principle of free evidence. The parties may present whatever evidence they desire. Evidence is only disallowed when the content or information contained in it is privileged based on a specific provision, the informant has a duty to keep the information privileged, or the evidence is illegally obtained. Specific evidence may be disallowed if it is too costly to present, if other types of evidence are more appropriate or relevant or if the evidence lacks relevance. The court is free to weigh and value the evidence as it chooses.

II. Fundamental Procedural Guarantees

50. In the Constitutional Reform of 2014, the provisions granting human rights were thoroughly modernized, and many new rights were introduced, among them the right to a fair trial. Section 95 of the Norwegian Constitution[21] reads:

> Everyone has the right to have their case tried by an independent and impartial court within a reasonable time. Legal proceedings shall be fair and public. The court may however conduct proceedings in camera if considerations of the privacy of the parties concerned or if weighty and significant public interests necessitate this.
> The authorities of the state shall ensure the independence and impartiality of the courts and the members of the judiciary.

51. The provision is very general, indicating key principles for regulating the organization of courts and court procedures. The provision does not explicitly regulate that courts must be established by law. Sections 86–91 of the Constitution specifically regulate the Court of Impeachment and the Supreme Court but have few specific rules for the Supreme Court in particular. Section 89 explicitly gives courts the right to judicial review.

52. Before the 2014 reform, important procedural rights were protected by the ECHR, which was given a semi-constitutional status by the 1999 Human Rights Act and by general principles of law, such as the principle of independent and impartial courts and basic civil procedural principles granting a fair trial in a reasonable time period. The CJA has specific rules on the organization of courts and the granting of independent and impartial courts.

21. *Kongerike Norges Grunnlov* 17 May 1814. Unofficial English translation is available at https://www.stortinget.no/globalassets/pdf/english/constitutionenglish.pdf.

53. The fundamental guarantees on procedural rights are loosely regulated in the Constitution. Section 95 provides only very basic guarantees. The provision is modelled after the ECHR, the UN Covenant on Civil and Political Rights and the EU Charter of Fundamental Rights, and its content is almost identical to these. As the provision has only been in force for a limited time, it is difficult to assess whether and how it differs from its international counterparts. Many of the principles of a fair trial have been developed through case law and doctrine.

54. Section 1-1 of the DA recaptures the main principles of civil procedure. It states that the purpose of civil procedure is to provide a fair and swift trial in legal disputes and provide for dispute resolution, and it grants the independence and impartiality of courts. Subsection (2) lists seven principles of civil procedure: proper and just proceedings, contradiction, orality, proportionality, balanced proceedings, reasoned rulings and the right to appeal.[22]

55. A principle of 'proper and just' proceedings (*forsvarlighetsprinsippet*) was introduced in the DA. It requires the judge to shape the proceedings so as to give the court a sufficient and justifiable ground for making sound, quality decisions. The principle of proper and just trials is a direct consequence of increasingly flexible rules and a countermeasure for the principle of proportionality, which stresses the importance of economizing and saving resources. The need to save time and money must be balanced against the need for proper, sufficient and just proceedings. Because flexibility and judicial discretion[23] are key values of civil proceedings, many rules are open, leaving ample room for adapting the proceedings to the particular case at hand. The principle of proper and just trials serves as guidance for the judge when exercising the discretion given in the flexible rules.

56. The principle of contradiction (*kontradiksjonsprinsippet, audiatur et altera pars*) has a central position in Norwegian civil procedure law. Both parties must be given an opportunity to be heard, and both parties must be given sufficient time and opportunities to prepare and present their cases. Parties must be treated equally and fairly.

57. As a general rule, civil proceedings are oral (*muntlighetsprinsippet*). Written proceedings are only allowed in particular cases for simplified proceedings or when written proceedings are superior to oral proceedings for some other reason, such as

---

22. Inge Lorange Backer, *The Norwegian Reform of Civil Procedure*, 51 Scandinavian Stud. L. (2007); Inge Lorange Backer, *The Reform of Norwegian Civil Procedure*, in *Reforms of Civil Procedure in Germany and Norway* (Volker Lipp & Halvard Haukeland Fredriksen eds, Mohr Siebeck 2011); Inge Lorange Backer, *Goals of Civil Justice in Norway: Readiness for a Pragmatic Reform*, in *Goals of Civil Justice and Civil Procedure in Contemporary Judicial Systems* (Alan Uzelac ed., Springer 2014).
23. Anna Nylund, *Preparatory Proceedings in Norway – Efficiency by Flexibility and Case Management*, in *Current Trends in Preparatory Proceedings* (Laura Ervo & Anna Nylund eds, Springer 2016) and Anna Nylund, *Norwegian Civil Procedure – How to Make Fast Even Faster*, in *Ways of Implementation of the Right to Civil Proceedings Within a Reasonable Time* (Aurimas Brazdeikis et al. eds, Vilinius Univ. Press 2016).

the nature of the case or to save resources. However, purely written proceedings usually require the consent of the parties. Oral proceedings also increase the publicity of proceedings, as representatives of the media and the general public may come to the courthouse to see justice being done.

58. Proceedings must be proportional, balancing the economic and non-economic values of the case with the resources used for resolving it (principle of proportionality, *proporsjonalitetsprinsippet*).

59. Associated with proportionality is the principle of balancing (some of) the differences in the parties' resources (*forholdsmessighet*). Balancing resources may not be done in a manner that endangers the impartiality of the court. Balance may be reached through a variety of methods, *inter alia*, the following: offering legal aid, restricting the number of witnesses or experts when one party is clearly more powerful than the other and giving more judicial guidance to self-represented parties.

60. Courts must give reasons for 'important rulings'. The duty to give reasons and the extent of the reasons depend on the type and content of the ruling and circumstances related to the case, such as the importance of the issue for the parties and for society at large and whether the ruling is final.

61. The right to appeal is granted against 'rulings of special importance'. Thus, although there is a general right to recourse against judgments, this right may be restricted to some types of rulings and some types of cases. The provision guarantees the first appeal only.

62. Apart from the aforementioned principles, which are found in many Western legal systems, Norwegian civil procedure thinking operates de facto with two additional principles. These are not recognized in doctrine as principles per se, but they serve as a basis of the system. The first principle is that of early resolution by settlement. Settlement provides swift resolution and allows the parties to create their own solution to the dispute. Settlement is achieved preferably out of court before legal proceedings are initiated through negotiation, mediation or other alternative dispute resolution (ADR) mechanisms. Judges also have a duty to encourage the parties to negotiate and, if appropriate, to provide for mediation during court proceedings.

63. The second principle is flexibility. Procedural norms should be flexible and give the judge discretion to adapt the proceedings to fit the needs of the parties and their particular case. Flexibility enables the judge to tailor the proceedings and provides for appropriate, expedient and proportionate proceedings.

Part I. Judicial Organization

Chapter 1. The Courts and Their Members

§1. COURTS

I. Structure of the Court System

64. The Norwegian court system (as shown in Figure 1) is a simple court system consisting almost exclusively of general courts. The first level consists of twenty-three District Courts (*tingrett*), the appellate level of six Courts of Appeal (*lagmannsrett*) and the final level of the Supreme Court (*Høyesterett*). There are no administrative courts and very few special courts. In addition to courts, Conciliation Boards (*forliksråd*) are the first instance for civil and commercial non-family cases.

65. The number of district courts was reduced from sixty to twenty-three in 2021, and the number of Land Consolidation Courts from thirty-three to nineteen. While the majority of legal professionals and judges were in favour of the reform, because it abolished small courts with only one permanent judge, the current government has taken steps to reverse the reform.

Figure 1   The Norwegian Court System

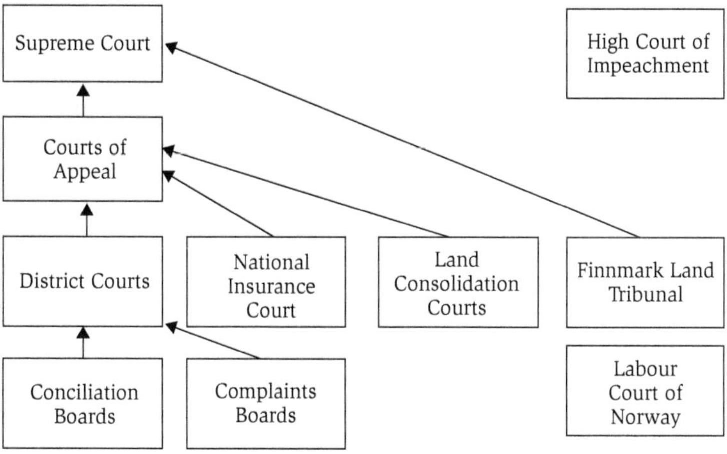

66. The Norwegian preference for a simple court system consisting of general courts, with few or no special courts, is strong. Consequently, there are only five types of special courts: the High Court of Impeachment, Land Consolidation Courts, the Finnmark Land Tribunal (*Utmarksdomstolen for Finnmark*), the Labour Court and the Insurance Court. Only the first two of these are mentioned as special courts in section 2 of the CJA. The Act mentions Consular Courts (*konsulrett*) as a special court, but these are not regular courts with the power to pronounce judgments.[24]

67. Land Consolidation Courts (*jordskifterett*) rule on the borders, ownership and use of immovable property. Their role has traditionally been important, as the borders of immovable property are often not properly decided upon in areas used for pasture in mountains and difficult-to-access areas. The Land consolidation courts follow the rules of civil procedure only partially, and the land consolidation judges must have a master's degree in land consolidation combining studies in geography, law and economy. The ruling is subject to appeal to the Court of Appeal. The Court of Appeal hears the case with one land consolidation judge and two regular judges.

68. The Finnmark Land Tribunal is a special court similar to the Land Consolidation Courts. Its task is to establish rights related to immovable property in the county of Finnmark. The indigenous Sami people have populated this area, where only a minuscule part of the land can be used for agriculture. Most of the area is state-owned but used by the Sami people for reindeer-herding. Rights to use of the land are still unclear. Three of the five judges of the Finnmark Land Tribunal are lawyers, and the two others are experts in archaeology, Sami culture or other relevant subjects.

69. The Labour Court of Norway has sole jurisdiction in matters relating to collective labour agreements, such as the existence, validation and interpretation of these agreements. Most of the judges work part-time and are appointed for three years by the nomination of working life organizations. Only the chief judge, deputy chief judge and a third judge are appointed on a permanent and full-time basis.

70. The Insurance Court (*Trygderetten*) decides disputes on social welfare benefits and publicly financed pensions. The judges are appointed part-time. The chair, the deputy and one other judge are judges in general courts; the other judges have education in medicine or rehabilitation. The rulings are subject to appeal to the Court of Appeal.

A. Complaints Boards

71. Specialization in society and the growth of regulatory law, partly due to EEA membership, have led to the establishment of administrative complaint boards. The

24. Anna Nylund, *Institutional Aspects of the Nordic Justice Systems: Striving for Consolidation and Settlements, in Rethinking Nordic Courts* (Laura Ervo, Pia Letto-Vanamo & Anna Nylund eds, Springer 2021).

boards are quasi-courts and, in a European context fall under the definition of tribunals in terms of both Article 6 of the ECHR and Article 34 of the EFTA Surveillance and Court Agreement. As the boards are not classified courts, their organization and the principles of the procedure involve a mixture of procedural law and administrative law. Typically, the majority of the judges are lawyers and are appointed for a limited period. Judges work part-time, and a secretariat consisting of full-time employees, many of whom are lawyers, assists the judges. The jurisdiction of the boards is generally mandatory; parties may initiate court proceedings only after having a final ruling from the relevant board.

72. The County Social Welfare Boards (*fylkesnemndene for sosiale saker*) decide cases on compulsory care for children, compulsory care of mentally ill persons and other issues related to compulsory social services. The judges are lawyers, and the rulings are subject to appeal to the District Courts. There are twelve County Social Welfare Boards.

73. The Market Board (*markedsrådet*) decides disputes related to marketing, particularly with regard to whether marketing is unlawful. The Norwegian Complaints Board for Industrial Property Rights (*klagenemnda for industrielle rettigheter*) and the Norwegian Complaints Board for Competition (*konkurranseklagenemnda*) have a similar composition and function in their respective areas. The Norwegian Complaints Board for Public Procurement (*klagenemnda for offentlige anskaffelser*) is also a quasi-court.

74. The Patients' Injury Compensation Board (*pasientskadenemnda*) decides disputes related to compensation to patients for injuries they have suffered during or due to medical care. Patients' organizations appoint some of their members. The Immigration Appeals Board (*utlendningsnemnda*) is a quasi-court with jurisdiction in immigration matters. It has a large corps of judges, called Board Leaders, which must have the qualification of a judge.

75. Consumer dispute resolution boards hear disputes related to contracts on consumer sales, consumer services or the right to repeal a consumer contract. The Norwegian Government has a policy to encourage the use of ADR to provide swift and cheap procedures. There are both private and public consumer dispute resolution boards.

76. The Consumer Authority (*Forbrukertilsynet*) is a government body that offers dispute resolution services in general consumer cases that are not covered by a specialized dispute resolution board. Additionally, the Authority hears disputes arising from the sale of goods between two natural persons who are acting outside their trade. The Consumer Authority does not have the competence to hear cases on healthcare services or secondary education. The process focuses on trying to find settlement. The settlement is not binding as a judgment. Previously, the Consumer Council (Forbrukerrådet) provided the services. To strengthen the organizational independence of the dispute resolution body, the competence to resolve these disputes was transferred to the Consumer Authority.

77. If the parties are not satisfied with the outcome from the Consumer Authority, they may bring the case to the Consumer Complaints Commission (*forbrukerklageutvalg*) within one month. The Commission provides inexpensive resolution of consumer disputes. The vast majority of consumers prefer the Commission to the courts, as it is inexpensive and simple. The Commission handles consumer purchases, cooling-off periods, credit purchases and handicraft services. It may also decide disputes between two private parties regarding a purchase. It offers mediation services to help solve disputes without the parties having to file a court case. The members are appointed for a four-year period. The chairs of each section must have a master's degree in law. The other members have expertise in consumer issues. The Commission issues a decision in the case, which is enforceable unless one of the parties brings an action to the District Court within one month (Consumer Commission Act section 7).[25]

78. There are private consumer dispute resolution bodies specializing in specific fields. Many of these have public approval, such as the complaint boards for banking, debt collection, travel, parking and insurance. For consumers, they are free of charge or charge only a nominal fee. The decisions of the boards are not enforceable.

79. Consumer dispute resolution processes hinder the parties from bringing an action to a court or the Conciliation Board (Act relating to authorization of alternative dispute resolution entities in consumer matters section 26).[26] Periods of limitation are halted during consumer dispute resolution proceedings (Limitation Act section 16).[27]

B. Conciliation Boards

80. Although the CJA does not classify Conciliation Boards (*forliksråd*) as courts, they function as de facto courts with adjudicative functions. The history of Conciliation Boards dates back to 1795, arising from the idea of lay judges settling and deciding small cases swiftly at the local level. Today, each municipality has a Conciliation Board consisting of at least three lay judges. The number of lay judges depends on the size of the municipality. The Conciliation Boards blend the three-tier structure of the courts, as they are in fact the first tier in cases in which they have jurisdiction. Their primary function is to provide default judgments for non-contested claims.

81. The Conciliation Boards have only limited jurisdiction in civil and commercial cases. Administrative and family cases and a number of other types of cases are exempt from Conciliation Boards, as are civil and commercial cases with a value

25. *Lov om Forbrukerklageutvalget* 2017 no 7.
26. *Lov om godkjenning av klageorganer forforbrukersaker* 2016 no. 29. Unofficial English translation available at https://lovdata.no/dokument/NLE/lov/2016-06-17-29.
27. *Lov om foreldelse av fordringer (foreldelsesloven)* 1979 no. 18.

above NOK 200,000 (approximately EUR 20,000) where both parties have a legal counsel. For small claims, the Conciliation Boards are in practice the mandatory first court. Thus, for small claims, the Norwegian court system is four-tiered. As the name suggests, Conciliation Boards strive for settlements between the parties, and they have only a limited right to decide the case. They can only decide cases at the request of both parties or at the request of one party if the case is sufficiently simple and clear. If the case is too complex for the Conciliation Board, it must reject the case and the parties may continue proceedings by initiating regular court proceedings at the District Court, since the content of the proceedings in Conciliation is limited.

82. Judgments and default judgments pronounced by the Conciliation Boards and settlements entered by the parties in the Conciliation Boards are binding and enforceable. They become res judicata on equal terms with judgments pronounced by courts. A party may seek recourse against a ruling of the Conciliation Board by initiating civil proceedings at the District Court.

83. Conciliation Boards are an issue of dispute in Norway. Many lawyers consider them outdated and consider the quality of service to be variable. In an increasingly complex legal system, lay judges have difficulties ruling on legal actions. The organization of the Conciliation Boards is also problematic, as the local enforcement authorities provide administrative services for Conciliation Boards. Hence, the secretariat is not professionalized, nor do lawyers advise the members of the boards. In 2001, the official report for modernization of the rules of civil procedure suggested making Conciliation Boards a voluntary service. The Ministry of Justice did not agree; consequently, Conciliation Boards have mandatory jurisdiction.[28]

C. District Courts

84. District Courts are the Courts of First Instance. Until 2002, the first courts were organized into two different entities with Rural District Courts (*herredsrett*) situated in small towns and rural areas and City Courts (*byrett*) situated in larger towns. Courts were referred to as enforcement courts (*namsrett*) in enforcement cases and as probate and bankruptcy courts (*skifterett*) in bankruptcy and probate cases, despite being the same court with the same judges. Except for Oslo, where bankruptcy, insolvency and enforcement cases are still under the Oslo Enforcement Court (*Oslo byfogdembete*), the different designations have been abolished, as have the differences in organization. Indre Finnmark District Court has particular expertise in Sami customary law and in the Sami language. Documents and evidence in the Sami languages are accepted, and the parties and witnesses may speak any Sami language in the hearings.

28. Anna Nylund, *Comparing the Efficiency and Quality of Civil Justice in Scandinavia: The Role of Structural Differences and Definitions of Quality*, 38 Civil Just. Q. 427–439 (2019).

85. There are twenty-three District Courts, all of which have a chief judge (*sorenskriver*) and two or more full-time judges. Additionally, all District Courts have one or more deputy judges. Oslo District Court has more than seventy judges and a total of two-hundred and fifty employees. In addition, the Oslo Enforcement Court has a staff of approximately twenty judges, making it one of the largest courts in Norway. Larger District Courts are organized into two or more divisions.

86. District Court judges are generalists and judge all types of cases: civil, commercial, criminal, administrative, insolvency and family law. In courts operating with divisions, certain types of cases are directed to a single division. In the largest courts, the divisions are even more specialized, as most cases are directed to a specific division or divisions. Judges rotate between the divisions, making them generalists.

D. Courts of Appeal

87. Six Courts of Appeal handle appeals from District Courts and special courts. The courts are Borgarting (seated in Oslo), Eidsivating (Hamar), Agder (Skien), Gulating (Bergen), Frostating (Trondheim) and Hålogaland (Tromsø). In addition to the chief judge (*førstelagmann*), there are also one or more senior judges (*lagmann*), some of whom chair a division of the court, and several other judges (*lagdommer*). In land consolidation cases, one of the judges in the panel of three is a land consolidation judge. Several Courts of Appeal have law clerks (*utredere*) who assist the justices in finding relevant information and preparing the cases.

E. The Supreme Court

88. The Supreme Court is situated in Oslo and handles appeals from the Courts of Appeal and the Finnmark Land Tribunal. The primary task of the Supreme Court is to ensure clarity by interpreting the law and to provide development of the law, i.e., to be a court of precedent. However, the rulings are not formally binding for lower courts, but lower courts treat them as de facto binding, diverting from them only if weighty reasons suggest the necessity of doing so. Access to the Supreme Court is limited and leave to appeal is granted in approximately 120 cases annually, half of which are civil cases. The rest of the cases are subject to limited, mostly written, proceedings. Leave to appeal is granted mainly for cases raising a matter of principle with interest beyond the specific dispute at hand.

89. The Chief Justice (*justitiarius*) is Toril Marie Øie, who is the first woman to hold the office. The court has a total of approximately eighteen to twenty justices (*høyesterettsdommer*) in two divisions. The Supreme Court has law clerks (*utredere*) who assist the justices in finding relevant information and preparing the cases.

90. The Appeals Committee (*ankeutvalget*) of the Supreme Court serves the role of the gatekeeper to the Supreme Court. It gives the final ruling in the majority of cases. The Committee consists of three justices, with a rotation system among the justices of the court.

II. Administration of the Courts

91. The Norwegian Courts Administration (NCA, *Domstolsadministrasjonen*) provides administrative support to judges and court staff. The NCA has steering functions, such as administering the distribution of resources between courts based on specific performance goals, making strategic plans and administering projects to increase the efficiency and quality of court services. The NCA provides training to judges and helps administer court buildings and other facilities and equipment needed in courts. The NCA is independent of the Ministry of Justice. The Ministry of Justice and the Norwegian Parliament set aims and objectives for the courts and make the annual budgets, but they cannot instruct the NCA in specific administrative matters.

III. Bench

A. Conciliation Boards

92. Conciliation Boards are quorate with a panel of three lay judges. The chief judge of the Conciliation Board has the power to rule on procedural grounds and make any procedural ruling necessary before the hearing. The chief judge may also give a default judgment when the defendant has not filed a statement of defence within the time limit.

B. District Courts

93. The District Courts are generally quorate with one professional judge in civil cases (DA section 9-12, CJA section 21). In some types of cases, the District Court is quorate with a professional judge and two lay judges. The provisions mandating the use of lay judges are found mostly in statutory substantive law. In labour law cases, the court has two lay judges, one chosen from a panel representing employers and the other from a panel representing employees. Both panels are administered by the NCA. In cases on guardianship, the court has two lay judges; in cases involving judicial assessment of the value of property, the division of property or expropriation, the court has two lay judges with expert knowledge in the relevant field.

94. The parties may request that the court consists of a panel of a professional judge and two lay judges. The court may include two lay judges if it finds it desirable to do so, but in practice, the court will do so only in exceptional cases and only when the court deems it necessary to invite experts as lay judges. Typically, lay judges sit in large cases involving complex facts, such as construction cases. The lay judges may be experts if the nature of the case requires it. The court may choose the persons it finds suitable to be expert lay judges. The NCA has lists of experts for fields where expert knowledge is required frequently, such as construction and psychological assessment. The expert lay judge may also be a lawyer with expertise in the field of law at hand.

95. If the case involves particularly complex legal or factual issues, the chief judge of the court may decide that the court will sit with more than one professional judge. In these situations, the panel of judges will consist of either three professional judges or two professional judges and three lay judges.

96. The parties have a right to agree that the court will sit with more than one professional judge. The court shall respect the agreement if the parties waive their right to appeal, and the amount in the dispute case may not be under the threshold value for cases requiring a leave to appeal, which is NOK 250,000 (approximately EUR 25,000). The same threshold is applicable to discern between the regular track and the small claims track. An agreement to waive the appeal and to have more than one professional judge mimics an arbitration agreement and functions as an alternative to arbitration. As the court can sit with expert judges, the parties may ensure that the panel has proper expertise, and the parties may suggest who could serve as an expert lay judge.

97. In extensive cases, the chief judge of the court may order a judge to serve as a substitute judge and to be present at the hearings without being a member of the panel. Should the ordinary professional judge hearing the case be unable to attend some of the hearings, the substitute judge will step in and judge the case. If there is more than one professional judge or if the panel has lay members, the court is quorate if no more than one professional judge, one lay judge or one member from both categories is unable to attend.

98. The judge managing the case during the preparatory stage has the right to rule on procedural issues without consulting the members of the panel (DA section 19-2). Procedural rulings may relate to admissibility and form of evidence, the duty to disclose evidence, the schedule of the proceedings, time limits, preclusion and other issues related to preparation of the main hearing. The case-managing judge may also dismiss the case on procedural grounds, *inter alia*, due to a lack of legal standing or the court lacking jurisdiction.

C. Courts of Appeal

99. The Court of Appeal is quorate with a panel of three professional judges (CJA section 12). However, in cases where lay judges are required in the District Court, the Court of Appeal must sit with a panel of three professional judges and two (expert) lay judges. In cases requiring special expertise or in which the parties request lay judges, the Court of Appeal has the discretion to hear the case in a panel with two lay judges (DA section 29-17). When lay judges have participated in the District Court, the Court of Appeal will usually follow suit. Although the District Court ruled on the case without lay judges, the Court of Appeal may opt to include lay judges. Lay judges participate in hearings only and are not included in the written procedure.

100. In extensive cases, the chief judge of the court may order a substitute professional judge to attend the hearings. The Court of Appeal is quorate with three professional judges. If lay judges attend the hearings, the presence of one lay judge suffices for the court to remain quorate.

101. The case-managing judge has the right to rule on procedural issues, such as evidence and setting time limits (DA section 19-2). However, the case-managing judge may not dismiss the case or the appeal or deny leave to appeal.

D. Supreme Court

102. The Supreme Court is quorate with a panel of five justices. The Supreme Court does not have lay judges. For cases raising questions of principle, cases in which the Supreme Court considers setting aside earlier case law and, in particular, cases where the Supreme Court performs judicial review of statutory law, the Court sits in a grand chamber of eleven justices or in a plenary session. Before the final stage of the proceedings, the Chief Justice has the power to decide that a grand chamber will hear the case. After the main hearing has commenced, and for cases with only written proceedings, after the parties have made their final submissions, two of the five justices on the panel may request that the grand chamber hears the case. If at least six justices make such a request, or the Chief Justice deems it necessary, the case is transferred to a plenary session.

103. The Appeals Committee of the Supreme Court (*ankeutvalget*) grants leaves to appeal in appeals against judgments. Further, the Appeals Committee hears appeals against court orders and decisions. The Appeals Committee consists of three justices who serve on the Committee on a rotating basis. The Committee is quorate with three judges. The Appeals Committee may transfer appeals against court orders and decisions involving a question of principle to a panel of five justices.

104. In time-consuming cases, the Chief Justice may order one or two justices to attend hearings. The justice attending the hearings steps in if one of the justices is absent. The grand chamber and the plenary session are quorate with a minimum of five justices. In the event of an even number of justices, the justice serving the shortest time must step down.

105. Similar to the situation in lower courts, the case-managing judge has the power to rule on procedural issues (DA 19-2). The judge can also refer a procedural issue to the Appeals Committee.

IV. Appointment of Judges

106. The Government appoints all permanent professional judges based on the recommendation of the Judicial Appointments Board (*Innstillingsrådet for dommere*), CJA section 55a. The Board is independent of the government and courts. The Government formally appoints judges based on the recommendation of the Board. The Board has seven members: of these, three are judges, one is an advocate, one is a lawyer employed by a public law body and two are non-lawyers. The Government appoints the members and their personal deputies for a four-year period. The NCA functions as a secretariat for the Board. For the appointment of the Chief Justice of the Supreme Court, an ad hoc procedure is set in place.

107. The Judicial Appointments Board decides temporary appointments for a duration of less than one year, and the chief judge of the court may decide appointments of less than six months and deputy judges. The Board may also assign a judge to serve temporarily at another court at the same level in the judiciary and may appoint retired judges to serve in a single case. A Court of Appeal may ask District Court judges in the district to serve temporarily at the Court of Appeal. Temporary appointments are only allowed when a judge is on leave, a position as a judge is open, a judge is declared disqualified, congestion occurs due to an unexpected number of cases or due to complex cases that require more judges, or when necessary due to reorganization of courts (CJA sections 55–55f).

108. In appointing judges, the Board strives for diversity in gender, age and previous work experience. It bases its recommendation on applications, interviews, references and a note from the chief judge of the relevant court. The lists of applicants and the recommendations of the Board are public documents.

109. The Bench consists primarily of full-time professional judges. A five-year university degree in law passed with excellent marks and Norwegian citizenship are required for judges. Judges are recruited broadly from private-practice lawyers, lawyers employed by the public sector, lawyers in the police and prosecution, and legal academics. Appellate courts recruit judges mostly from outside the courts. The minimum age is 25 for judges, 21 for deputy judges and 30 for Supreme Court justices and judges in appellate courts. However, in practice, most judges receive their initial appointment at 45–50 years of age. Judges must retire at age 70. Retired judges may serve as extraordinary judges appointed for specific cases until age 74.

110. The District Courts appoint deputy judges (*dommerfullmektig*) for a two-year period. The period may be extended for one additional year, for a total of three years. Deputy judges are newly educated lawyers who serve as trainee judges, with powers limited to small and easy cases initially. Deputy judges do not hear complex cases and may not hear cases in a panel consisting of more than one professional judge.

111. The Supreme Court has court clerks, who are lawyers early in their careers. They assist the justices, particularly in the selection of the cases to which a leave to appeal should be granted. In recent years, the Courts of Appeals have employed clerks to assist the judges, particularly during the early stages to select cases in which a leave to appeal should be granted and to help identify cases lacking any reasonable prospect of success.

112. The council of each municipality appoints lay judges for two pools of equal size: one for women and one for men. The size of the pools depends on the anticipated number of cases, as each lay judge should serve on two cases annually. Each pool is appointed for a four-year period. The members of the pool should be representative of the general population. Lay judges for a specific case are drawn randomly from the pool.

113. Specialist lay judges are recruited either from a pool of specialists who have indicated their interest in serving as specialist judges or, if a pool for the specific type of expertise does not exist, by suggestion of the parties. The NCA maintains the pools or lists of persons interested in serving as specialist lay judges.

114. Conciliation Boards consist of lay judges, who must be at least 25 and no more than 70 years of age at the time of appointment. The judges must be 'well-suited' for the position and have a good command of Norwegian. Knowledge of the law is not required. The judges serve for a four-year period and may be re-elected. The council of each municipality elects the members of the Conciliation Boards and appoints the chair. There are three judges and three deputy members. In large municipalities, the Conciliation Board consists of two or more departments, each of which consists of three members and their deputies, with one of the members acting as the chair. The members receive a two-day training on procedural principles and rules.

115. Judges on the Conciliation Boards serve part-time. The Conciliation Boards convene once per month, except for the month of July. If required, the Boards have bi-weekly or even weekly hearings.

116. Cases are distributed to the judges according to the principle of randomness. However, the many exceptions to the principle of randomness diminish its strength. Many courts practice some form of moderate specialization, where cases requiring knowledge of or experience in a specific area are assigned only, or primarily, to certain judges. For instance, cases related to children or complex commercial cases may be assigned to certain judges. Complex cases are assigned to more experienced judges, as are cases requiring a specific type of knowledge. Moreover, the chief judge must take into account the workload of each judge.

§2. Members of the Judiciary

I. Incompatibilities

117. Judges are not permitted to have appointments that are incompatible with their profession, CJA sections 121a–121k. There are four categories of appointments: those that are always permitted without being registered, those that are permitted but need to be registered, those that require prior permission and those that are prohibited. Permitted appointments that are not registered include, *inter alia*, leadership positions in organizations with less than 100 members, membership in religious organizations and occasional lectures. Permitted appointments that are registered include leadership positions in organizations with more than 100 members and regular teaching assignments. Activities requiring prior permission include, *inter alia*, participating in arbitration tribunals and dispute resolution bodies and participating in business activities. Any activities that may potentially be incompatible with being a judge require permission.

118. The general rules on impartiality prohibit a person from acting as a judge or juror in cases involving relatives, involving a company where that person has or has had certain leadership positions and where he or she has acted on behalf of a party or acted as an arbitrator (CJA section 106).

119. CJA section 108 contains a general provision on impartiality of judges. It states that a person may not serve as a judge 'when other special circumstances exist that are capable of undermining confidence in his impartiality'. Once there are objective grounds on which the partiality of the judge can be questioned, the judge must refrain from deciding the case. The provision captures the idea that justice not only must be done but also must be seen to be done.

II. End of Functions

120. Judges end their functions at retirement, which occurs at or before the age of 70. Judges may not be dismissed or relocated unless the dismissal is a result of criminal proceedings and the dismissal is based on a legal provision.

III. Discipline

121. The Supervisory Committee for Judges considers complaints against judges. Parties, legal counsel, witnesses, experts, the chief judge or justice of the court where the judge is appointed, NCA, the Ministry of Justice and the Norwegian Bar Association may file a complaint if a judge has wilfully or negligently breached the obligations or the proper conduct of judges. The Committee may issue a critical assessment or a warning as a disciplinary measure, but it does not have the power to dismiss a judge. If the complainant or the judge is dissatisfied with the decision of the Committee, he or she may initiate legal proceedings within two months.

Chapter 2. The Bar

§1. Exercise of the Legal Profession

122. The legal profession consists of licensed lawyers, who may use the title of advocate (*advokat*). Lawyers who have obtained their licence retain it even if they are employed as in-house lawyers or by the government. However, judges, lawyers in the public prosecution service and certain civil servants may not practice as lawyers outside their positions. Young lawyers work as junior lawyers (*advokatfullmektig*) under the supervision of an experienced licensed lawyer. Most advocates are members of the Norwegian Bar Association (*Den Norske Advokatforening*), but membership is not mandatory.

I. Conditions for Admission

123. The Supervisory Council for Legal Practice (*Tilsynsrådet for advokatvirksomhet*) is responsible for granting and withdrawing licences to practise law. It oversees advocates and acts as a disciplinary board. The Lawyer Licencing Board (*Advokatbevillingsnemnden*) of the Supervisory Council grants licences and authorizes lawyers to practise as junior lawyers and advocates based on the recommendations of the Supervisory Council. The Supervisory Council is financed by membership fees.

124. The conditions for admission to the bar are a five-year integrated master's degree in law and at least two years of relevant work experience as a junior lawyer under the supervision of an advocate, as a (deputy) judge, as a lawyer in the public prosecution service or as a teacher of law at a law programme at a university. The candidate must have represented a party in three main hearings in civil cases. One of the civil cases may be substituted with a criminal case and one with court-connected mediation. Further, a course in advocate ethics and skills is required, and candidates for admission must present their criminal records.

125. Lawyers from other EEA countries are allowed to practise law in Norway and gain membership in the Norwegian Bar Association in accordance with the free movement of workers and services.

126. Advocates need permission to represent parties in the Supreme Court. The Supreme Court grants permission when the advocate has practised law independently (i.e., holding the title of advocate) for at least one year and the advocate has successfully argued two cases before the Supreme Court. The justices hearing the cases decide whether the advocate has demonstrated a sufficiently high level of relevant skills.

II. Rights and Duties

127. Advocates have a monopoly to offer legal services and advice, CJA section 218. However, persons holding a five-year degree in law who are not advocates may provide legal advice; thus, advocates have essentially lost part of their monopoly. However, only advocates have the right to represent or assist parties in court. Further, certified auditors or controllers may provide limited legal services related to taxes. Several universities have legal clinics where law students offer limited legal advice free of charge. Furthermore, all individuals have the right to represent close relatives regardless of professional background.

128. An advocate may use a junior lawyer to perform duties out of the court and in the District Court. Permission is required for an assistant lawyer to act in the Court of Appeal. The junior lawyer must have an authorization in order to be permitted to act on behalf of the advocate.

129. Advocates must provide a security, in practice a document stating that the advocate has a sufficient insurance, to cover any liability they may incur when providing legal services, unless the advocate is employed by the State or a municipality. Advocates have a duty to provide services diligently, conscientiously, expediently and ethically. They must act in the interest of their clients. The Supervisory Council for Legal Services monitors the conduct of advocates.

130. The Norwegian Bar Association publishes Standards on Good Legal Practices, which the Ministry of Justice confirms. The Standards are binding for all advocates, and they set the standard of conduct.

131. Advocates have several privileges. Legal aid is provided only to persons represented by an advocate, and courts delegate the administration of bankruptcies to advocates only. The duty and the privilege of confidentiality are central to all advocates and providers of limited legal aid.

III. Discipline

132. The Supervisory Council for Legal Services oversees advocates. Advocates are obliged to give the Council access to information. The Council may issue reprimands and warnings for conduct in breach of ethical rules or laws. Based on the recommendations of the Supervisory Council for Legal Practice and the Disciplinary Board of the Norwegian Bar Association, the Lawyer Licensing Board may revoke a licence and issue a ban prohibiting a person from membership in the Bar Association if the person is deemed unfit or unworthy due to a breach of the rules or a criminal record. A decision to issue a reprimand or a warning may be appealed to the Lawyer Licensing Board. Further appeal to courts is possible. Normally, clients contact the Disciplinary Board of the Bar Association, but clients may also contact the Supervisory Council. The Board oversees persons offering limited legal advice in addition to advocates. Offering unauthorized legal advice is a criminal offence punishable by a fine or imprisonment for up to three months.

133. The Disciplinary Board hears complaints on lawyers' fees. Should the Board find that a lawyer has claimed an excessively high fee, it shall determine the reasonable fee for the case and order the advocate to return the excess amount.

§2. Private Organizations

134. More than 90% of advocates are members of the Norwegian Bar Association (*Advokatforeningen*). In 2018, the total number of members was 9,317, and the number of trainee lawyers was 1,608.[29]

135. The Bar Association has issued the Standards on Good Legal Practice (*Regler for god advokatskikk*) and a commentary to them. There are also standards for particular groups of lawyers, particularly defence lawyers and lawyers representing victims of crime. The Ethics Board (*etikkutvalg*) issues recommendations on the interpretation of the Standards or how to solve a particular ethical issue when a member or the board of the Bar Association requests a recommendation or advice. Further, the Bar Association helps its members to obtain the required security and necessary insurance for malpractice.

136. The Bar Association has a discipline system with a discipline committee (*disiplinærutvalg*). The local discipline committee is the first step when a client is unsatisfied with the services an advocate has provided or considers the fees excessively high. The decision of the local discipline committee is subject to appeal to the Disciplinary Board (*Disiplærnemnda*), which may criticize or reprimand the advocate or issue a warning. The disciplinary organs may also adjust the fee. In severe cases, the Disciplinary Board may ask the Supervisory Board for Legal Services to withdraw the licence.

137. Members of the Bar Association use the abbreviation MNA after their titles or in the name of their law offices.

29. Annual Report of the Norwegian Bar Association 2018, https://www.advokatforeningen.no/contentassets/0c5dbe102b8a43e5ba9976f09bf43501/arsrapport_2018_endelig.pdf.

Chapter 3. The Bailiffs

§1. Exercise of the Profession

I. Process Servers

138. The process server has the task to serve documents when other methods of service, usually postal service, have not been successful. The local chief enforcement officers and heads of police stations are chief process servers. Other persons, usually enforcement officers or police officers, may also be appointed as process servers by the local District Court (CJA section 63).

II. Enforcement Authorities

139. The enforcement authorities are part of the civil organization of the police force. The civil services of the police force are organized in Sheriff's Offices (*lensmannskontor*) in rural areas and Enforcement Offices (*namnsfogdekontor*) in urban areas (EA Chapter 2). Sheriff's Offices perform tasks related to civil administration in addition to investigation and law enforcement in criminal cases. The functions of Enforcement Offices are limited to civil administration, in particular enforcement of civil rights and obligations, serving legal documents and handling debt restructuring. The Sheriff's Offices and Enforcement Offices also serve as the secretariat for Conciliation Boards.

§2. Public Institutions and Private Organizations

140. State civil servants and police officers carry out the functions of the bailiff. Private persons can also serve documents. There are, however, no professional bailiffs in the private sector. Debt collection agencies provide services for debt collection, but their powers are limited to urging a person to pay voluntarily.

Part II. Jurisdiction

Chapter 1. Domestic Jurisdiction

§1. Subject Matter Jurisdiction

I. Factors to Be Taken into Account in Determining Jurisdiction

141. Since Norway has a unitary court system that consists of general courts, issues related to subject matter jurisdiction are rare. Administrative cases are considered civil cases but have some special regulations, including rules on subject matter jurisdiction. In some types of cases, particularly cases related to administrative matters, parties must first go through an administrative complaint board before initiating court proceedings. In other cases, such as consumer cases, the use of consumer resolution boards is optional.

142. The main division is between cases in which the interest is primarily economic and those with a primarily non-economic interest. A claim is characterized as economic when it is related primarily to an economic interest, and non-economic interests are secondary. The viewpoint of the claimant is decisive for the classification of the case. In an employment case on unlawful notification, the primary interest of the employee is non-economic, as a notification may hinder or impair future employment. The same case has a primarily, or exclusively, economic value for the employer. In this example, the District Court has jurisdiction if the employee is the claimant, and the Conciliation Board has jurisdiction if the employer is the claimant.

143. Chapter 17 of the DA regulates the valuation of the claim. If the prayer for relief consists of payment of a specific sum of money, the sum is used to determine the interest at hand. If the case is not pecuniary, the claimant must provide information on an estimated value of the subject matter. For instance, if ownership is contested, the estimated value of the object in question must be presented to the court. For claims consisting of payments running at specific intervals, the value of the claimed amount is multiplied by the number of times it is still to be paid. If the payments run indeterminately, the maximum amount is ten times the annual payment. Typically, only the disputed amount is determinant for jurisdiction and for other situations in which the amount in question determines the proceedings, such as the small claims track and access to the Court of Appeal. If the defendant admits a claim partially, the admitted amount will be subtracted. The court may set aside the estimation of the value as presented by the parties if the court deems the estimated value to be incorrect.

II. Main Claims and Ancillary Claims

144. Subject matter jurisdiction in civil cases follows the main claim, unless one of the ancillary claims has mandatory jurisdiction. For instance, if the Conciliation Board does not have jurisdiction over the main claim, then the party may bring any ancillary claims directly to the District Court, although the ancillary claims are under the jurisdiction of the Conciliation Board. Should the main claim and the ancillary claim be divided, the District Court may rule that the Conciliation Board has jurisdiction on the ancillary claim or may rule that it keeps jurisdiction itself. The value of all the claims, both main and ancillary, is calculated to determine the jurisdiction. If a party introduces a new claim or extends the claims to a new party, then the new claim or party is exempted from the Conciliation Board.

145. Both main and ancillary claims are included in the calculation of the value of the claim. If there are several claims, the value of the claims is cumulated. Interests accrued before the case became pending are only calculated if they are contested. Counterclaims are not deducted from the contested amount.

III. Overview of the Jurisdiction of the Different Courts

146. The main question related to subject matter is the division between the District Courts and Conciliation Boards.

147. Conciliation Boards have jurisdiction in civil and commercial cases. The Conciliation Boards lack jurisdiction in the following matters (DA section 6-2):

- cases with a primarily non-economic interest;
- family law cases, except for financial matters between spouses related to separation and division of travel costs arising from contact arrangements for children;
- cases against public law bodies and civil servants, unless they are entirely of a private law character;
- cases on intellectual property rights;
- cases concerning the validity of an arbitral award or in-court settlement;
- cases decided on by a tribunal or dispute resolution body if it is provided by statute that the rulings of the tribunal shall be binding on the parties; and
- other cases where a statutory provision mandates that the case is not subject to their jurisdiction.

148. Conciliation Boards do not have jurisdiction on matters related to child maintenance, but only on the division of travel costs in conjunction with the child having contact with a parent. As spousal maintenance is almost non-existent in Norway, cases related to the economic relationship between the spouses after separation usually occur only once between the same parties (i.e., shortly after separation).

149. As Norway has no administrative courts, administrative law cases are considered civil cases. They start directly at the District Court. Even though the public law element is limited and/or subordinated to the private law element of a case, Conciliation Boards lack jurisdiction in these cases because a public law element is present.

150. Cases with a primarily economic value are exempted from Conciliation Boards if:

- The amount in dispute is at least NOK 200,000 (approximately EUR 20,000) and both parties are assisted by a lawyer. The statement of claim must be signed by the legal counsel of the claimant, and the defendant must have received legal advice before the statement of claim was filed (e.g., during negotiations to reach settlement).
- Out-of-court mediation pursuant to DA Chapter 7 has been attempted.
- A tribunal or dispute resolution body has heard the case on the merits.
- A new claim or party is introduced through a joinder of cases after the summons has been served.

151. In case a tribunal or dispute resolution body has heard the case on the merits, the hearing must have been based on the consent of the opposite party, or the tribunal or dispute resolution body must be publicly approved based on statutory law. In consumer law, the Consumer Complaints Board and several private consumer dispute resolution bodies are publicly approved through the Consumer Complaints Commission Act[30] and Act on Approval of Consumer Disputes.[31]

152. In practice, where the disputed value is above the threshold of NOK 200,000, parties have legal counsel, as a rule, and are consequently exempted from Conciliation Boards.

153. In Oslo, the Oslo Enforcement Court (*Oslo byfogdembete*) has exclusive jurisdiction on bankruptcy, insolvency and enforcement cases. The Oslo District Court does not have jurisdiction in these matters. The two courts must transfer matters between them if the receiving court lacks jurisdiction.

154. For some administrative law cases decided by a tribunal, the Court of Appeal serves as the Court of First Instance.

30. *Forbrukerklageloven* 2017 no. 7.
31. *Lov om godkjenning av klageorganer for forbrukersaker* 2016 no. 29. Both acts implement the Directive 2013/11/EU of 21 May 2013 on alternative dispute resolution for consumer disputes.

§2. VENUE (TERRITORIAL JURISDICTION)

I. Factors to Be Taken into Account

155. The domicile of the defendant is, as a rule, decisive for the venue. However, the parties have the right to choose from a range of options depending on the claim. There are a few exceptions that protect the weaker party and that concentrate cases requiring special knowledge to a single District Court. The rules are based on the Lugano Convention, but they are far less detailed than the rules of the Convention.

II. Main Claims and Ancillary Claims

156. The main claim is decisive for rules on venue. Ancillary claims and counterclaims will follow the main claim, unless there are specific rules for sole mandatory jurisdiction for the ancillary claim or counterclaim. When another court has sole mandatory jurisdiction on one of the claims or a counterclaim, the court where the action is pending may transfer the case to the court with sole jurisdiction or split the claims to separate actions.

III. Overview of the Different Rules

157. The main rule for territorial jurisdiction is that the domicile of the defendant (i.e., 'the ordinary venue') is decisive (DA section 4-4). The domicile is usually decided based on data from the National Register of Persons or the business register. However, if a person does not de facto reside at the indicated address, the de facto place of residence serves as the domicile. Registered business entities have their ordinary venue where the head office is situated and foreign business entities where the agency, branch or similar place of business is situated. The ordinary venue of the State of Norway is Oslo. The ordinary venue for county and municipal offices is at the main administrative centre of the county or municipality. Other undertakings and organizations that are not registered business entities have their ordinary venue where the person upon whom the summons is to be served has his or her ordinary venue.

158. DA section 4-5 offers a range of alternative venues for particular types of claims. Actions relating to real property may be brought where the real property is situated. Claims related to contractual relationships may be brought where the contractual obligation has been or is to be performed. Damages in tort may be brought where the damage originated or where it has occurred or will occur. An employee may bring an action against the employer at the place of work or where the employee normally performs his or her work. In maritime relations, the action may be brought at the vessel's port of registry. Actions against heirs may be brought at the place where the deceased had his or her last ordinary venue. A consumer may bring an action against a tradesperson at the consumer's own ordinary venue.

Actions against the State and county authorities may be brought at the claimant's ordinary venue. Actions against insurance companies for payment of insurance claims may be brought at the ordinary venue of the claimant.

159. Despite the fact that DA has no mandatory rules on venue for any specific type of case, mandatory rules on venue are found in other statutes. For instance, the Oslo District Court has mandatory jurisdiction on claims related to patents and patent infringements (Patent Act, *patentloven* 1967 no. 9 section 63), and claims related to the Business Entity Register must be lodged at the domicile of the National Business Entity Register. Some types of administrative claims, such as claims related to immigration, have a mandatory venue in Oslo.

160. The parties may also enter into agreements on jurisdiction. There are no specific requirements for jurisdiction clauses, except that jurisdiction clauses between a trader and a consumer must be in writing. However, clauses on international jurisdiction must be in writing (DA section 4-6). Consumers are not bound by jurisdiction clauses that they have entered into before the dispute has arisen.

§3. Resolution of Jurisdiction Conflicts

161. Jurisdiction conflicts arise mainly between District Courts and Conciliation Boards, as well as among District Courts. If an action is filed at a court lacking territorial jurisdiction, the court shall refer the case to the court with territorial jurisdiction (DA section 4-7). If more than one court has jurisdiction, the court must first ask the claimant which of the courts the claimant prefers and act accordingly. The court must also hear the court to which it wishes to transfer the case and, if applicable, the opposing party (CJA section 38). If the receiving court opposes the transfer of the case, the Court of Appeal decides on jurisdiction. The ruling on competing jurisdiction is not subject to appeal. The case remains lis pendens during the transfer.

162. Jurisdiction conflicts between District Courts and Conciliation Boards are solved by the District Court. If the claimant brings an action at the District Court, but the claim belongs under a Conciliation Board, the District Court shall transfer the case to the competent Conciliation Board. If the Conciliation Board does not have jurisdiction, it must summarily dismiss the case (DA section 6-3 subsection 4) or, when applicable, transfer it to the Conciliation Board having territorial jurisdiction.

163. A court may also transfer a case to another court when it considers that hearing the case in the other court is more appropriate or necessary (CJA section 38). This may be done only under special circumstances, such as when taking of evidence will be decisively easier at the other court. Courts have the power to transfer cases even if a valid, exclusive jurisdiction exists.

164. General courts may only transfer a case to another general court, and Land Consolidation Courts only to another Land Consolidation Court, not a special court or quasi-court. Special courts and quasi-courts are barred from transferring cases, with the exception of Land Consolidation Courts. Court must dismiss a case filed in the wrong branch of courts.

165. Rulings in which a general court declares itself to lack jurisdiction are binding for general courts on the same and subordinate levels (CJA section 35). The same rule applies to Land Consolidation Courts. A ruling on jurisdiction is not binding for special courts, such as the Labour Court. Consequently, parallel proceedings could arise. However, as the competency of the Labour Court is different from that of general courts, neither the ambit of the dispute nor the parties would be identical even when the dispute arises from the same facts. In Rt. 1987 p. 98, the Supreme Court found that an employee could bring an action on unlawful dismissal against the employer in a general court, although the Labour Court had ruled on issues arising from the same dismissal. The employees' organization and the employers' organization were parties to the case in the Labour Court, and the legal dispute was related to the right to dismiss the employee, as he was a union representative.

Chapter 2. International Jurisdiction

§1. Rules Applicable in the Absence of a Treaty

166. Norwegian courts have international jurisdiction only in cases that have a 'sufficiently strong connection' to Norway (DA section 4-3). This requirement is usually fulfilled when the defendant's ordinary venue is in Norway, and the case has an additional connection to Norway, such as the contractual obligation or tangible parts of it are to be fulfilled in Norway, HR-2018-936. When these two criteria are not fulfilled, the rule has been interpreted to have both a positive and a negative aspect, as described below.

167. The positive aspect enables courts to establish Norwegian jurisdiction even when the defendant's ordinary venue is not in Norway and an alternative venue pursuant to section 4-5 does not exist in Norway. Since the threshold for establishing international jurisdiction is high, this rule applies only in exceptional cases. In a few cases from the 1960s,[32] Norwegian courts established jurisdiction in family cases even when the spouses did not have their domicile in Norway. One case concerned child abduction and the other right to divorce. The circumstances were exceptional in both cases.

168. In *Centrebet* (Rt. 2010 p. 1197), a Norwegian consumer sued the Australian Internet betting company Centrebet in Norway. The consumer had lost a large sum of money on betting. Centrebet had neither a branch nor employees in Norway or could any betting be done in Norway. Nonetheless, the Supreme Court assumed jurisdiction based on a sufficiently strong connection to Norway, because Centrebet clearly directed its marketing to the Norwegian market by offering web pages in Norwegian, offering customer service electronically in Norwegian and offering a free Norwegian telephone number to its customer service.

169. If a case is subject to Norwegian jurisdiction, but no venue is established pursuant to sections 4-4 and 4-5, then the District Court in Oslo has jurisdiction. If the defendant has sufficient assets in Norway, then the place where the assets are located is an alternative venue to Oslo.

170. The negative aspect of the requirement of a 'sufficiently strong connection' allows Norwegian courts to reject jurisdiction even when a venue can be established in Norway. Thus, establishing territorial jurisdiction does not suffice. The requirement of a 'sufficiently strong connection' is related to forum non conveniens, because it is essentially a flipped version – a requirement of *forum conveniens* – particularly in commercial cases. Unless the case has strong connections to Norway, Norwegian courts do not have international jurisdiction.

---

32. Rt. 1960 p. 188 and Rt. 1960 p. 1403.

171. *Svalbard Plane Crash*, *Trico Subsea* and *Samsung* illustrate the high threshold. In the *Svalbard Plane Crash* case (Rt. 1998 p. 1647) an aeroplane from a Russian airline crashed on Svalbard, a Norwegian territory in the Arctic. The family members of the deceased victims sued the insurance company of the airline in Norway. The Supreme Court found that the crash on Norwegian territory did not establish a sufficiently strong connection to Norway.

172. In *Trico Subsea* (Rt. 2012 p. 1951), Raffles Shipping Project, a shipbroker based in Singapore, sued Trico Subsea AS, a company registered in Norway, for payment of brokerage. The contract between the parties had no connection to Norway. The Supreme Court found that the threshold for rejecting jurisdiction is normally high if the ordinary venue of the defendant is in Norway, as it was in this case. In spite of this comment, it argued that the threshold for Norwegian jurisdiction is generally high in commercial cases. The Supreme Court assumed ultimately Norwegian jurisdiction, since the ordinary venue of the defendant was in Norway.

173. In *Samsung* (Rt. 2015 p. 1040), CKT Marine Services, a company registered in the Netherlands, initiated proceedings for provisional measures against Samsung, which is domiciled in Korea, and a Belgian financial institution. CKT Marine Services and Samsung had agreed on arbitration in Stavanger. The contract between CKT and the Belgian financial institution had a clause indicating Stavanger as the venue. The Supreme Court rejected Norwegian jurisdiction in both cases, since a sufficiently strong connection to Norway had not been established. The court argued that the threshold for establishing a sufficient connection is high in commercial cases and particularly high for provisional measures. It disregarded Article 31 in the Lugano Convention, which establishes jurisdiction for provisional measures at the place of arbitration and at the court agreed upon by the parties, and the rules in the ArbA.[33]

174. Based on *Trico* and *Samsung*, one may contend that the threshold for establishing Norwegian jurisdiction is particularly high in commercial cases, unless the ordinary venue of the defendant is in Norway.

175. In cases with an international element where Norwegian courts appear to lack international jurisdiction, the government is entitled to intervene by filing an objection against Norwegian jurisdiction. In such cases, the government must submit an appeal to the Supreme Court, and the Supreme Court rules on the international jurisdiction (CJA section 37). The right to intervene is narrow and is not dependent on the status of the government as a party to the case or the government's interest in the outcome. The government has used this power only in two cases, one of which the Supreme Court rejected.

---

33. *See* Anna Nylund, *Norway: An Insider Outside – Or an Outsider Inside – European Civil Justice*, in *The European Union and National Civil Procedure* (Anna Nylund & Bart Krans eds, Intersentia 2016).

§2. INTERNATIONAL TREATIES

176. The Lugano Convention is, in practice, the most important international treaty regulating international jurisdiction. The Convention serves as *lex specialis* to the DA and thus has priority over the Act (DA sections 1-2 and 4-7).

177. Norwegian courts apply the Convention regularly and refer to case law from the European Court of Justice in doing so. However, the Supreme Court consistently interprets the scope of the Convention to include only cases where both the claimant and the defendant are domiciled in a Convention state. In *Trico Subsea* (Rt. 2012 p. 1951), the Supreme Court discussed whether the Convention was applicable in light of the *Owusu* case. The majority of the three justices found that the Lugano Convention was not applicable.[34] The minority of two justices found that the Convention was applicable. In *Samsung* (Rt. 2015 p. 1040), the Supreme Court did not even discuss whether the Lugano Convention was applicable. When the Supreme Court and other courts have found that the Lugano Convention is applicable, they interpret it in light of case law from the European Court of Justice.

178. Norway is also a party to the Nordic Convention on Provisions of International Private Law Aspects of Marriage, Adoption and Guardianship of 1931 and the Convention on Jurisdiction, Applicable Law, Recognition, Enforcement and Co-operation in Respect of Parental Responsibility and Measures for the Protection of Children of 1996. The Conventions have preference over the rules in the DA (DA section 1-2), but they have a weaker status formally than the Lugano Convention.

---

34. *See ibid.*, p. 105, in particular references in footnote 34.

Part III. Actions and Claims

Chapter 1. Actions

§1. Definition

179. Actions are brought by submitting a statement of claim (*stevning*) to the court. The content of the statement of claim is regulated in detail (DA section 9-2). The statement of claim must state the name of the court and the names and addresses of the parties and when applicable, their representative and legal counsel. The claimant must state the specific claim and relief, as well as the cause of action and legal grounds upon which the claim and prayer for relief are based. The statement of claim must indicate which evidence will be invoked in a tentative list of evidence that names the pieces of evidence the claimant wishes to present and the persons to be heard. If the basis of the court's jurisdiction is not clear, the claimant must indicate it. The statement of the claimant must also communicate the claimant's view on how the court proceedings should be conducted.

180. The claim, including the particular prayer for relief, and cause of action must be stated in sufficient detail for the court to be able to assess whether it has jurisdiction and to ensure prima facie that the case is not manifestly ill-founded. Further, the statement of claim shall give sufficient information for the court to engage in case management, including, *inter alia*, an assessment of whether the claim should be directed to the small claims track, whether court-connected mediation is appropriate and whether preparation should be written, oral or a mixture of both. However, the claimant should not present more details than necessary so as to avoid frontloading the case.

181. The statement of claim is submitted in writing. Formally, the court must also accept oral statements of claim when a party is self-represented (DA section 12-1). In practice, the court will recommend that the party engages a legal counsel to receive help to put the statement in writing.

182. The requirements for the statement of claim (application for conciliation proceedings) for Conciliation Boards are slightly lower (DA section 6-3). The statement of claim must state the name of the Conciliation Board, the names and addresses of the parties and their legal counsel. The claimant must also state the prayer for relief, the exact amount claimed and a short description of the cause of action. The statement of claim does not have to identify the legal grounds for the claim. The claimant must provide copies of documents upon which the claim is directly based. The claimant is not required to provide a tentative list of other evidence.

183. A party seeking review of an enforceable judgment of the Conciliation Board or of a tribunal (usually an administrative complaints board) must file a statement of claim fulfilling the requirements of a statement of appeal (DA section 9-2 subsection 4). The party initiating the action must submit the judgment and a statement requesting that the court reviews the judgment and stating the amendment requested.

§2. Admissibility

184. Norwegian law distinguishes between general and special and between absolute and relative criteria for admissibility. The general criteria for admissibility apply to all cases, whereas the special criteria apply only to certain cases. Absolute criteria must be fulfilled in all cases, and the court has a duty to enforce the criteria on its own motion. The court investigates relative criteria for admissibility only if a party claims the criterion is not fulfilled. All general criteria for admissibility are absolute, with the exception of territorial jurisdiction of general courts. The defendant establishes territorial jurisdiction for the court by entering an appearance without contesting the territorial jurisdiction.

185. Some criteria fall between the categories of absolute and relative, since the court must investigate them on its own motion, yet the opposite party may consent to admissibility. The time limit for initiating proceedings against decisions of taxation may be extended if the defendant consents. The court must make the defendant aware of the lacking criterion on admissibility and ask if the defendant consents to the action despite this.

186. The criteria for admissibility must be fulfilled when the proceedings are initiated (i.e., when the statement of claim arrives at the court). Most of the criteria of admissibility must be fulfilled throughout the proceedings. The main exceptions are the criteria for territorial jurisdiction and for the value of the case. The court has discretion to allow the parties to amend their statements of the case if one of the parties ceases to exist or to have a capacity to sue or if the disputed object is destroyed or materially changed.

I. General Criteria for Admissibility

187. The *general criteria* for admissibility are the capacity to sue; the capacity to act in proceedings; that the claim is characterized as legal; that the claimant has a genuine need to have the claim determined against the defendant; and that the issue is not res judicata or lis pendens. Further, a Norwegian court must have territorial jurisdiction on the matter and the claimant must be present at court hearings.

A. Both Parties Have the Capacity to Sue

188. All natural persons have the capacity to sue and to be sued (*partsevne*) (DA section 2-1). The capacity to sue and be sued for legal persons varies: full capacity, broad partial capacity, limited capacity or no capacity. Natural persons, the Norwegian State, municipalities, county authorities, limited liability companies, general partnership companies, limited partnership companies, cooperative societies, savings banks and foundations all have full capacity to sue. Further, estates in bankruptcy and estates of deceased persons under public administration and other organizations have full capacity when the law states so.

189. Partial and limited capacity is determined based on the organizational structure, formalized membership and the funds available. The more formalized the organizational structure is, the more formalized membership is and the more funds the organization has, the more likely it is that the organization will have a broad capacity to sue, and vice versa. For an organization with partial capacity, the capacity is limited to actions where the subject matter naturally falls within the purpose of the organization. For example, a sports association with a register of members paying membership fees, a board of directors, and assets in the form of bank accounts, a club house and equipment will have a broad capacity to sue. In the *Fosen* case HR-2021-1975-S, a Sami *siida*, a group of Sami people who herd nomadically their reindeer together, rather than its members, had a limited capacity to sue due to the collective nature of herding rights in traditional Sami culture. A neighbourhood association with a less formalized membership, only occasional board meetings and very limited assets has a limited capacity to sue. A Facebook group is not a sufficient organization to have limited capacity to sue, Rt. 2012 p. 901.

B. Both Parties Have the Capacity to Act in Proceedings

190. The capacity to act in proceedings includes the capacity to file the statement of the case and to act on one's own behalf in court proceedings (*prosessdyktighet*) (DA section 2-2). Persons lacking the capacity to act in proceedings must have a representative. The representative attends to all the rights and obligations of the party (DA section 2-3).

191. Persons aged 18 and above have the capacity to act in proceedings, unless they are not able to safeguard their own interests due to a lack of mental ability, either temporarily or permanently. The mental ability of a person depends on the person's ability to understand the case, not on a diagnosis of illness or developmental issues. A person with a moderate intellectual disability may be able to understand a simple case but lack the ability to understand a more complex case. Conversely, a person of a very high age, although in good general health, may lack the ability to understand a complex case. If the person does not have a guardian, the court must appoint a guardian *ad litem* (provisional guardian) for the party.

192. Minors and persons under guardianship have limited procedural capacity in issues on personal circumstances, as provided in statutory law. These include, *inter alia*, cases on mandatory care of children, cases related to rights of the patient in medical care and cases on compulsory care for persons with mental health disorders or substance abuse problems. In most cases, the custodial parents are the representatives of children (DA section 2-4). Children over the age of 15 have the right to receive notice of court hearings and to attend them. The guardian is the representative for persons of age under guardianship.

193. The representative of a legal person is the person who has the authority to accept service on behalf of the party (DA section 2-5), usually the chairperson of the board of the legal person (CJA section 191). The board may delegate the power to one of its members other than the chairperson. Government bodies abide by rules found in various statutes. The representative has the right to delegate the power to act as a representative to an employee or to a person associated with the legal person. Delegation must be in writing, and it may apply to an individual case or to a specific type of case.

194. For persons with a partial or limited capacity to sue, the board is the representative in court proceedings. If the organization lacks a board, the members act as the representatives together.

195. The party representative is not the party counsel. Legal counsel is not mandatory. In-house counsel may have delegation to act as a representative of the party or may be appointed as legal counsel. A person may not act as a representative and legal counsel simultaneously.

C. The Court Has Jurisdiction on the Claim

196. The court must have functional, subject matter and territorial jurisdiction to hear the case.[35] If Norwegian courts lack international jurisdiction or general courts lack jurisdiction, the case is dismissed. If Norwegian general courts have jurisdiction, then the case is transferred to the court having jurisdiction.

D. The Claim Is of a Legal Nature

197. Legal standing requires that the claim is of a legal character and that the claimant has 'a genuine need to have the claim determined against the defendant' (DA section 1-3). Admissibility of the case depends on a total assessment of the character of the claim, the relevance of the claim and the connection between the claim and the parties. Although one of the requirements is only partially fulfilled, the court may conclude that the claimant has legal standing.

35. The basis for jurisdiction is discussed in Part II *supra*.

198. First, the claim must be of a legal nature (*rettskrav*). The legal character is determined primarily on whether the issue at hand is regulated by law (i.e., by statutory law, case law or principles of law). The claim must have direct legal consequences for the legal rights and obligations of the claimant. The claimant may request that the court establish that the defendant is liable for the damage, but the claimant may not restrict the claim to cover only the issue of causality between an act and the associated damage, as causality does not have direct legal consequences. Membership in an association may be a legal claim if membership entails particular privileges or if exclusion could amount to discrimination. A father who was excluded from a sports association for repeated inappropriate and violent behaviour during his children's practices did not have a sufficient legal interest to render the exclusion a claim of legal nature (HR-2021-639-A). For example, membership in a yacht club is a legal claim if the yacht club operates a marina, membership is a requirement for a permanent spot at the marina, and there are in practice no alternatives to the marina.

199. The claim may either indicate a positive obligation or negate an obligation. For instance, a party may claim that he or she is not liable for the damage as long as the parties in the case have a genuine ongoing dispute on liability. The claim may be of either a declaratory nature or a claim for performance. The claimant may, for instance, choose to claim that the defendant is liable for the damage instead of claiming compensation for the damage. Negative claims and declaratory claims require that a ruling on the claim will provide clarification of the claimant's legal rights and obligations and must have a practical consequence for the claimant. Further, the prayer for relief must be precise and unambiguous. This requirement is heightened for claims for performance, as the claim must be enforceable.

200. A claim is legal only if it relates to a specific legal issue related to a specific set of facts. This definition excludes the *actio popularis* type of litigation, as a question of general interpretation of a law is not related to a specific set of facts. However, there are some exceptions to the rule to allow courts to rule on the validity of statutes when the claimant shows there is a particular need to do so.

E. The Claimant Has a Current and Genuine Need to Have the Claim Determined Against the Defendant

201. An action may only be brought on current issues. Past issues are subject to litigation only when brought within a reasonable period of time from the event and are contingent on the judgment having tangible impact for the claimant. In Rt. 2010 p. 897, an employee sued the employer for wrongful termination of employment two years after the termination occurred. The Supreme Court found that the issue of termination was raised unreasonably late and thus had lost its relevance. It held, however, that a claim for compensation for unlawful termination was still timely. Claims for future issues are subject to litigation only if the claimant has a pressing need for clarification of his or her rights. In claims for performance, the duty of the defendant must as a rule be due, or if the defendant has a duty to refrain from doing something or to endure something, the case is ripe when the defendant has acted in breach of this duty.

202. One may only initiate proceedings on one's own behalf. The court may make an exception when the claimant has a strong direct interest in the outcome, or, if an indefinite group of persons shares a collective right, an organization or an individual may bring an action on behalf of the group. The same is true if no individual holds the right individually, such as in the case of animal rights. An organization or an individual may bring an action claiming the owner of a factory must stop certain activities causing environmental pollution. In the *Climate* case HR-2020-2472-P, several environmental organizations had the right to sue the Norwegian Government for issuing oil and gas production licences. In the *Acer* case HR-2021-417-P, Nei til EU (No to EU) challenged a decision by the Norwegian Parliament regarding vesting power in ACER, the EU energy agency, on the grounds that it was made with simple, rather than qualified, majority. The Supreme Court found that the association had legal standing even if the decision as such did not have direct effects for it. An organization or association may only bring actions related to matters that fall within its purpose and scope (DA section 1-4).

203. Proceedings may only be initiated against the person having the right or the obligation in question or upon whose rights the claim will have a direct impact. Sometimes several persons must be sued concurrently (mandatory joinder of persons), as the claim will have a direct impact on the rights of several individuals. For example, a claim that shares were registered on the wrong person in the shareholder register of a limited liability company must be directed both against the company and against the person registered as the owner of the shares in question (Rt. 2002 p. 816).

204. The requirements for legal standing are discretionary and depend on a concrete assessment of the totality of the factors in the individual case. Small differences in the facts of the case may be decisive for whether the claimant has legal standing.

F. The Case Is Not Lis Pendens or Res Judicata

205. The case or particular claims may not be lis pendens or res judicata. A claim is lis pendens if it is brought between the same parties on the same subject matter as a pending case (DA section 18-1). This rule also applies to foreign proceedings, if the ruling will be final and enforceable in Norway. A case becomes lis pendens when the statement of claim or the application for conciliation proceedings arrives at the court or the Conciliation Board. Cases pending at dispute resolution boards, including consumer resolution boards and (administrative) tribunals, are also lis pendens. However, if the board or tribunal does not resolve the case within six months, a party has the right to start regular civil proceedings (DA section 18-2). Once the tribunal has decided the case, the parties may initiate court proceedings or review proceedings at court.

206. A claim is res judicata if a court has given a final ruling on the same issue between the same parties. The ruling becomes final when it can no longer be challenged by the use of ordinary legal remedies. If a claim is res judicata, the court dismisses it summarily (DA section 19-15 subsection 3).

207. The identity of the case covers both the parties and the subject matter. The parties are identical only if they are the same parties as in the first case. In a situation with a joinder of parties, lis pendens and res judicata exist only between the parties that are the same in both cases. For example, if A brings an action against C, and later A and B bring an action against C and D on the same issue, lis pendens exists only between A and C. Thus, A can sue D, and B can sue C and D in the new action.

208. Determination of the identity of the subject matter is contingent on a comprehensive assessment of five factors. These factors, discussed below, are:

(1) whether the claims have a similar character;
(2) whether the claims are based on the same legal rules or regulations;
(3) whether the claims are based on the same factual grounds;
(4) whether the justifications behind the rules are similar; and
(5) whether it is reasonable and natural to consider the situations identical.

209. First, claims of a similar character are considered identical. The similarity is determined based primarily on the criteria that must be fulfilled for the court to find for the claimant. A claim for ownership is different from a claim on right of use. A claim on unlawful termination of an employment contract is different from a claim on unlawful resignation from an employment contract, because resignation and termination are based on different types of considerations and are allowed under different circumstances. A claim for damages based on breach of contract is considered to be the same claim as a claim for damages based on the opposite party having presented wrongful information to a court, tribunal or arbitration tribunal in a case where the party claimed damages based on breach of contract. The objective of the claims is the same: to claim damages based on the same breach of the same contractual obligation (Rt. 1993 p. 10 A).

210. Second, the legal grounds for the claims must be similar in order for the cases to be identical. Damages related to direct economic loss have different legal grounds than damages related to non-economic harm, since they are regulated differently. However, both economic and non-economic damages for defamation are regulated by the same provision and are thus considered to have the same legal grounds.

211. Third, the factual grounds for the claims determine identity. The factual ground refers primarily to the cause of action, but the concepts are not identical since the factual grounds are more detailed whereas the cause of action is more abstract. If the same facts or the same incident serves as the origin of the case, the cases are identical. A leaky roof resulting in problems in the attic is identical to damage in the walls caused by the same leaky roof. However, damages arising from a deficient ventilation system are not considered the same issue as problems arising from the leaky roof, since they are based on different facts.

212. Fourth, the justification for the legal rules on which the claims are based determines identity. Defects in the formation of contracts due to duress or misrepresentation are considered to have the same justification, whereas rules on competency have a different justification. A claim on monetary compensation and a claim on termination arising from breach of contract are covered by the same justification and are thus considered to be identical.

213. Fifth, the court must consider what is reasonable and natural to consider as identical. The court must, *inter alia*, appraise if it is natural to require the claimant to include all possible grounds for defects in the formation of a contract at once, or to include all possible (including future) consequences of a breach of contract in one case. Many of the considerations depend on case law. For instance, strict liability is considered identical to a claim for damages on negligence. The decision is based on weighing and balancing arguments rather than on a strict rule.

214. Although the rules on lis pendens and res judicata are very similar, some differences remain. First, a ruling is also binding for third parties who would be bound on contractual grounds. For example, if the owner of a property sues the owner of a neighbouring property claiming a right of way, the ruling will be binding on a new owner of each property. Second, rulings on the merits have full power of res judicata, but the res judicata for other types of rulings may be limited. If the court dismisses an action because the claim is filed too early and is not ripe, the claimant may bring a new action once the claim is ripe.

215. Third, facts and circumstances occurring after the ruling are pronounced (*facta supervenientes*) could nullify the res judicata effect. For example, a court may pronounce a termination of a contract unlawful. After the ruling, a party to the contract may terminate it based on circumstances that have taken place after the ruling. In this case, res judicata does not hinder admissibility if the new case is based on the new termination. The Damage Claims Act section 3-8[36] and the Water Resources Act section 52[37] have special provisions reducing the force of res judicata for compensations for losses that could not have been foreseen at the time when the amount of compensation was determined. A party may file a new claim for compensation for the same injury if his or her health deteriorates considerably.[38]

---

36. *Lov om skadeerstatning* 1969 no. 26.
37. *Lov om vassdrag og grunnvann* 24 Nov. 2000 no. 82.
38. *See also* res judicata in Part IV Ch. 3, §1, I, C, 5, *infra*.

216. The identity of the case is determined in a similar manner in a number of other contexts as well, such as the end of a period of limitation or other time period; the ambit of the dispute (*ne ultra petita partum*); the difference between adding a new claim through joinder of cases and amendment of claims; and the difference between withdrawal of an action and limitation or withdrawal of a claim.

G. The Claimant Must Be Present at Court Hearings

217. If the claimant, or his or her legal counsel, is not present at court hearings, the court must dismiss the claim (DA sections 6-6 and 16-9). The requirement to be present is considered a criterion for admissibility. Sanctions for procedural irregularities are discussed in more detail in Chapter 3 *infra.*

II. Special Criteria for Admissibility

218. Special criteria for admissibility are limited to a specific category of cases. There are numerous special criteria for admissibility, many of them related only to administrative cases or to legal costs. The character of special criteria for admissibility depends on whether the criterion at hand serves primarily a private or public function. If the criterion serves primarily a private function, then it is a relative criterion, or one that can be rebutted by consent. If the function is primarily public, then the criterion is likely to be absolute. For example, the time limit to initiate proceedings against decisions made by the shareholders' meeting of a limited liability company is an absolute criterion, since it protects third parties, particularly investors and employees. Conversely, the time limit for initiating proceedings to contest termination of an employment contract is relative, as it primarily protects the private interest of the employer.

219. Since Norway does not have administrative courts, administrative law cases are considered civil cases. In administrative cases, the parties, particularly the private party, must usually first exhaust all administrative recourses against an administrative decision. Administrative recourses consist of administrative appeals boards, tribunals and quasi-courts. If the private party has not exhausted the administrative recourses, the case is not admissible in court.

220. In some types of cases, court proceedings must be initiated within a certain time limit. This applies, *inter alia*, to dismissal from employment and termination of tenancy agreements, appeals against tax assessments and appeals against rulings of the Insurance Court.

221. If the claimant is not domiciled in Norway or in an EEA country, the defendant has a right to demand that the claimant provides security for the potential liability of costs (DA section 20-11). The court has discretion to waive the requirement if providing security would deprive the claimant of the right of access to justice or if it would be disproportionate for other reasons. Such reasons include situations in which the claimant has sufficient property in Norway to cover the costs or in which the case is indispositive.

III. Procedural Questions Related to Admissibility

222. The court must investigate the requirements for admissibility on its own motion as soon as it receives the statement of claim (DA section 9-6 subsection 3). This investigation is done prima facie, based on the statement of claim. When necessary, the court must reassess whether the criteria for admissibility are fulfilled after the defendant has submitted the statement of defence. The defendant must substantiate a claim contesting the admissibility. The court may postpone the assessment of admissibility to a later stage of the proceedings if the assessment is strongly related to contested substantive issues. If it is clear that the claimant does not have any reasonable chance of success on the substantive issues, and an issue of admissibility is unclear, the court has the option to rule for the defendant without ruling on admissibility.

223. A party must raise an objection to a lacking relative admissibility criterion as soon as possible (DA section 9-6 subsection 2). If the defendant does not raise an objection in the statement of defence, he or she is considered to have consented to the proceedings.

224. Proceedings on admissibility are normally written, but the court must hold a hearing if it is required to achieve a fair process and sufficient argumentation. A court order on admissibility is subject to appeal.

IV. Pre-action Obligations

225. The parties have an obligation to attempt to resolve the case early through negotiation, mediation or other ADR proceedings (DA section 5-4). The claimant-to-be must notify the future defendant of the intention to initiate litigation and relevant evidence (DA sections 5-2 and 5-3).[39] Pre-action obligations are not formally a condition for admissibility, nor does the failure to fulfil the duties result in dismissal. Failure to meet the requirements only results in a duty to compensate the opposite party for any additional costs that occurred.

§3. Vexatious Litigation

226. A court may dismiss a case if it is beyond reasonable doubt that the case does not have a sensible purpose and it is brought by a person repeatedly bringing such cases in a vexatious manner (DA 2-2 subsection 5). In Rt. 1995 p. 1113, the

39. For more details, *see* Part IV Ch. 1, §1 *infra.*

Supreme Court found that a person initiating more than 100 unfounded cases lacked the capacity to act in proceedings. In Rt. 2000 p. 1379, the Supreme Court upheld a ruling to dismiss a case on damages due to unlawful surveillance and bugging, where the claimant could not render any concrete incident when the alleged activities would have taken place. The claims were deemed a result of paranoia.

227. Vexatious litigation may also consist of bringing a claim without a good reason when the opposite party accepts the claim at the earliest opportunity (DA section 20-4). A failure to fulfil pre-action duties may constitute bringing an action without good reason. Omissions of other kinds and any types of delaying tactics may be sanctioned when the omission is grossly negligent or the delaying tactic is obvious. The sanction is a liability for legal costs incurred by the omission or delay.

Chapter 2. Claims and Defences

§1. Definition

228. Norwegian law recognizes three types of claims: declaratory claims (*fastsettelsessøksmål*), claims for performance (*fullbyrdelsessøksmål*) and constitutive claims (*rettsendringssøksmål*). The first group of cases is characterized by the claimant requesting that the court establish whether a right or obligation exists, such as that the claimant has a property right to a specific object. In claims for performance, the claimant wants the court to establish that the defendant must do something, endure something or refrain from doing something. Constitutive claims are possible only if a specific provision provides for them. These actions are reserved for situations in which the court has the sole mandate to alter the legal status or rights of a person. Proclaiming a missing person dead is an example of an action for changing legal status. Constitutive claims are diminishing, as administrative agencies decide most of these matters.

§2. Distinctions

I. Elements of Actions

229. Norwegian law distinguishes between prayer for relief (*krav*) and the precise amount claimed (*påstand*). The prayer for relief indicates the disputed legal circumstance, such as ownership or liability for a damage. The identity of a claim is discretional and depends on the factual and legal conditions for invoking an outcome; the character of the outcome; and which interests the specific legal rule or principle protects. Changing the cause of action results in a change of the identity of the case.

230. The amount claimed relates to the particular outcome requested by the party, such as payment of a specific sum or identification of the specific object that the defendant must return. The terms *claim* and *prayer for relief* are sometimes used interchangeably, and the exact notion of a claim depends on the context and circumstances. The court is bound by the claim and the prayer for relief and may not go beyond them in its judgment (*ne ultra petita partum*).

231. The term 'cause of action' (*påstandsgrunnlag*) refers to the circumstances upon which a party bases its prayer for relief and claim. The circumstances that constitute the cause of action must directly fulfil the conditions set in a legal norm. For a claim on compensation for breach of contract, the cause of action could be the existence of a written contract that entails specific obligations for the parties and the act or omission constituting the breach of contract.

II. Main Claims and Ancillary Claims, Primary Claims and Subsidiary Claims

232. The distinction between the main claim and ancillary claims is contextual and discretional. Claims for interest, late payment interest, compensation for economic and non-economic loss, and so on are often ancillary to the main claim, but they are accumulated with the main claim in calculating the value of the case. Claims related to interest are an exception, as they are not included in the value of the claim unless the opposite party has explicitly disputed them. The court may split the case and hear ancillary claims in a separate hearing.

233. In addition to primary claims, the party may bring subsidiary claims. A party may, *inter alia*, have a primary prayer for relief of ownership and have a subsidiary prayer for relief of right to use. Parties may also present alternative remedies in addition to the primary remedy when alternative remedies are foreseen, such as delivery of substitute goods as the primary remedy and reduction in price as the alternative remedy.

III. Defence on the Merits and Procedural Defences

234. The defendant may present procedural and material defences. Procedural defences related to relative admissibility criteria must be presented as soon as possible (DA section 9-6).

235. Defences on the merit could result in the court ruling for the defendant, thus disapproving the claimant's claim. A defence on the merits can be based on legal or factual arguments or on both. Factual defences consist of counter-facts or denial of the factual basis of the claim.

§3. Joinder of Claims

I. Principles

236. Norwegian civil procedure is flexible for joinder of causes and joinder of parties (*kumulasjon*). Joinder is considered efficient and expedient, since it allows the parties and the court to consider the same evidence and the same legal argumentation at once. The risk of contradictory judgments is avoided when the claims are concentrated in one court and one case file. As joinder of cases could amount to increased complexity or delay, flexible rules are necessary to enable the court to weigh the benefits and drawbacks in each case.

237. Joinder is possible when Norwegian courts have international jurisdiction on all claims and the court has territorial jurisdiction for at least one of the claims. The claims must be heard pursuant to the same procedural rules and with the same composition of the panel of judges (DA section 15-1 subsection 1). Thus, a case on parental responsibility and a claim falling under the general procedural norms cannot be joined, since special procedural rules apply to parental responsibility cases.

238. A party wishing to introduce new causes of action or new parties after the proceedings have been initiated must do so in the form of a statement of claim or orally during a hearing (DA section 15-4). The new claims are exempted from proceedings at the Conciliation Board regardless of their character and value.

239. The court does not have the power to formally oppose joinder when all parties involved agree to joinder. Nonetheless, the court has discretion to split the proceedings with respect to one or some of the claims or issues in the case even in the case of joinder of claims. Thus, when the court considers joinder inappropriate, it will immediately split the cases. Additionally, the court has power to rule separately on one or more of the claims (DA section 16-1).

240. As an alternative to formal joinder of cases, the court can consolidate cases for a joint hearing (DA section 15-6). Consolidation differs from joinder, as the cases are not formally united and the parties or causes remain independent actions. Consolidation is an option when the parties in two or more cases are only partially overlapping, or when the causes of action are only partially overlapping.

II. Joinder of Causes

241. The claimant may bring several causes of action against the same defendant in the same action. The defendant may bring counterclaims against the claimant if the general conditions for joinder are fulfilled (DA section 15-1). There are no requirements that the causes of action be similar or arise from the same or similar circumstances.

242. Before closing the preparatory stage of proceedings, the parties may introduce new causes of action at their own discretion. The court has discretion to reject joinder by splitting the case if it finds that joinder is not appropriate. After the closing of the preparatory stage two weeks before the main hearing, new causes of action are subject to preclusion (DA section 9-16). [40] The rejected claims become a separate action, unless both parties agree to the amendment and the court does not consider joinder inappropriate. The court has the power to allow joinder by letting a party introduce a new cause of action even against the wishes of the opposite party, when the amendment could result in a significant loss for the party and the delay and other disadvantages are not significant.

243. The court applies the rules on joinder on its own motion. A ruling on joinder is subject to appeal. Joinder of causes is also possible in appellate proceedings,

40. Preclusion is discussed in more detail, §4 *infra*.

even if the new cause of action has not been subject to earlier proceedings (DA sections 15-1 and 29-4). Thus, the new cause of action is heard directly in appellate proceedings, skipping the first instance.

III. Joinder of Parties

244. Joinder of parties is possible when the general requirements for joinder of claims are fulfilled and no party objects (DA section 15-2). If a party objects, the court has discretion to allow joinder when the claims are so closely connected that joinder provides for efficient proceedings or avoids contradictory judgments. The norm is open and gives the court ample discretion.

245. Joinder of parties may be accomplished in the statement of claim, in the statement of defence or at a later stage of the proceedings. The claimant and the defendant have equal opportunities to draw in new parties. Joinder of parties is not subject to restrictions as to the relationship between the parties. If a party loses the capacity to sue, the opposite party may avoid dismissal of the case by introducing a new party with the capacity to sue. If the defendant is not the correct party for the current claim, the claimant may introduce the correct person as a new defendant. Introducing new parties is possible until the court has made a final ruling dismissing the case.[41]

246. Before the closing of the preparatory stage of proceedings, the parties may introduce new parties at their own discretion. After the closing of the preparatory stage, two weeks before the main hearing, introducing new parties is subject to preclusion (DA section 9-16).[42] However, the court may disallow joinder of parties if the claim against the third party would considerably delay or complicate the proceedings.

247. A ruling to reject or allow joinder of parties is subject to appeal. Joinder of parties is not allowed in appellate proceedings, unless a change of circumstances necessitates it. For example, if the claimant has claimed compensation for damages resulting from a falling roofing tile, and the defendant who owns the building sells the building during the proceedings, the claimant may require the new owner join the action.

248. A third party has the right to join the proceedings (*intervensjon*) when the general requirements for joinder are fulfilled and the third party intends to submit a claim that has the same cause of action as or is so closely connected to the original claim that the claims ought to be heard in the same proceedings (DA section 15-3). This rule is discretionary and allows the court to find the most appropriate ruling to achieve expedient and economic proceedings.

---

41. Rt. 2009 p. 655 and Rt. 2011 p. 1345.
42. *See* §4 *infra*.

249. Joinder of parties is mandatory if the claim has a direct impact on the rights of several individuals (*litis consortium necessarium, tvunget prosessfellesskap*). In Rt. 2002 p. 816, a claim that shares were registered on the wrong person in the shareholder register of a limited liability company had to be directed both against the company and against the person registered as the owner of the shares in question.

250. Each party is regarded as independent of the other parties (DA section 15-5). If one of the parties admits the claim partially, the admittance does not bind the other parties, or if one party appeals the ruling, the appeal is not binding for the other parties. Evidence is binding for all parties and must be given the same weight for all.

251. If the same ruling must be passed for all parties, the procedural steps taken by one party will be binding for the other parties. This applies in all cases with mandatory joinder and cases with an extended res judicata. The same is true for other situations in which goods or rights are indivisible or the ruling in the case must cover a range of legal subjects. For instance, the procedural steps taken by one co-owner are binding for all co-owners in disputes against third parties, and opening of bankruptcy proceedings is binding for all creditors.

§4. Amendment of Claims, Causes for Action and Legal Grounds for Claims

252. During the preparatory stage, parties may amend their claims for relief, the cause of action and legal grounds for the claims and may introduce new evidence without restrictions. The court has discretion to set a time limit for amending the prayer for relief, cause of action and introduction of time-consuming or expensive evidence. Setting a time limit is particularly useful to avoid that the parties request the court to appoint an expert or to inspect an object that cannot be brought to the courtroom shortly before the main hearing is scheduled to start.

253. Preclusion occurs at the conclusion of the preparatory stage, two weeks before the main hearing (DA section 9-16). At the conclusion of the preparatory stage, both parties file closing submissions. The closing submissions summarize the claims for relief, the specific amount claimed, the cause of action and the legal basis for the claims. They must also include a list of all evidence the party wishes to invoke (DA sections 9-10 and 21-6). This document forms the backbone of the main hearing, and any subsequent changes are subject to preclusion. The court has discretion to set a time limit for providing the information at an earlier stage of the proceedings (DA section 16-6).

254. Amendments resulting in a party dropping a cause of action, dropping or reducing the precise amount claimed or reducing a prayer for relief, or dropping arguments and evidence are admissible without any restrictions at any time. However, the court has discretion to sanction late amendments with a liability for costs if the party making the amendment could have been reasonably expected to make the amendment earlier.

255. Preclusion is dependent on the other party opposing the amendments; as a rule, the court does not enforce preclusion on its own motion. The rules for preclusion are discretionary, and the court must assess all relevant circumstances before it precludes amendments. In particular, it should aim to achieve expedient and cost-efficient proceedings. If an amendment results in a short delay but saves significant costs for the parties and the court or significantly improves the likelihood of the court arriving at the substantively correct outcome, the court should allow the amendment.

256. After the preparatory stage has been concluded, but before the main hearing has started, the party may make amendments that result from the closing submissions, or the opposite party agrees to the amendments. The court has discretion to allow amendments even when the other party disagrees provided that party making the amendment cannot be reproached for the amendment not having been made earlier, or that it would be unreasonable to refuse the amendment. Further grounds for amendment include cases in which there is no need for an adjournment of the main hearing and cases in which the opposite party has sufficient opportunity to defend his or her rights by presenting new arguments or evidence. The court must also allow an amendment if a refusal could lead to unreasonable loss for the party. The court may order the party requesting the amendment to be held liable for all extra costs incurred to the other party.

257. The court has the right to enforce preclusion on its own motion if the progress of the case or other important considerations suggest otherwise. Courts seldom enforce preclusion on their own motion, and, in practice, courts have taken a lenient stance towards preclusion.

258. Once the main hearing has been opened, the court may only allow changes if the party cannot be reproached for the late amendment, if the opposite party has sufficient opportunity to defend himself or herself, or if the refusal could lead to unreasonable loss.

259. Although the rule on amendments applies to the claim, prayer for relief, cause of action and evidence, it is applied differently for each category. In most situations, a change in the cause of action results in altering the identity of the action. Different causes of action usually make different facts and legal arguments relevant and require that the parties present different evidence. A modification of the prayer for relief is a less profound change. Allowing new evidence to be presented is likely to result in a slightly longer main hearing but not in a significant delay.

260. Courts are more inclined to reject an amendment of the claim when the amendment would result in changing the identity of the case than when it would not.

However, the decision depends on the extent to which the amendment requires the parties to present new evidence and new legal and factual arguments. The court must also assess whether the new claim and prayer for relief are res judicata in relation to the original claim, since rejection of the amendment could result in irretrievable loss when res judicata covers both.

261. Similarly, an amendment of the prayer for relief and claim could have a major or modest impact on the cause of action and legal argumentation in the case. The court assesses the potential drawbacks and benefits of allowing the evidence in making its decision. Courts seldom disallow amendments due to the fact that postponing the main hearing for a short period to enable the parties to prepare arguments and evidence for the amended case results in faster resolution than requiring the parties to file a new case.

262. Adding new evidence is the most common amendment made. Courts generally allow new evidence unless there is a particular reason not to do so. New evidence will seldom result in significant adjournment.

263. Legal arguments are not subject to preclusion. The parties are free to change their legal argumentation at any point. New legal arguments are admissible at all times, even if the amendment would result in an adjournment of the main hearing.

Chapter 3. Sanctions on Procedural Irregularities

§1. Formal Requirements

264. If a statement of claim, statement of defence or written submission is deficient, the court shall notify the party and exhort the party to rectify the deficiency within a given time limit (DA section 16-5). The court must indicate the nature of the deficiency and how it needs to be rectified. The court must also give information on the consequences of failure to rectify. For instance, if the claimant has indicated a one-person business as the defendant, the statement of claim must be rectified to the owner, as the one-person business lacks the capacity to sue, and the identity of the parties will not change, *see* HR-2019-2118 where the claimant had sued the Norwegian branch of a foreign company, which lacked capacity to be sued, to the foreign company itself, which had capacity to be sued. The court shall indicate that the owner of the business is the correct defendant. The court has a duty to give the parties guidance on procedural rules and routines to prevent and rectify errors (*prosessuell veiledning*) (DA section 11-5 subsection 1).

265. The court dismisses the statement of claim, statement of defence or written submission if the party does not rectify the deficiency within the time limit. Hence, if the claimant does not rectify the statement of claim, the case is dismissed and if the defendant does not rectify the statement of defence, the defendant is considered not to have submitted the statement, viz., he or she is considered to be unlawfully absent. If the party tries to rectify the deficiency but the rectification is not successful, the court has discretion to give new instructions and set a new time limit. However, a second rectification is only possible in special circumstances, such as for self-represented parties or when the issue to be rectified is complex. After rectification, the court disregards the original deficiency, and the case is treated as if it were initially correct.

266. A party who can be strongly reproached for a deficiency shall only be allowed to rectify it if there are weighty reasons for rectification (DA section 16-6). The threshold for considering a deficiency as strongly reproachable is high.

267. If the deficiency is not reparable, the court dismisses the case or rejects the brief. If the deficiency emanates from a circumstance for which the opposite party should bear the risk, the court shall not dismiss the case or reject the brief. For example, if a business entity wilfully evades the action by hiding information on its representatives or address, the court shall not reject the statement of claim although it lacks the said mandatory information.

§2. Time Limits

268. Norwegian civil procedural law operates with few pre-set time limits. Courts have discretion to set the length of most limits and to extend them if appropriate.

269. Omission of a procedural step within the time limit may constitute unlawful absence (*fravær*). Exceeding the time limit for payment of court fees; provision of a security pursuant to DA section 20-11; submission of the statement of defence; and submission of the statement of appeal or other recourse against a ruling amount to unlawful absence (DA section 16-7). The court has the power to order a party to take a procedural step within a time limit. If the party fails to do so, the court may sanction the failure to comply as an unlawful absence. The prerequisite for this sanctioning is that the step is of material importance for the opposite party or necessary for the proper conduct of the case. In complex litigation, the court may require the parties to provide a summary of facts, or to identify the key legal issues, before the end of the preparatory stage. Failure to comply will be considered unlawful absence.

270. Absence from the main or other hearing also constitutes unlawful absence (DA section 16-8). It is sufficient that either the party in person, its representative or the legal counsel is present. If the personal presence of a party is required at the hearing, the court will order the party to attend the hearing (DA section 23-1). The absence of the party will in these situations amounts to unlawful absence regardless of whether or not the legal counsel is present at the hearing. The presence of the legal counsel is only mandatory if the court has explicitly obliged the party to have representation pursuant to DA section 3-2. A party is considered to be absent should he or she leave the hearing without permission; refuse to discuss the subject matter of the hearing; be banned from addressing the court or expelled due to contempt of court; or attend without counsel despite an obligation to have counsel under DA section 3-2.

271. If the court has reason to believe that the party has a lawful reason to be absent or to fail to comply with a time limit, the court shall give the party an opportunity to apply for reinstatement. Illness and conditions outside the control of a party that make it impossible or disproportionately onerous to act in time or to be present at a court hearing constitute lawful absence (DA sections 16-12 and 13-4). Accidents, natural disasters, strikes affecting public transportation and breakdowns of telecommunication systems are typical examples of conditions amounting to lawful absence. The court has discretion to decide if a given situation falls under lawful absence.

272. For the claimant, the sanction for unlawful absence is dismissal of the case (DA section 16-9). Dismissal is possible only if the court has made the claimant aware of the consequence of absence or omissions. The ruling dismissing the case bars the party from commencing new proceedings on the same subject matter against the same defendant. However, when the case has been dismissed due to a failure to pay court fees or to provide a security pursuant to DA section 20-11, the claimant is allowed to bring a new action. To avoid dismissal, the claimant must apply for reinstatement.[43]

---

43. *See* Part IV Ch. 3 §2 *infra.*

273. For the defendant, the sanction for unlawful absence is a default judgment finding for the claimant (DA section 16-10). The claimant must request a default judgment in order for the court to have power to pass it.

274. The court has discretion to disallow a procedural step when allowing it would result in adjournment of a court hearing or in a significant delay (DA section 16-6 subsection 3). This applies in particular when the court has set a time limit for altering the claim, the prayer for relief, the cause of action or the legal grounds for the claims and a party invokes changes after the time limit has passed. It is not entirely clear whether the court has power to disallow amendments and additions in the absence of a time limit when the amendments would amount to significant delay and the benefits of such amendments are limited. The rule in DA section 16-6(3) is closely related to preclusion and extends the power of the court to disallow amendments so as to achieve timely and cost-efficient proceedings.

Part IV. Proceedings

Chapter 1. Overview of Norwegian Proceedings

275. Ordinary proceedings in the first instance consist of four stages: the pre-action stage, the pleadings stage, the preparatory stage and the main hearing. The DA introduced the pre-action stage; specifically, it introduced the concept of pre-action obligation and reduced the status of Conciliation Boards to quasi-courts. The Conciliation Boards function as first courts for small claims, although they have limited power to rule on the merits. Because they are not formal courts, proceedings before the Conciliation Boards are classified as pre-action proceedings. This text follows the national classification of proceedings.

276. The pre-action stage aims at narrowing and clarifying the issues and helping the parties settle the dispute. The pleadings stage consists of the filing of the statement of claim, the registration of the statement of claim and service of the summons. The preparatory stage starts when the summons is served on the defendant and may be written, oral or a combination of both written and oral elements. The concentrated main hearing is the centre stage of civil proceedings. First instance proceedings are visualized in Figure 2.

Figure 2 First Instance Civil Proceedings

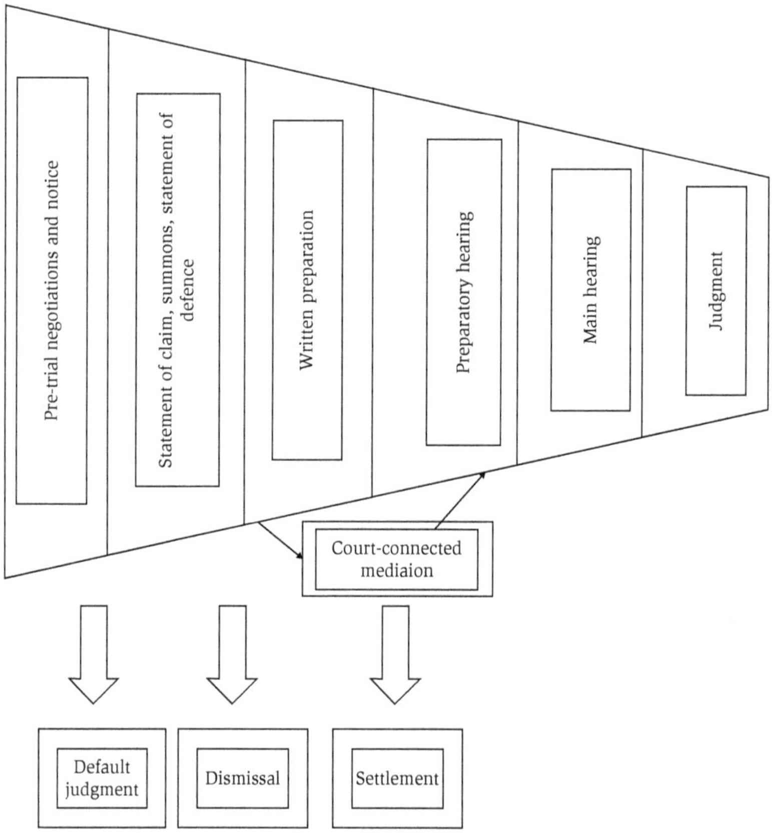

277. Proceedings in Courts of Appeal and the Supreme Court have the same structure as in District Courts. The proceedings consist of a pleadings stage, a preparatory stage and a main hearing. Written proceedings are more prevalent in appellate courts than in District Courts. Written proceedings consist of two stages: the pleadings stage and the written preparatory stage.

Chapter 2. Pretrial Proceedings

§1. Pre-action Obligations

278. Making courts a last resort for dispute resolution is a long-term policy in Norway. The multiple dispute resolution boards are the primary tool of achieving the goal. The DA is a further step in the strategy, as it mandates that the parties must attempt to solve the dispute, or at least parts of it, before beginning court proceedings. Additionally, DA requires the parties to exchange information and negotiate prior to bringing an action.

279. A party has the duty to give notice in writing to the person against whom the party intends to bring legal action (DA section 5-2). The notice shall include information about the claim, the cause of action and the legal basis for the claim and must indicate information about important documents and other evidence of which the opposite party may not be aware (DA section 5-3). The opposite party must respond to the notice within a reasonable timeframe. If the opposite party contests the claim completely or partly, he or she shall specify the basis for the contestation. If the opposite party has a counterclaim, the party must notify the opposite party of the counterclaim.

280. The parties have a duty to attempt to reach an amicable solution of the dispute before bringing legal action (DA section 5-4). Parties may engage in negotiation, out-of-court mediation or other dispute resolution processes to fulfil their duties. The parties have discretion to decide which method of dispute resolution is the most appropriate. Participation in dispute resolution does not have to be extensive; good faith participation in negotiation is sufficient. In some cases, the parties may discover early that negotiations will not be fruitful and proceed promptly to file a statement of claim.

281. The pretrial obligations are not formal criteria for admission: the sanction is limited to a duty to carry additional costs arising from the failure to fulfil the obligations. If the defendant admits a claim or parts of it immediately and the claimant has not fulfilled the pretrial obligations, the defendant will not be liable to compensate the claimant for the legal costs arising from the admitted claim.

§2. Proceedings at the Conciliation Board

I. The Functions and Aims of Conciliation Boards

282. The role of Conciliation Boards is to provide swift and inexpensive dispute resolution services through judgment or settlement. The Conciliation Boards function as a first court with limited jurisdiction. Most cases are disposed of with a default judgment or a judgment based on the defendant admitting the claim: the Conciliation Boards function as simplified proceedings for uncontested claims. The Conciliation Board has a mandate to facilitate settlement (conciliation, *forlik*). As proceedings are swift and the members of the Boards have no formal legal training and are only offered minimal training, the Conciliation Boards have a limited opportunity to actively promote settlement. Conciliation Boards have only limited power to issue rulings in disputed cases.

283. For claims of a primarily economic character for less than NOK 200,000 (approximately EUR 20,000), the Conciliation Board functions as the first instance, unless the case is exempted.[44] Conciliation Boards are not mentioned as courts in the CJA, but for small claims they are de facto courts, and their use is mandatory for cases falling under their jurisdiction. The proceeding before Conciliation Boards is regulated in DA Chapter 6. The remaining provisions are applicable to Conciliation Boards if and to the extent that they are appropriate considering their organization, goal and functions. The procedural rules are designed to accommodate self-represented parties.

II. Initiation of Proceedings

284. The claimant initiates proceedings at the Conciliation Board by filing an application for conciliation proceedings. In practice, the application for conciliation proceedings is a simplified statement of claim (DA section 6-3). The claim may be submitted in writing, or orally at the secretariat of the Conciliation Board. Professional creditors may register at the Norwegian National Collection Agency (*Statens innkrevingssentral*), a government organization specializing in debt collection for public organizations, in order to be able to file applications electronically.

285. The application for conciliations proceedings shall state:

- the name of the Conciliation Board;
- the names and addresses of the parties and, if applicable, the legal counsel and party representative;
- the claim that is being made and a prayer for relief which clearly states the result the claimant is requesting by way of judgment; and
- the cause of action, which must always contain a concise description of the facts upon which the claim is directly based.

286. Copies of documents upon which the claim is directly based shall be attached to the application. If the claimant claims compensation for cost incurred by debt collection, the request for payment pursuant to the Debt Collection Act section 10[45] must be attached.

44. Rules on the jurisdiction of Conciliation Boards are discussed *supra* Part II Ch. 1 §1, III.
45. *Inkassoloven* 1988 no. 26.

III. Initial Stage of the Proceeding, Service and Defence

287. When the application for conciliation proceedings arrives at the Conciliation Board, it is registered and the criteria for admissibility are checked by the staff. If all criteria for admissibility are not fulfilled, the case is dismissed, unless the error can be rectified. If rectification is possible, the secretariat requests that the claimant makes the necessary changes within a time limit. If the claimant does not rectify the application within the given time limit, the Board dismisses the case. In terms of jurisdiction, the case may be dismissed on the grounds that the Conciliation Board lacks functional jurisdiction. If the Conciliation Board lacks territorial jurisdiction, it may refer the case to the appropriate Conciliation Board (DA section 6-3). The court fee must be paid in advance for the case to be admissible.

288. The summons is served on the defendant together with an order to file a reply within a time limit (DA section 6-4). The limit is normally two weeks, but the Conciliation Board has discretion to set a longer or shorter time limit. The order to file a reply includes instructions on the mandatory contents of the reply and on the sanctions for failing to submit a reply. Conciliation Boards serve the summons by ordinary mail without a slip of receipt (CJA section 163 letter a). Thus, sometimes service is considered successful when the defendant does not actually receive notice of the proceedings, due to the summons being sent to the wrong address. The time of service is also unclear if no slip of receipt is used. The use of ordinary mail has been criticized, but the rule has not been abolished.

289. The reply shall indicate whether the defendant accepts or contests the claim and, if the defendant contests the claim, a brief account of the grounds of the contestation and any important documents supporting the contestation (DA section 6-4). The defendant must also state whether he or she objects to the jurisdiction of the Conciliation Board, as the Conciliation Boards have limited jurisdiction and limited capacity to decide cases. The reply may be filed in writing or orally at the secretariat.

IV. Written Stage of Proceedings

290. In most cases, the defendant does not file a reply. As a result, the Conciliation Board issues a default judgment, as long as the Board can find in the favour of the claimant fully or in the main (DA section 6-4 subsection 3). If there is reason to believe that the failure to file a reply is due to lawful absence, the Conciliation Board shall either set a new time limit or summon a hearing.

291. If the defendant admits the claim in the reply, the Conciliation Board issues a judgment finding for the claimant. The same applies when the defendant objects to the claim but the grounds for contestation are clearly without any prospect of success.

292. Conciliation Boards have authority to decide only simple cases. If the case is either factually or legally complex, or if hearing witnesses or experts is required, the Conciliation Board must terminate the proceedings (DA section 6-11). If the Conciliation Board deems that the parties may reach settlement in the case and the parties agree to the Conciliation Board hearing the case, a hearing may be held even if the case is complex.

293. The Conciliation Board must terminate the proceedings if one of the parties initiates proceedings at a tribunal or other dispute resolution board (e.g., a consumer dispute resolution board). The proceeding may be resumed once the other proceedings have ended.

294. There are no preparatory proceedings at the Conciliation Board, as the proceedings are intended for simple cases. The proceedings continue with a hearing, which shall be held within three months after the Conciliation Board received the application for conciliation proceedings (DA section 6-5). The Conciliation Board summons the parties to a hearing. The summons must be served on the parties at least two weeks before the hearing. The summons includes an invitation to submit copies of any new documents to the Conciliation Board and the opposite party. The parties shall submit the documents at least one week before the hearing. The summons also includes information that the party must give notice no later than one week before the hearing if he or she wishes to call witnesses or wishes to use a legal counsel or if the party has initiated proceedings in a tribunal or dispute resolution board.

295. Failure to provide information on documents and witnesses may result in adjournment of the hearing, and the party providing late notice may become responsible for the costs arising from the adjournment (DA section 6-8). If the evidence is of material importance and presenting it will not result in undue delay, the Conciliation Board has discretion to allow the evidence.

V. Attendance and Representation

296. The parties have a duty to attend the hearing in person if the hearing is held in the municipality where the party is domiciled or in the neighbouring municipality (DA section 6-6). Only lawful absence is a valid excuse. If the case concerns the business that which the party runs personally, the party may send one of the employees as a representative. Legal persons must send a representative as provided in statutory law. If the ordinary venue of the party is not in the same or a neighbouring municipality as the Conciliation Board hearing the case, the party may use a legal counsel or other representative.

297. Although representation in court is limited to licensed lawyers and advocates, the rules are more lenient for Conciliation Boards. Specifically, the party may also use:

- a provider of legal services who has a five-year master's degree in law, an auditor, another person who has limited right to provide limited legal services, or a person employed by a provider of legal services;
- a licensed debt collector;
- a spouse or domestic partner, a child or grandchild, a parent or grandparent, or a sibling;
- an employee or another person affiliated with the business undertaking that is a party; or
- another suitable person, with the approval of the Conciliation Board.

298. The Conciliation Board has a board of permanent representatives from which the parties can choose a member to act as counsel at the hearing. The members of the board of permanent representatives are citizens over the age of 25 with a good knowledge of Norwegian society and the Norwegian language. The municipality appoints the board of permanent representatives.

VI. The Hearing at the Conciliation Board

299. Hearings at Conciliation Boards are designed to be short and efficient. The usual length of a hearing is fifteen to thirty minutes. However, in rural areas, the hearing may be considerably longer, because the Board hears few cases and because the parties are willing to allow the Conciliation Board rule on their dispute even though the members of the Board lack legal training. If the case is not mature for judging after three hours and the parties have not reached settlement, a party can request that the proceedings be terminated (DA section 6-11 subsection 4). The hearing should take place within three months after the complaint is submitted (DA section 6-5). If the hearing has not taken place within three months of the service of the summons, a party may request that the proceedings be terminated. Hearings are open to the public.

300. At the beginning of the hearing, the parties present their claims and their views on the case and are allowed to respond to the presentation of the opposite party. Normally, the parties should primarily present the case themselves, even when they have a legal counsel. The Conciliation Board has the power to prohibit the legal counsel from speaking during the presentation of the case (DA section 6-8 subsection 2). The rationale for this approach is to facilitate settlement by letting the parties express their personal views in lieu of the legal version presented by their legal counsel.

301. Two tracks are available for the rest of the proceedings depending on whether the parties want the Conciliation Board to make a final ruling. If the parties do not want the Conciliation Board to rule on the claims, the Conciliation Board proceeds to quasi-court-connected mediation, a proceeding that mimics court-connected mediation (DA section 6-8 subsection 1). The Board is allowed to suggest solutions and express its views on the dispute. However, the Conciliation Board shall not have private meetings (caucuses) with the parties. In quasi-court connected mediation the Board has the power to bar the public from the hearing.[46]

302. If the parties have declared that the Conciliation Board is allowed to pass a final judgment or have not expressed their views on the issue, the proceedings are similar to those of the District Court (DA section 6-8 subsections 2–7). The Conciliation Board shall promote settlement between the parties. However, it may not suggest solutions or express its views. The Board may, *inter alia*, suggest that parties find a mutually agreeable solution, encourage negotiation or discuss the advantages of settlement, but it may not recommend a specific solution.

303. If the parties do not settle, the Conciliation Board may allow them to present evidence. The case may not be unduly delayed by the taking of the evidence. As the competence of Conciliation Boards is limited to factually and legally simple cases, and as proceedings should be swift and inexpensive, evidence is limited, particularly in urban areas. The parties shall present the documents they wish to use as evidence. The Board can reject evidence of which the party has not given notice at least one week in advance of the hearing. The need for extensive evidence is a hallmark of a case that is unsuitable for the Conciliation Board, and thus proceedings should be terminated in such cases. The hearing can only be adjourned if there is reason to believe that the case will be concluded by judgment or settlement at or before the new hearing. New essential evidence may qualify for the case to be adjourned, as may the wish of the parties to engage in negotiations.

304. The Conciliation Board cannot appoint experts, nor can it compel witnesses to appear or compel someone to disclose evidence. Hearing witnesses is dependent on the witness cooperating. Witnesses are not heard under oath; they are only encouraged to tell the truth.

VII. Conclusion of the Proceedings

305. The proceedings are concluded by settlement, judgment or termination.

306. If the claimant fails to attend the hearing, the Conciliation Board shall dismiss the case. If the defendant fails to attend, the Conciliation Board shall pronounce a default judgment. The condition for ruling on the case based on absence is that the Conciliation Board finds that the decision is not contrary to any public policy consideration. A default judgment is only possible if the Conciliation Board finds it can rule for the claimant in full or in the main. If the case cannot be decided based on absence, the case shall be adjourned, and the parties must be summoned to a new hearing. The party present at the hearing may demand that the proceedings be terminated (DA section 6-6 subsection 3).

46. The conduct of court-connected mediation is discussed in Part XI Ch. 5 *infra*.

307. If the parties reach an agreement, they may either withdraw the action or enter into an in-court settlement. An in-court settlement is included in the court records, and both parties and the members of the panel hearing the case sign the settlement agreement.[47]

308. If the parties do not oppose the option that the Conciliation Board rules on the case, the Board must assess its competence to judge the case on the merits to do so. The case must be both legally and factually fairly simple, and the parties must have presented sufficient evidence and arguments to give the Board a sound basis for a ruling (DA sections 6-8 and 6-10). If the case is not sufficiently simple or requires evidence not available to the Board or extensive legal arguments, then the Conciliation Board does not have an adequate basis for its ruling, and the case is discontinued.

309. All three members of the panel must agree that the basis is adequate for the Board to have the power to decide the case. If the members agree that the basis for the ruling is sufficient, then the Board shall ask the parties whether they consent to the Board deciding the case (DA sections 6-8 and 6-10). If both parties agree, the Conciliation Board may pass a judgment. If only one party agrees, then the Conciliation Board may pass a judgment only if the claim is primarily of an economic nature and the value of the claim is less than NOK 200,000. If the Conciliation Board receives permission to pass a judgment, it must give the parties an opportunity to give final statements before passing the judgment. In calculating the value of the claim, the sum the defendant has acknowledged is deduced from the sum the claimant has claimed (DA section 17-2).

310. The Conciliation Board must terminate the procedure on its own motion as soon as it finds the case is not sufficiently simple in terms of legal or factual issues or the evidence needed (DA section 6-11). If the parties have declared that they do not wish the Conciliation Board to pronounce a judgment, the case is terminated at the end of the hearing, unless the parties have reached settlement. The defendant may demand that the proceedings shall be terminated if the parties have initiated proceedings at a publicly approved dispute resolution board or tribunal. Further, the parties may request that the proceedings be terminated when the hearing has not been closed within three hours or when the proceedings at the Board have not been concluded within three months.

311. After the case has been terminated, the parties may proceed to use other dispute resolution mechanisms or to file a statement of claim at the District Court. The parties may bring the case before the Conciliation Board again after twelve months have elapsed or with the consent of the opposite party. If the proceedings have been terminated because a party has initiated proceedings before a publicly approved dispute resolution board or tribunal, the case may be brought to the Conciliation Board after the proceedings before the dispute resolution board have been concluded.

---

47. For more details on in-court settlements, *see* Part IV Ch. 3 §1, I, C, 7 *infra.*

VIII. Rulings

312. Rulings shall state the name of the Conciliation Board, the time and place the ruling was pronounced, the judge or the members of the panel making the ruling, the names of the parties and the reference number for the case (DA section 19-6). The ruling must be in writing and signed by all members of the panel. The ruling shall state whether it is unanimous. If there are dissenting votes, the ruling shall state who is in dissent and the issues to which the dissent relates.

313. A judgment on the merits is brief, but it must state the cause of action, the claims and prayers for relief, and the factors relevant to the Board's ruling in the case. The judgment must also state the provision in statutory law on which the outcome is based. This final requirement may be difficult, as the members of the panel are not lawyers and hence have a limited knowledge of law. The judgment is pronounced within one week of the closing of the hearing (DA section 6-12).

314. Other rulings, such as rulings to terminate the case, are given in the form of a decision. The Conciliation Board does not give grounds for the ruling, but it must state the provision on which the ruling is based.

IX. Costs

315. Compensation of costs for the Conciliation Board is limited to the court fee, legal assistance (limited to up to four times the court fee) and limited travel expenses (DA section 6-13). The court fee is 1.1 times the general court fee, which is NOK 1,223 as of 2022, that is 1,358 NOK (approximately EUR 140). Compensation for legal costs is limited to four times the court fee (4,892 NOK in 2022). Travel expenses are covered in full for parties who have an obligation to attend the hearing in person and to an amount up to a half court fee for others, such as witnesses. The claimant may also claim compensation for costs incurred in debt collection, but a claim for debt collection efforts reduces the compensation for legal assistance to one court fee.

X. Recourse Against the Ruling

316. The recourse against a ruling of the Conciliation Board is to instigate regular proceedings in the District Court under which the Conciliation Board is situated. A party that wants the District Court to review the judgment must file a simplified statement of claim within one month of the date the judgment was served on the party. The proceedings at the District Court are regular first instance proceedings, not appeal proceedings, despite the fact that the District Court is de facto the second court.

317. The recourse against a default judgment of the Conciliation Board is reinstatement (DA section 6-14 subsection 4). The rules on reinstatement are more lenient for Conciliation Boards than for regular courts because the case must be reinstated at the request of the defendant. The reason for this is that the summons is served by regular mail without a slip of receipt. Thus, the summons may have been served at the wrong address, in which case the defendant has not been aware of the proceedings for a valid reason. The decision to grant reinstatement is not subject to appeal. The defendant is only allowed reinstatement once during the proceedings. The defendant can choose to file for proceedings in the District Court instead of filing a request for reinstatement.

318. The recourse is an appeal only if the recourse is limited to rulings on costs and rulings to rectify or amend a judgment beyond what is permitted by DA sections 19-8 and 19-9.[48] The statement of appeal is made in simplified form, and the proceedings in the District Court are conducted according to the rules on appeals proceedings. The District Court rules on the merits of the issues subject to appeal.

319. Judgments of the Conciliation Board may be reopened by application to the District Court pursuant to the provisions of DA Chapter 31.

48. For the power of courts to amend rulings, *see* Part IV Ch. 3, §1, I, C, 6 *infra.*

Chapter 3. Proceedings in First Instance

§1. Adversarial Proceedings

I. Ordinary Proceedings

A. Statement of Claim

1. Statement of Claim

320. A civil action starts when the claimant files the statement of claim. The statement of claim shall state the following:

- the name of the court;
- the names and addresses of the parties, their representatives and legal counsel;
- the claim, including prayer for relief sought;
- the cause of action and legal grounds for the claim;
- a tentative list of evidence upon which the party relies;
- the grounds for the jurisdiction of the court if the jurisdiction of the court is not clear; and
- the claimant's view on how the proceedings in the case should be organized.

321. The statement of claim must be sufficiently detailed to identify and individualize the parties and the claim. The purpose of the statement of the claim is also to enable the court to manage the case. Based on the statement of claim (and statement of defence), the court assesses, *inter alia*, whether the claim shall be diverted to the small claims track, the extent and form of the preparatory stage, the prospective time frame of the case, the need for expert evidence, the prospects of settlement and whether court-connected mediation is appropriate. The parties have a right to influence the proceedings; the parties can jointly request that the proceedings are fully or partially written. The court is usually bound to follow a request for the District Court to hear the case in a panel of three judges. The court needs information on the parties' views in order to exercise case management.

322. The statement of claim must contain sufficient information related to jurisdiction to allow the court to determine whether it has jurisdiction. When the prayer for relief is non-pecuniary, the claimant must argue why the interest at stake is primarily non-economic or give information on the value of the object of dispute.

323. Furthermore, the statement of claim must be sufficiently detailed to enable the court to determine the identity of the case, to determine whether it is lis pendens, and to issue a default judgment. The defendant must be able to prepare a proper defence. However, the claimant must limit the information on the cause of action and legal grounds for the claim to an outline, leaving out details that are not necessary at the early stage of the proceedings. This rule aims at requiring the parties to identify the core legal and factual issues at the beginning of the proceedings, since overly detailed information could result in the core of the case being lost.

Similarly, the list of evidence is tentative and brief: it should be limited to an identification of the main evidence (documentary, real, witness, etc.) on which the claimant intends to rely and a description of which disputed fact(s) the claimant intends to prove with each specific piece of evidence.[49]

324. When a ruling from a Conciliation Board, a dispute resolution board or tribunal whose rulings are enforceable already exists in the matter, a simplified statement of claim suffices. The statement of claim must include the name of the court; the names and addresses of the parties, their representatives and legal counsel, if applicable; the ruling of the board or tribunal; and the amendment to the ruling that the party requests. Furthermore, the party must expressly request that the District Court review the ruling. The District Court obtains the ruling of the board, which serves as the primary source of information for determining the claims, prayers for relief, the cause of action and legal basis of the claims.

325. The statement of claim is filed either by mail or at the registry at the District Court. Members of the Bar Association are expected to use an electronic portal to file cases and documents. Self-represented parties can only use the portal to view their case, not the associated documents. The District Court registers the case on the day it is received, and the case becomes immediately lis pendens. The DA recognizes oral statements of claim; however, in practice, courts will strongly encourage the claimant to engage a legal counsel.

326. Self-represented parties must pay the court fee before initiating proceedings, while parties with representation may postpone payment until the end of the proceedings.[50] The court fee covers the proceedings in the first court, including the first day of the main hearing. The fee is five times the basic fee (the basic fee is NOK 1,223 as of 2022, so the total fee is NOK 6,115, or approximately EUR 5,610). When the main hearing lasts longer than one day, each additional day results in a fee of three basic fees per day. After five days, the daily fee increases to four times the basic fee. Hence, when the main hearing lasts for three days, the court fees amount to eleven times the basic fee and a hearing lasting seven days costs twenty-five times the basic fee. If the court dismisses the case or if the parties withdraw the action or settle no later than four weeks before the main hearing (i.e. no main hearing is held), the fee is reduced to twice the basic fee. Settlement later than four weeks before the main hearing results in a fee of 2.5 times the basic fee and settlement during the main hearing in the court fees being reduced by half (e.g., settlement during the second day of the main hearing results in court fees of four times the basic fee). Any excess fees paid in advance will be returned.

---

49. Anna Nylund, *Norwegian Civil Procedure – How to Make Fast Even Faster*, in *Ways of Implementation of the Right to Civil Proceedings Within a Reasonable Time* (Aurimas Brazdeikis, et al. eds, Vilinius Univ. Press 2016).
50. Court Fee Regulation s. 3-1, *Forskrift etter rettsgebyrloven* FOR-1983-02-15-86.

2. Notice

327. Once the court receives the statement of claim, it makes a prima facie assessment of it to ensure it fulfils the criteria for admissibility. If all criteria are fulfilled, the court issues the summons, which is served on the defendant. The court exhorts the defendant to give a statement of defence (reply) in writing within a time limit (DA section 9-3). In small claims cases and cases requiring swift proceedings, the court may exhort the defendant to reply at a court hearing. The time limit for the reply shall normally not be shorter than three weeks. In complex or cross-border cases, the time limit can be significantly longer. The court must indicate the sanctions for failure to submit an incomplete statement of claim and for failure to submit the statement of claim during the time limit.

328. The summons is served on the defendant. Service by post (CJA section 163a) is the usual method of service, either by using a receipt of service, which the defendant is obliged to sign and return to the court, or by sending a recorded delivery. If service by post is not appropriate or if it fails, a process server serves the letter. The District Sheriffs, enforcement officers and the chief inspector at police stations are process servers. District Courts may appoint deputy process servers from among police and enforcement officers. The process server serves the summons personally to the defendant or, if the defendant does not have capacity to act in the proceedings, to the lawful representative.

329. If the process server is unable to find the defendant, the summons may be served on a member of the household of the defendant. The member of the household must be of age and present at the domicile of the defendant. Children, parents and domestic partners are members of the household. The process server may also serve the summons to a tenant when the landlord is the recipient, and vice versa, when the tenant and the landlord live in the same building. At the place of employment or place of business, the process server may serve the summons to an employee or to the employer or the manager of an employee. If the defendant has a business, the summons may be served at the place of business; if there is no place for business, the summons may be served on a person of age at the last place of business. If the defendant has neither a domicile nor a workplace in Norway, and the process server does not find the defendant, the summons may be served at the current place of residence of the defendant on an adult member of the household of the defendant or to a member of the household of the host (CJA sections 168–171).

330. If the defendant or the legal counsel of the defendant is registered in the electronic portal established in a pilot project on electronic communication with courts, and the respective court is part of the pilot, service may be done through the portal. An electronic signature is needed to verify service (CJA section 197a).

331. If the defendant rejects the summons, the process server may deposit the summons at the nearest court office, post office or other appropriate place. When a person belonging to the household of the defendant or a person at the workplace of the defendant refuses to accept service, or when a suitable person is not found, the process server shall leave a written notification that the documents may be collected from the court office, post office or other appropriate place (CJA sections 175 and 176).

332. When service cannot be performed in any other way, the court may decide to post information about the summons and a notice indicating where the summons can be collected. A notification is also published in the Norwegian Public Advertiser and in one or more local newspapers at the last known residence of the defendant. A notification should also be left at the last known residence of the defendant (CJA section 181).

333. If a party has a legal counsel with an ordinary power of attorney, the service shall be addressed to the legal counsel (CJA section 193). Some documents, including a summons to appear in court, must be served on the party and may not be served on the legal counsel. Documents may be served directly to the legal counsel in a simplified manner (CJA section 179). Service to the counsel is done by regular postal service, and the legal counsel must return a slip of receipt.

334. Norway is a party to the Hague Convention on Civil Procedure (1 March 1954), the Hague Treaty on Service of Documents in Cases and Matters of Civil or Commercial Nature (15 November 1965), the Nordic Convention on Mutual Assistance in Judicial Matters (26 April 1974) and Protocol 1 on certain questions of jurisdiction, procedure and enforcement to the Lugano Convention. Service to Norwegian citizens is done through Norwegian Embassies (CJA section 180). Postal service is used if the country where service takes place is a party to the Nordic Convention, the Hague Convention of 1965 or the Lugano Convention, and the country accepts service by post. Otherwise, signatories to these Conventions accept direct contact between authorities. In other cases, service takes place through the central authorities or, if no Convention is applicable, through the Ministry of Justice. Norway also has some bilateral agreements on judicial cooperation, and some international treaties have rules on service of documents.

3. Summary Judgment

335. If a party obviously lacks legal standing, or if any of the other requirements for admissibility are lacking, the court must dismiss the case. If the requirement for admissibility can be corrected, the court must first exhort the party to correct the problem within a time limit set by the court. The court has discretion to determine the length of the time limit.

336. If the defendant does not file a statement of defence within the time limit and the claimant requests a default judgment, the court will issue a default judgment. A default judgment is contingent on there being no public policy issue requiring full proceedings and on the court being able to find in favour of the claimant in full or in the main. The facts must not appear to be clearly incorrect.

337. The court must find for the claimant if the defendant admits the claims (DA section 9-7). If the defendant admits some or parts of the claims, the court may postpone the ruling on the admitted claims. If the parties settle the claims, they may request that the court pass a judgment identical to the settlement. If the parties agree on or settle some, but not all, of the issues, the court may postpone the ruling of the claims on which the parties agree.

338. If it is evident that a claim cannot succeed either in full or in part, or if it is evident that the objections to the claim cannot succeed, the court may, upon the application of a party, determine the claim by judgment (DA section 9-8). The judgment is passed after simplified proceedings. Simplified proceedings may only be used if the case clearly lacks any reasonable prospect of success, viz., if it is manifestly ill-founded, *see* Rt. 2003 p. 301. This provision is applied with caution. It is particularly useful in cases in which the procedural issues related to the criteria for accessibility are unclear but the outcome of the substantive issues is clear. The court avoids spending resources on procedural issues by ruling on the merits.

339. The decision to have simplified proceedings is not subject to appeal in itself. However, the ruling on the merits taken in simplified proceedings is subject to appeal.

B. *Progress of Proceedings*

1. Introductory Hearing and Case Management

a. Goals of the Introductory Stage

340. The introductory, or preparatory, stage of civil proceedings starts when the court receives the statement of claim and ends two weeks before the main hearing.

341. The purpose of the preparatory stage is to ensure that the case is 'heard in a swift, cost effective and sound manner' (DA section 9-4). The goal of the preparatory stage is early settlement of the case and achievement of substantively correct results in expedient and cost-efficient proceedings through a concentrated, appropriate main hearing. Concentration is twofold. The main hearing is to be concentrated to a single session, preferably taking a single day rather than several consecutive days. The main hearing should be concentrated on the disputed core legal and factual issues.[51] Identification of the core disputed issues facilitates settlement, provides a fertile ground for the court to achieve the substantively correct result as to both facts and law and contributes to concentrated proceedings.

342. Two of the basic principles governing the preparatory stage are flexibility and cooperation. Flexibility provides tools for the court to tailor the proceedings to

51. Anna Nylund, *The Structure of Civil Proceedings – Convergence Through the Main Hearing Model?*, Civil Procedure Review 13–39 (2018) and Anna Nylund, *Case Management in a Comparative Perspective: Regulation, Principles and Practice*, 292 *Revista do Processo* 377–398 (2019).

each case. Judges have a duty to actively manage the case in order to expedite the proceedings while still providing for correct results.

343. Cooperation between the court and the parties is a prerequisite for tailoring the proceedings. The parties decide the scope and object of the proceedings, as they have the sole right to decide on the prayers for relief and to introduce the facts and the main legal arguments. The case-managing judge discusses the organization of the proceedings with the parties (usually their legal counsel) to achieve the most favourable design. The parties and the judge also cooperate to clarify the case and to identify the main legal and factual issues and the disputed facts and legal arguments.[52] In practice, judges and the parties discuss primarily procedural issues during the preparatory hearing.

b. Statement of Defence

344. The statement of claim must identify the case, the parties and their legal counsel and indicate whether the defendant accepts or contests the claims and whether the defendant objects on procedural grounds to the court dealing with the case (DA section 9-3). Additionally, the defendant shall state the precise claim, prayer for relief sought, the cause of action and the legal grounds upon which the claim and prayer for relief are based. The statement of defence must indicate which evidence will be invoked by presenting a tentative list of evidence. The statement of defence must communicate the defendant's view on how the court proceedings should be shaped. Once the court has the statement of the defence, it may start planning the conduct of the preparatory stage.

345. Any claims, including the particular prayer for relief, cause of action and the legal grounds for it must be stated in sufficient detail so as to allow the court to manage the case properly, including, *inter alia*, to assess whether the claim should be directed to the small claims track, whether court-connected mediation is appropriate and whether preparation should be written, oral or a mixture of both. However, the defendant should not present more details than necessary, so as to avoid frontloading the case and thus causing the main arguments to disappear in the details.

346. The judge must check that the statement of defence fulfils the requirements of the law. If the defendant admits all claims, the court finds for the claimant. If the defendant does not file a statement of defence, the court issues a default judgment at the request of the claimant. If the defences presented are manifestly ill-founded, the court may find for the claimant.

---

52. For further details, *see* Anna Nylund, *Preparatory Proceedings in Norway – Efficiency by Flexibility and Case Management*, in *Current Trends in Preparatory Proceedings* (Laura Ervo & Anna Nylund eds, 2016).

c. Oral and Written Forms of Preparation

347. The case management hearing (*planmøte*) constitutes the core of the preparatory stage. The hearing should be conducted as a remote hearing in the form of a conference call with the judge and the legal counsel attending. However, the judge has discretion to extend the preparatory stage and to choose between written and oral preparatory proceedings or to choose a mix of both. Written proceedings are less expensive and are therefore preferred.

348. The case management hearing is formally a court hearing (*rettsmøte*). However, court hearings entail several obligations for the court, such as to document the meeting and to ensure the presence of the parties, and the public normally has access to the hearing. A court hearing takes place either in the courtroom or as a remote hearing where both parties are present on the telephone or through video link. Alternatively, one party may be present in the courtroom while the other is present via telephone or video link. If the judge only calls to schedule a meeting or to address some other purely technical question, then the telephone call is not a hearing. Other types of *ex parte* communication are not allowed. Because preparatory hearings conducted as remote hearings are not open to the public and most case management hearings are conducted remotely, case management hearings do not fulfil the criterion of a public hearing in practice.

349. During the case management hearing the judge and the legal counsel discuss, *inter alia,* whether court-connected mediation is appropriate and the schedule and conduct of the main hearing, whereas substantive matters receive little attention. On average, the preparatory hearings last approximately one hour in total.

350. Parties with legal counsel are usually not summoned to attend preparatory hearings. The party should be available via telephone on short notice to ease discussion between the party and the counsel. The party may wish to drop or amend a claim or to settle the case fully or partially, either during or after the preparatory hearing. Thus, communication between the party and the counsel may be necessary.

351. The court can schedule a preparatory hearing which the parties attend, for instance, to hear a procedural issue (e.g., to determine whether the court has territorial jurisdiction). A full preparatory hearing may also be needed to prepare the main hearing in a highly complex or extensive case.

d. Measures During the Introductory Stage and Case Management

352. Norwegian courts have five main methods of achieving early resolution and preparing a concentrated main hearing. These are (procedural) case management, procedural guidance, clarification, judicial guidance and promotion of settlements.

353. The judge in charge of preparing the case must be involved in active procedural case management (*aktiv sakstyring*) so as to ensure timely and appropriate proceedings (DA section 11-6). Time limits are a central tool to enhance clarity and expediency. The judge discusses the following issues as part of case management (DA section 9-4):

- whether court-connected mediation[53] and judicial settlement efforts should be attempted;[54]
- whether the case should be heard pursuant to special provisions (e.g., as a class action);
- whether a preparatory hearing should be held and whether it could be appropriate to rule on the case following such a hearing;
- whether the parties shall make written submissions and whether these shall form part of the basis for ruling on the case;
- whether the proceedings in the case should be split;
- how evidence should be presented, secured or produced and the use of expert witnesses;
- whether lay judges or expert judges should participate in deciding the case;
- whether the parties shall submit closing statements;
- scheduling of the main hearing (i.e., dates and estimated duration of the hearing); and
- other issues of importance.

354. The judge has discretion to tailor the proceedings to the case in cooperation with the parties. The statement of claim and statement of defence serve as starting points for case management. The judge shall make a plan for the proceedings after having consulted with the parties by telephone, in writing or even in person. The judge can later amend the plan after having heard the parties' views.

355. One of the goals of the preparatory stage is to make a plan for the main hearing. The judge must plan for the main hearing in consultation with the parties. A timetable should be drafted to set the approximate times for presentation of the case, testimony, hearing of witnesses and experts, discussion of written evidence and closing arguments. The order of the witnesses should be decided in addition to the approximate duration of the hearing of each witness. The parties may opt to set time limits for the presentation of cases and closing arguments. The parties submit their suggestions for the timetable with the written closing submissions.

356. Second, the court may provide the parties with procedural guidance to prevent errors and to enable the parties to attend to their interests in the case (DA section 11-5 subsection 1). The court must provide self-represented parties in particular with sufficient information on procedural rules and consequences of non-compliance with these rules and court orders. Furthermore, the court must inform the parties about local practices when appropriate. If there are considerable differences in power between the parties, the court should, to some extent, try to level the playing field by giving more guidance to the weaker party. Guidance does not mean

53. For further details on court-connected mediation, *see* Part XI Ch. 5 *infra.*
54. For further details on judicial settlement efforts, *see* Part IV Ch. 3 §1, I, B, 1, f *infra.*

that the court can give advice to the parties on which procedural steps or position they should take. However, the court may ask whether a party has evidence to prove a claim, thus inducing the party to present new evidence. The proceedings are party-initiated, and the parties determine which claims, defences, contentions and evidence they provide.

357. Third, the judge has a duty to clarify issues including, among others, the specific claims, prayers for relief the parties pursue, the cause of action and the legal argumentation on which the claims are based and the evidence the parties intend to present (DA section 11-5 subsections 2-5). Clarification refers to the judge addressing incomplete or unclear claims and arguments. For instance, when a party alludes to a fact or argument without making clear whether the party invokes the fact or argument, the judge must ask questions for clarification. Similarly, the judge must intervene when a party in a tort case addresses negligence but is silent on causation. The rationale for this is to make parties aware of misunderstandings or errors at an early stage. Moreover, early identification of key disputed issues is an incentive for the parties to make adjustments and modifications to claims, the cause of action, legal grounds for claims and evidence at an early stage well in advance of the main hearing.

358. The 2008 reform aimed at extending clarification to include identification of core disputed factual and legal issues to define and narrow the ambit of the dispute. By separating disputed legal and factual matters from undisputed matters and central issues from peripheral, or even irrelevant, matters, the court proceedings, in particular the main hearing, become more concentrated in time and scope. The parties can thus focus on presenting evidence related to core disputed facts and on the legal arguments related to the main disputed legal aspects of the case while spending less time on marginal issues. Concentrating the case to the main issues gives the court a better basis for reaching a sound conclusion, since material of limited relevance is not a source of distraction. Identification of the core of the case provides a sound basis for procedural case management, since the court has a good basis for tailoring the proceedings and assessing the suitability of measures available.[55] In practice, the reform has been relatively unsuccessful, which can be attributed partly to the short duration of case management hearings and that judges limit their scope primarily to procedural aspects of the case.

359. Identification of the essential disputed issues also serves as a foundation for rejecting irrelevant and disproportionate evidence (i.e., evidence that does not appreciably strengthen the case of the party or evidence that is not proportionate with the case) (DA sections 21-7 and 21-8). Proportionate and relevant evidence saves both time and costs for the parties and the court.

360. However, the DA does not clearly mandate the court to actively assist the parties in identifying the core disputed issues. Rather, it tacitly assumes the parties are able to do so. The case management hearing concentrates on procedural issues,

55. *See* Nylund (2019).

not substantive law or facts. Hence, the parties are sometimes able to pinpoint the key issues only during – or sometimes even after – the main hearing.

361. Fourth, the court has discretion to exercise judicial guidance (*materiell veiledning*), which refers to the court giving the parties hints and feedback[56] to ensure that the claims, cause of action and legal grounds for the claims are presented as intended by the parties and to ensure that the parties have not unintentionally omitted something or claimed something other than they intended. The court has only a right, not a duty, to provide judicial guidance. When giving guidance, the court must refrain from actions that may interfere with its impartiality. The balance between giving enough guidance and ensuring impartiality may sometimes be difficult to strike. The tone of voice or the choice of wording of a question could be decisive in whether or not the court is impartial.

362. Several factors influence whether the court should provide judicial guidance and how invasive the guidance should and can be. Judicial guidance is more acceptable in the early phases of the preparatory stage than during the main hearing. Self-represented parties often need information on legal rules, whereas the legal counsels are expected to provide their clients with sufficient expertise. The subject matter is also important: a more invasive approach is needed in cases where mandatory rules are applicable. In certain consumer law cases, the Court of Justice of the European Union (CJEU) case law mandates national courts to apply EU law on their own motion, which entails an obligation to provide judicial guidance.[57] The same applies to cases concerning rights derived from the European Convention on Human Rights.

363. In indispositive cases, the court has a duty to ensure that the outcome is correct (DA section 11-4). The court also has a duty to ensure that the relevant public policy considerations, circumstances and evidence are discussed. Thus, the court has a duty to provide judicial guidance when it considers it necessary to do so in order to achieve these goals.

364. Clarification, identification of the core disputed issues and judicial guidance are often most easily done during a court hearing, either a remote or a preparatory hearing at the courthouse. When both parties have a legal counsel, clarification can be done in written proceedings. Self-represented parties will more often benefit from a preparatory hearing, as will cases with many or complex issues in need of clarification.

365. Fifth, the judge must assess whether promoting settlement is appropriate (DA section 8-1). The judge may, *inter alia*, encourage the parties to use mediation and other alternative means of dispute resolution before they file the case. Settlement is a goal in itself. Settlement may be a bi-product of clarification, as a result

56. This is similar to the concept of *die materielle Prozessleitung* in German law. *See also* Fredriksen and Strandberg (2019).
57. *See* Fredriksen and Strandberg (2019).

of which the parties perceive the gap between their positions as narrower than they did previously and comprehend the advantages of settling the case. The court can encourage the parties to negotiate or divert the case to court-connected mediation, or the case-managing judge or the presiding judge can promote settlement. Promoting settlement often necessitates a hearing in which the judge can pinpoint the main advantages of settlement, the disadvantages of continuing the proceedings, and the nature and size of the gap between the parties' positions.[58]

366. Although the court has five main methods for preparing the case, the DA sanctions directly only for the failure to provide procedural case management. The chief judge has a duty to ensure that the judges comply with the duty to provide active case management (DA section 11-7). In the event that the judge responsible for case management fails to fulfil his or her duties, a party can demand that the chief judge intervenes. The chief judge shall transfer the case to another judge or take over the case him- or herself. If the chief judge is the case-managing judge or is disqualified for other reasons, a superior court rules on case management.

367. If the court decides to have a preparatory hearing, it has the power to give a ruling on the merits after the hearing, provided that it has a solid basis for its ruling and the parties have consented (DA section 9-5 subsection 4). The parties must have had a sufficient opportunity to present evidence when relevant. If a preparatory hearing has been held, the court may have sufficient information to decide the case. Deciding the case during the preparatory hearing occurs mainly in simple cases and cases that became simple after partial settlement or successful clarification.

368. The preparatory stage closes two weeks before the main hearing (DA section 9-10). The parties file closing submissions in which the case is 'cemented' for the main hearing. Preclusion occurs at the closing of the preparatory stage. Amendment of the cause of action, claims for relief, ground for the claims or evidence requires the consent of the opposite party or the court.[59]

e. Closing Submissions, Summaries and Briefs

369. The parties must submit written closing submissions at the end of the preparatory stage, two weeks before the main hearing, unless the court decides otherwise. The closing submissions must outline the claims of the parties, including the relief sought, cause of action, the legal rules invoked and which pieces of evidence the party will present (DA section 9-10). The closing statement should not exceed one page. In complex cases, the closing submission should not exceed two pages. The statements form the basis for the main hearing. They set the legal and factual limits of the case and define the dispute. The closing submissions can be very brief, consisting primarily of keywords briefly stating the main points. The closing submissions help the parties and the court prepare the main hearing by informing them

58. For further details on promoting settlements, *see* Part IV Ch. 3 §1, I, B, 1, f *infra*.
59. For further details on preclusion, *see* Part III Ch. 2 §4 *supra*.

of which claims and defences will be evoked, which factual and legal questions are disputed, and which pieces of evidence will be presented. After the time limit for the closing submissions has passed, the parties may amend their submissions and offer new evidence when the amendments ensue from the closing submissions of the opposite party. Other amendments are allowed unless the other party or the court opposes them.[60] A tentative schedule for the main hearing should be attached to the closing submissions.

370. In complex cases, the court has discretion to set a time limit for providing the information earlier than two weeks before the main hearing. After the first time limit has elapsed, the parties make changes induced by the submissions of the opposite party and file final closing submissions two weeks before the main hearing.

371. The closing submissions combined with the two-week period between the end of the preparatory stage and the main hearing are among the main tools available to combat problems of the parties amending the claims, prayers of relief, cause of action and legal grounds for the claims throughout the proceedings in the District Court. The closing submissions allow the parties to prepare the main hearing in an efficient way. At the same time, the period is a procedural void between the preparatory stage and the main hearing stage of the proceedings. The closing of the preparatory stage is closely connected with preclusion.

372. In complex cases, the court may order the claimant to submit brief chronological or other systematic summaries of the facts of the case (DA section 9-9 subsection 4). To avoid unnecessary costs, this opportunity is limited to cases with complex facts. The defendant must submit a reply stating which parts of the summary of facts are accepted and which parts are contested. The defendant must give a brief account of the contested facts. The court may encourage the parties to cooperate by making a single summary of the facts, in which disputed facts are clearly labelled and provided in two different versions.

373. The summary of facts helps to cement the main disputed and undisputed facts of the case. Once the main facts are presented in a systematic manner, the undisputed facts of the case are set. The summary of facts gives the parties and the court the opportunity to evaluate whether the disputed facts are essential or incidental to the case and what evidence is needed to prove the disputed facts. The court and the parties may also compare the facts with the claims and the legal argumentation: Are the claims appropriate for the cause of action, or should they be adjusted or even dropped? Does the argumentation of the parties fit the cause of action and the claims?

374. If there are many pieces of written evidence, the court may request that the parties provide these in a booklet with consecutive numbering. This makes it easy to find a given document referred to by one party during the main hearing.

---

60. *See* Part III Ch. 2 §4 *supra.*

375. In particularly complex cases, the court may order the parties to provide a brief on a specific issue. If the legal question is complex, the parties can be ordered to provide an overview of preparatory works, case law and legal literature on the topic. In a case with complex technical details, the parties can be ordered to provide an overview of these details to help the court understand the case. In addition, the material provided can be actively used in the main hearing. The parties can refer to the material, knowing that the opposite party and the court have access to the same documents. The documents are usually numbered sequentially, helping the parties and the court identify them easily.

f. Judicial Settlement Efforts

376. The judge has a duty to consider the possibility of a full or partial settlement at each stage of the proceedings (DA section 8-1). If the court considers settlement possible, it must promote settlement (*ordinær mekling*) during the preparatory hearing, during the main hearing or in its other contact with the parties. The court may engage in promoting settlement at more than one stage of the proceedings but may not exert pressure on the parties to settle. The efforts to find settlement may be limited to part of a claim or some of several claims. The court should not promote settlement if the nature of the case or other circumstances, such as the relative inequality between the parties or mandatory rules protecting the weaker party, suggest otherwise.

377. In its settlement efforts, the court may, *inter alia*, pinpoint the common ground, facilitate negotiations for settlement, point out the advantages of settlement vis-à-vis continuing litigation and suggest the parties consider settlement. The judge can emphasize the benefits of a settlement or stress the risks of the court ruling on the main issues. However, the judge must refrain from actions endangering impartiality. The court may not hold separate meetings (private meetings, caucuses) with the parties, present proposals for a solution, offer advice or express points of view that could impair its impartiality. The court also may not receive information that cannot be communicated to all parties involved (DA section 8-2). However, the court may point out the size of the gap between the parties' claims relative to the size of the claims or relative to the cost and duration of court proceedings. It may also suggest that the parties consider certain types of solutions, including solutions that the court could not include in a ruling. For instance, in an employment dispute, the court may suggest that the employer should write a letter of recommendation for the former employee as part of the settlement agreement. The judge or panel of judges promoting settlement shall hear the case if the parties do not reach settlement. Hence, the impartiality of the judge is paramount when promoting settlement. When intensive methods to promote settlement are called for, the judge may suggest that the case be transferred to court-connected mediation.

378. The outcome of judicial settlement efforts may be settlement, partial settlement or no settlement. If the case is not settled, or the parties reach a partial settlement, regular court proceedings continue on the issues that are not subject to settlement.

379. If the parties reach full or partial settlement, they may ask the court to enter the settlement into the court records as an in-court settlement (*rettsforlik*) (DA section 19-11). The judge may help the parties with the wording of the settlement. The court must ensure that the settlement states precisely what the parties have agreed upon and that the settlement is not contrary to public policy considerations. The settlement agreement must fix time limits for compliance in order for it to be enforceable. When the settlement is entered into court records, it becomes an in-court settlement, which is binding and enforceable as a judgment. If the settlement agreement does not include provisions on the allocation of the costs, the court then rules on the costs at the request of a party. An in-court settlement is not subject to appeal. A party may bring an action to declare the settlement invalid, or to amend it, pursuant to the rules for invalidity and amendment of contracts. The action must be brought at a District Court within six months of the date the party became aware of or a party acting diligently ought to have become aware of the alleged grounds for invalidity. The action cannot be brought more than ten years after the settlement was finalized (DA section 19-12).[61]

380. In-court settlements are not mandatory. If the parties chose not to register the settlement in the court records, the settlement is binding as a contract and subject to rules regarding contracts. The parties are then considered to have withdrawn the action or claims concerned.

381. The content of the settlement and the role of the judge have been discussed vis-à-vis whether the judge can contribute to a settlement that provides remedies that would not be available in a court ruling. Naturally, the content of the settlement does have to be identical to the probable outcome if the case were decided by the court. Rather, the disputed issue is how much the settlement can depart from the law before the judge must withdraw from the case, tell the parties that the negotiated outcome is not in accordance with the law or reject the possibility to register the settlement as an in-court settlement. Different views on this issue have been expressed; most commentators are quite liberal but emphasize that public policy considerations and the protection of the weaker party constitute restrictions.

2. Written Proceedings

382. There are several grounds for concluding the case in purely written proceedings. A default judgment can be given against a defendant who does not file a statement of defence or who does not file a brief when the court has requested one. The court may dismiss the case if the claimant does not file a brief when the court has requested one.

383. If the case is dismissed on procedural grounds, usually due to lacking one or several criteria for admissibility, proceedings are, as a rule, written (DA section

61. For further details on challenge of in-court settlements, *see* Part IV Ch. 4 §3 *infra*.

9-6 subsection 4). A hearing is necessary only if the right to fair and reasonable proceedings requires it. The same rule applies to simplified proceedings in cases in which it is evident that the claim cannot succeed or that the objections to the claim cannot succeed (DA section 9-8).

384. If the parties settle, oral proceedings are not necessary (DA section 9-7). The parties may either withdraw the action or request that the court establish the settlement as an in-court settlement. An in-court settlement is binding and enforceable in the same manner as a judgment.

385. The parties may further agree on written proceedings with the consent of the court. The parties may also agree to have partially written proceedings, in which the court rules on some issues based on written material only (DA section 9-9 subsection 2). The court may give its consent to fully or partially written proceedings only if they are more efficient than oral proceedings. Fully and partially written proceedings based on the agreement of the parties are very rare in practice.

3. Trial

a. Principles of the Main Hearing

386. The principles of a fair trial and proper conduct of the case are central to the main hearing. The court is responsible for gaining an adequate and satisfactory basis for its ruling. The proceedings should be proportionate and balance the importance of the case with the resources the parties and the court expend on it.

387. The main hearing adheres to the principles of concentration, orality, and immediacy. Concentration refers both to conduct of the main hearing in a single session and to concentration of the issues discussed to core disputed issues. During the COVID-19 pandemic lockdowns, main hearings have been conducted remotely, either with the judge and the parties participating via video link or partly remotely with the judge and the parties present at the court, and all or some witnesses and the audience gaining access via a video link.[62]

388. The main hearing is conducted over one day or two or more consecutive days. In large cases, the hearing is scheduled four days a week. Sometimes, the court decides to adjourn the hearing for one day to enable the legal counsel to prepare their final submissions.

389. Concentration of issues refers to the allocation of time between different issues. Central issues should receive more time than peripheral ones, complex issues should receive more time than easy ones, and undisputed and irrelevant issues should not be discussed unless strictly necessary. Further, the court should avoid unnecessary repetition and overlaps (DA section 9-13). The court may set timeframes for hearing witnesses or party presentations and is responsible for enforcing

62. Nylund, Anna, *Covid-19 and Norwegian Civil Justice*. Eleven 2021.

the timeframes. The quality of the preparatory stage is an essential factor for successful concentration of issues. However, in practice, too little time is generally devoted to the identification of core disputed issues to allow for concentration of the main hearing. Inadequate preparation results in late amendments and excessive time spent on peripheral issues.

390. The main hearing is independent of the earlier stages. In the main hearing, the parties and their counsel must repeat the essence of the case and state their claims, including the prayer for relief, the cause of action and the legal grounds for the claim. The judge hearing the case in the main hearing may or may not be the judge who managed the case during the preparatory stage.

391. Proceedings are strictly oral and immediate: parties may not refer to written materials that they have provided earlier but must present them orally to the court. Parties may not allude to what they have said during a preparatory hearing. All relevant information must be presented in the main hearing.

392. Parties, their counsel, experts, and witnesses may not read from a prepared manuscript. However, they may use notes or other supporting documents as an aid for recounting facts and details and to provide an outline for their oral arguments or presentations. The level of detail allowed in such documents depends on the purpose and content of the presentation: in general, the more complex and detailed is the necessary information, the less the court will restrict the use of notes. Information in briefs and other written documents must be stated orally (DA section 9-14). A witness who uses notes must state when, for whom, by whom, and for what purpose the notes were prepared (DA section 24-9). The notes of the witness are not part of the case documents and may not be used as evidence in the case (DA section 9-14).

393. Written evidence must be presented orally; that is, the parties must read the relevant passages of the document, such as (parts of) the contract clause in dispute. With the consent of the court, the parties can agree that part of the written evidence be presented in writing only.

394. Extensive expert reports can be exempted from oral presentation when the written format is deemed more appropriate due to the content of the report (e.g., complex technical data). However, the expert must still appear in court for oral examination.

b. Determining the Trial Date

395. The trial, or main hearing, shall be held within six months of filing of the case (DA section 9-4). Not all cases are disposed of within six months, due to court congestion, holidays, illness and case complexity. The average time for processing cases is approximately six months; thus, courts usually meet the set time limit. The managing judge has the duty to set dates as early as possible to enable a swift proceeding.

396. The court has an obligation to make a plan for the proceedings in the initial phase of the preparatory stage. The court must schedule the date for the main hearing no later than the first meeting with the parties. The main hearing must be scheduled even if the case is directed to court-connected mediation so as to avoid additional delay should mediation fail.

397. If necessary, the main hearing may be rescheduled (DA section 16-3). Rescheduling may be necessary to ensure the proper proceedings, particularly in complex litigation where the parties need time to explore factual and legal issues and to obtain reports from experts. Negotiations on settlement or (court-connected) mediation may render rescheduling necessary. Unforeseen incidents, such as sudden illness of a legal counsel or a judge, or other unforeseen circumstances may also result in rescheduling.[63]

c. Preparation for the Main Hearing

398. During the two-week period between the closing of the preparatory stage and the main hearing, the parties and the court prepare for the main hearing. The court shall set the final timetable for the main hearing based on the timetables the parties have suggested in their closing submissions. The court has the power to set binding timeframes for the parties' submissions, testimony of parties and other presentations of evidence if the timeframes are reasonable and appropriate (DA section 9-11). However, binding timeframes are seldom used. The parties and the court also agree on how the factual and legal background of the case is presented, such as whether the court or the parties read the parties' closing submissions aloud or whether another document is used as the basis for the presentation of the case.

399. The court summons the parties to the main hearing, and the legal counsels summon witnesses. The court may oblige a party or representative to summon witnesses, if appropriate. If necessary to ensure compliance with the summons or for other reasons, the court can summon witnesses. As a rule, witnesses must be summoned one week in advance of the hearing, but they may be summoned on shorter notice if necessary and if doing so does not require the witness to 'neglect important tasks' (DA section 13-3).

400. The court has power to split the main hearing or proceed to the main hearing for one or some of the claims or disputed issues when appropriate (DA section 16-1). For example, the court may hear issues related to liability in a separate hearing and afterwards continue the preparatory stage for the issue of compensation.

401. The presiding judge should prepare for the hearing by reading the case file, and other members of the panel should read the summary of facts and closing submissions provided by the parties. In most cases, the presiding judge has managed the case during the preparatory stage and therefore has sufficient information well in advance of the main hearing.

63. *See* Part V Ch. 3 *infra.*

d. Conduct of the Main Hearing

402. The use of legal counsel is not mandatory at the main hearing. Even when the party has a legal counsel, parties are usually summoned to the main hearing. When a party has been summoned to the main hearing, failure to attend the hearing amounts to unlawful absence even if the legal counsel is present (DA section 16-8).

403. The court opens the main hearing and verifies that the parties are present and that case is ripe for the main hearing (DA section 9-13). The court clarifies the prayer for relief, the cause of action, the legal grounds for the claims and the evidence the parties have announced they intend to present (DA section 9-15). The closing submissions serve as a background for the clarification of the claims and their background; the court can either read these or provide its own summary of the case. The introduction allows the court and the parties to mutually ensure that all involved persons have the same understanding of the case and to correct any misunderstandings.

404. Next, the claimant gives a brief presentation of the case, the prayers for relief, the cause of action, the legal grounds of the claims, and the evidence. Additionally, the claimant presents written evidence and other objects, images, documents and so forth that will not be presented at an on-site inspection. The defendant is then given an opportunity to do the same. The defendant shall confine the presentation as much as possible to correcting and supplementing the views of the claimant. The aim of the 2008 reform was to provide for succinct and pertinent – not circumstantial or extensive – presentations. The reform has had modest effects on concentrating the main hearing to key disputed issues. The parties shall present the relevant legal issues, but the main legal argumentation is presented at a later stage. The format of the presentation of the defendant depends on whether the defendant has presented counterclaims.

405. The court has discretion to organize the initial presentation in another way, *inter alia,* to separate the presentation of written evidence from the initial presentation or to merge the initial presentation and the closing arguments.

406. The third step consists of the parties' testimony. The claimant testifies first, followed by the defendant, unless the court finds it more appropriate to hear the defendant first. The legal counsel examines the party first, then the counsel of the opposite party examines the party, and finally the court may examine the party. If a party is self-represented, the court examines the party first. The court may also decide to merge the initial presentation and the testimony of a self-represented party if it finds it appropriate to do so. Normally, the party begins by giving an account of the facts. Afterwards, the examining party may ask detailed questions.

407. After both parties have testified, the witnesses testify. Each witness is called in, and the court controls that the person present is the witness by asking the witness to state his or her name, date of birth, occupation, address, and relationship to the parties (DA section 24-8). The witness must pledge to tell the truth and not conceal anything. The witness is first examined by the party who summoned the witness, then by the opposite party and finally by the court (DA section 24-9). A party may ask the court to examine the witness for him or her. The examination starts with the witness giving an account of the facts. Then the party who called the witness and the opposite party may ask more detailed questions. The court must intervene if the witness is asked questions that are not pertinent. Questions suggesting a certain answer are not admissible, unless they are part of a cross-examination of a witness.

408. The next step is hearing experts and presentation of written evidence, other documents, and objects. In this step, the parties present written evidence by describing the content and relevance of each piece of evidence and by reading the core parts of the content of the document to the court.

409. The final stage of the main hearing is the closing arguments. In this stage, both parties have two opportunities to address the court. The claimant generally gives his or her closing arguments first, unless the court determines otherwise for special reasons. The closing arguments are based on the initial presentation of the parties and the evidence presented, but often there is a considerable overlap between the two presentations. Parties should not repeat arguments or information presented earlier. The main purpose of the closing arguments is to allow the parties to present their legal arguments and to argue their case. The court should intervene if the speech is repetitious or if the party introduces new issues. The second round of speeches should be limited to brief comments with regard to the first speeches. The court may intervene by asking the parties questions. Usually, the legal counsels deliver the arguments while the parties remain silent.

410. The court has ample discretion to organize the main hearing as it finds appropriate. The court and the parties may agree to merge parts of the presentation or to present evidence and arguments related to a claim or an issue and then proceed to the presentation of evidence and arguments related to another claim or issue. The closing arguments should be kept as the last item on the agenda insofar far as possible. The court may postpone taking some of the evidence to a later stage of the main hearing if it is not possible to hear all the evidence at once.

e. Closing of the Main Hearing

411. When the case is ready to be ruled on and the parties have given their closing arguments, the court declares the case closed for judgment (DA section 9-17). After the hearing has been closed, the parties are not allowed to bring additional arguments.

412. If the court concludes that the case was not sufficiently argued, the court may resume the main hearing to ensure a proper basis for its ruling (DA section 9-17 subsection 2). Reasons for this may include a change of circumstances, new evidence or a party having forgotten to mention something of vital importance. The court may uncover a possible legal basis for the judgment that has not been discussed during the main hearing. The court can resume the case only in exceptional circumstances.

C. Judgment

1. Deliberation

413. Courts rule based on the arguments and evidence presented at the main hearing, or, when no main hearing is held, based on the arguments presented at the most recent hearing. In written proceedings, the written documents delivered to the court form the basis of the ruling. Only judges present at the hearing may rule on the case. The preparatory judge rules on procedural issues during the preparatory stage, unless the panel of judges has been present at the hearing. If a prompt ruling is required and the preparatory judge is not available, the chief judge or a judge appointed by the chief judge has the power to decide procedural issues (DA section 19-2).

414. If the court sits with more than one judge, the judges shall deliberate the outcome as soon as possible after the main hearing (DA section 19-3). Normally, the deliberation is held immediately after the hearing or on the next day. If lay judges are part of the panel, a formal deliberation session must be held. If the panel consists of professional judges only, the court has more discretion. For instance, one of the judges could write a draft ruling which the rest comment in writing, or the judges could deliberate remotely via telephone or electronic communication. However, each member of the panel has the right to demand final deliberations.

415. A panel of judges must always vote on each claim and contested procedural issue separately. If the judges are unanimous, there is no formal voting, as unanimity is expressed directly in the judgment.

416. If there are several grounds for dismissing, quashing or staying a case or claim or for applying for reinstatement, the court must vote separately on each ground. The same rule applies to appellate courts voting on setting aside an appealed ruling or on reopening. If a judge is outvoted on a procedural issue, that judge shall take part in deliberating and voting on the other issues. For instance, a judge who votes for dismissing a case on procedural grounds must participate in voting on the ruling on the merits.

417. On rulings on the merits, the court rules only on the outcome, not the cause of action or legal grounds for the claim. Any disagreement on the cause of action or legal grounds for the claim will only be expressed in the reasoning of the judgment. The claimant demands that the defendant shall pay NOK 5 million based on a contract. Judge A finds for the claimant, judge B finds for the defendant since he or she is convinced that the contract is null and void and judge C finds for the defendant since he or she is convinced that the claimant demanded payment too late. As a result, the court will find for the defendant although the grounds judges B and C base their findings on differ. The same applies to procedural rulings. However, if there is more than one ground for rejecting, dismissing or staying a case, each of the grounds shall be voted on separately. Thus, if judge A believes the case should be rejected due to one of the parties lacking the capacity to sue, judge B believes general courts lack jurisdiction and judge C thinks the claim does not have legal character, the case will not be rejected, unless at least two of the judges agree on the same ground for rejection. The same applies to setting aside on appealed ruling, reinstatement and reopening.

418. The court reaches its ruling by a majority. Thus, two lay judges form the majority even if the professional judge dissents, and the professional judge and one of the lay judges form the majority when a lay judge dissents. Unanimity is required for some rulings, such as rulings to split the case when one of the parties opposes splitting (DA section 16-1), to reject a clearly unmeritorious appeal (DA sections 29-13 and 30-4) and to reject the reopening of a case (DA sections 31-8 and 31-9).

419. If one of the members of the panel falls ill and cannot participate in the hearing or the deliberation, then the panel has an even number of members and the presiding judge has the casting vote.

420. If there is no majority for any outcome when a sum of money or other quantity is determined, the principle of *maius includit minus* applies. If the first judge votes for NOK 800,000, the second judge for NOK 600,000 and the third judge for NOK 500,000, then the outcome is NOK 600,000, because the vote for NOK 800,000 is interpreted to be in favour of any sum below it as well. The highest amount is cumulated with the second highest amount and so forth until majority is reached. Hence, the first and the second judge have a majority for NOK 600,000.

2. Different Kinds of Rulings

421. There are three types of rulings: judgments, court orders and decisions (DA section 19-1). Judgments (*dom*) are final rulings on the merits: the court rules on the claims and prayers for relief (the substantive issues). A judgment may be partial if the court decides to rule on only one or a few of several claims. Partial judgments may also be used to rule on the question of liability for damage. The determination of the size of the damages is then postponed to a later hearing.

422. Court orders (*kjennelse*) are rulings on procedural matters. Court orders are used to dismiss a case on procedural grounds, including rulings on the admissibility of a case and rulings on the admissibility of evidence and the duty to provide evidence.

423. Rulings on procedural issues have the form of decisions (*beslutning*) if the statutes do not require the ruling to be a court order. Rulings granting and refusing leave to appeal are always decisions.

424. The ruling on an appeal on a judgment has the form of a judgment, and the ruling on an appeal on a court order has the form of a court order. This applies unless the court rules on an appeal on procedural grounds, such as when the court finds that the appeal is inadmissible.

425. The content of the ruling is decisive, not the label of the ruling. Thus, a judgment wrongly labelled a court order must be treated as a judgment, not as a court order, when determining its effect and the right of review. Judgments and court orders are always subject to review. Decisions are only subject to review when the court has interpreted incorrectly which types of rulings it has power to decide, or on the grounds that the ruling is obviously unsound or unreasonable (DA section 29-3).

3. Formal Aspects of the Ruling

426. Rulings shall state the name of the court, the time and place at which the ruling was pronounced, the judge or the members of the panel making the ruling, the parties and the court reference number for the case (DA section 19-6). The ruling must be in writing and signed by all members of the panel. The ruling shall state whether it is unanimous. If there are dissenting votes, the ruling shall state who is in dissent and the issues to which the dissent relates.

427. Judgments and court orders contain a short account of the case that includes information identifying the matter and delimiting the factual background of the case. The account gives the necessary factual basis for understanding the court's reasoning. The length of the account depends on the complexity of the facts and on which facts are disputed. Often the court starts by stating the core issue of the case in one or two sentences.

428. The ruling must also identify the claim, prayers for relief, the cause of action and the legal grounds. It may also be necessary to include central procedural issues.

429. District Courts also give a brief account of the proceedings and describe the evidence that was presented. Appellate Courts and the Supreme Court give a short presentation of the most important elements of the proceedings in lower courts, particularly the claims, the prayers for relief and a brief account of the ruling.

430. The grounds for the ruling are given after the case and the proceedings have been described. The length of the grounds depends on, *inter alia*, the complexity of the case, the number and nature of the disputed issues and the importance of the case. The court must give grounds regarding both how it has decided disputed facts and how it has interpreted and applied the law. The court must decide all claims, unless the ruling is a partial ruling or a court order.

431. If a panel of judges decides the case, the panel gives only one set of grounds. However, any dissenting judges or judges who concur on the outcome but not the grounds must write a separate opinion. An opinion may also be partly concurring or dissenting. Judges strive to keep the number of opinions as low as possible. In the Supreme Court, the first voting judge writes the opinion in his or her name, with other judges concurring or dissenting. The first dissenting judge writes a dissenting opinion, striving to reach unanimity among the dissenting judges. In rare cases, the ruling will have several dissenting opinions.

432. The final part of the ruling consists of the outcome of the case. If the court finds against the defendant, the outcome indicates that that the defendant is obliged either to pay a certain amount or to do or refrain from doing something else, at a certain time to a specific person. Alternatively, the court may find for the defendant. Further, the court may rule on legal costs, if the parties have requested compensation for them.

433. Decisions often relate to simple 'managerial' issues, in which case the court does not have a general obligation to give grounds for its decision. However, if the issue is more complicated or is of particular importance to one of the parties, the court must give brief grounds for the decision. Some rules specifically mandate the court to give grounds for certain types of decisions, *inter alia*, decisions ending proceedings in the Conciliation Board (DA section 6-12 subsection 4) and decisions to refuse leave to appeal on the grounds that the case is manifestly unmeritorious (DA section 29-3 subsection 5).

4. Notice and Service

434. A ruling is pronounced in writing when it is signed by the judge or all the members of panel of judges deciding the case (DA section 19-4). The ruling shall be pronounced within four weeks after the main hearing is closed. If a single judge has heard the case, the time limit is two weeks. If the court is not able to adhere to the time limits, it must state the reason for the delay in the ruling. The ruling becomes binding for the court and the parties when it is pronounced.

435. The court announces the expected date for the ruling in the main or preparatory hearing, if the case has proceeded to a hearing. Otherwise, the parties are given notice in a written format.

436. The ruling is pronounced either orally by a judge who reads it aloud at a court hearing or in writing. When the judgment is pronounced orally, the parties must be summoned to a court hearing where the main parts of the judgment are read aloud. The ruling is considered served at the hearing to all parties successfully summoned to the hearing. A written version of the ruling must be available no later than the day after the hearing. However, if the court pronounces a default judgment at the hearing where one of the parties is absent, it is not considered served upon the defendant. Most rulings are pronounced in writing. If a party has a legal counsel, the counsel obtains the judgment. Self-represented parties are served by mail.[64]

437. Rulings that do not conclude the court proceedings (e.g., rulings on admissibility of evidence) do not have to be served formally. In such cases, the court notifies the parties of the ruling.

5. Res Judicata

438. The ruling becomes res judicata and enforceable when the parties can no longer seek regular recourse against it. The time of res judicata is determined separately for each claim. Thus, in a case that consists of several claims, a claim dismissed on procedural grounds or a claim the court has ruled on in a first partial ruling becomes res judicata before the rest of the claims do so (DA section 19-14).

439. The time limit for appeal is calculated from the time the ruling was served on the party. Thus, the ruling may become res judicata at an earlier time for one of the parties than for the other.

440. Legal doctrine has identified four dimensions of res judicata; these are codified in DA section 19-15. The first two dimensions are the positive and negative functions of res judicata. The negative function refers to the rule that a court must, on its own motion, dismiss an action between the same parties on a claim that has been decided in a final ruling. The positive function of res judicata refers to the obligation of courts not to try a claim that has been decided on in a final ruling. For instance, in the first proceedings between A and B on ownership of a building, the court finds that A is the rightful owner of a building. In a second case where B claims A is liable to pay compensation for damage resulting from a roof tile falling from the building, the court may not try the question whether A owns the building. There are exceptions to both rules if one party proves there is a significant change of circumstances (*facta supervenientes*). For instance, in the first ruling, the court found the termination of a contract unlawful. After the judgment, a party to the contract terminates it based on circumstances that have taken place after the ruling. Res judicata does not hinder the parties to the contract from commencing new proceedings.

441. Positive and negative res judicata is limited in certain types of cases where the court rules on circumstances in the future. Personal injury cases are the paramount example of rulings with limited res judicata. The health of the injured person could deteriorate or improve unexpectedly; hence, res judicata is limited. Parental responsibility cases are another example: the best interest and the circumstances of the family may alter significantly over time. These cases are not formally res judicata.

---

64. For further details on service, *see* Part IV Ch. 3 §1, I, A, 2 *supra*.

442. The third and fourth dimensions of res judicata are the subjective and objective aspects. Res judicata applies only to the parties. However, some types of rulings, including many family law issues and mortification of documents, have an *erga omnes* effect.

443. The subjective aspect of res judicata is extended to third persons in some cases. First, the ruling is binding on third parties who would be bound by a corresponding agreement on the subject matter of the action. A judgment on ownership of an object is binding for a person who subsequently acquires ownership from a party of the original case. For example, the aforementioned case where the court found A to be the lawful owner of a building, A sells the building to C. In the second case, B claims damages due to a falling roof tile, the court may not try the question of whether C is the lawful owner of the house. If a general partnership is a party to the case, the ruling is binding on the partners.

444. The objective dimension of res judicata is defined by the claim, the prayer for relief, the cause of action and the legal grounds for the claim. The outcome of the ruling as stated in the final part of the ruling is decisive; however, to determine the dimension and identity of the case one must supply it with information gained from the rest of the ruling. The identity of the case is determined by a comprehensive evaluation of five factors:[65]

(1) whether the claims have a similar character;
(2) whether the claims are based on the same legal rules or regulations;
(3) whether the claims are based on the same cause of action;
(4) whether the justifications behind the rules are similar; and
(5) whether it is reasonable and natural to consider the situations identical.

445. The factors are prima facie identical for every aspect of the identity of the case, including lis pendens, but the application of the criteria may differ from one context to another. In terms of enforceability and res judicata, the interpretation must be slightly narrower than in other contexts, such as determining whether the judge is giving guidance within the boundaries of the case. Res judicata requires foreseeability and thus a narrower interpretation.

446. Res judicata is limited to issues on which the court has explicitly ruled. If the claimant demands payment based on a contract, the court will rule only on the obligation to pay; the question of the validity of the contract is not subject to res judicata. If the defendant claims set-off, the debt used for the set-off is not subject to res judicata. A defendant who wants the debt to be covered by res judicata must file a formal counterclaim. Res judicata is limited to the time of the ruling. If the court rules that A is the owner of the property in 2020, the question of ownership in 2016 may not be subject to res judicata. Res judicata depends on the issues and facts on which the court explicitly ruled in the first case.

65. For a detailed discussion of the factors, *see* Part III Ch. 1 §2, I, F *supra*.

447. Rulings dismissing the case on procedural grounds have only limited res judicata. The boundaries of res judicata depend on the grounds for dismissal and the possibilities to remedy the procedural deficiency.

6. Interpretation and Rectification of Rulings

448. Norwegian law does not allow actions where a party seeks clarification to a ruling. The outcome of the ruling should be specific enough to identify the rights and obligations arising from it. The description of the cause of action, the prayer for relief and the cause of action as described in the ruling guide the interpretation of the ruling. If the ruling has serious defects, it is null and void. In Rt. 2005 p. 362, the Supreme Court declared a ruling of the Conciliation Board against a person lacking the capacity to sue null and void.

449. The court has a right to rectify a ruling if it contains spelling or arithmetic errors, misunderstandings, oversights or other clear errors and the ruling consequently does not reflect the intended outcome (DA section 19-8). The court has the right to rectify all parts of the ruling, including the outcome. The error must be clear, but it does not have to be obvious. The court may not change the intended outcome of the case. An analysis of the description of the claims, prayer for relief, cause of action, legal grounds for the claims and the reasoning of the court reveals the intended outcome. For example, if the reasoning of the court indicates that the court has allowed set-off or has included interests in the claim, but the outcome does not reflect the set-off or the interests, the court may rectify the outcome. The court may rectify the ruling on its own motion or by application of a party. Rectification is not dependent on a time limit.

450. The court may make a supplementary ruling if it has neglected to rule on an issue (DA section 19-9). Typically, the court has not ruled on legal costs although the parties may have claimed them. A party to a case with an incomplete ruling must apply for a supplementary ruling before the time limit for appeal.

451. The court may reverse a decision and a court order when the ruling does not end the proceedings, if a fair and expedient trial requires doing so and if the decision is not disproportionately onerous for a party that has acted in reliance of the ruling (DA section 19-10). The court may, *inter alia*, reverse rulings allowing or disallowing certain evidence, rulings stating that the proceedings are to be written, rulings allocating the case to the small claims track and rulings joining or separating cases. The court may also reverse a ruling on the admissibility criteria and dismiss the case in the new ruling; however, in these situations, the threshold for reversing the ruling is higher than for rulings on evidence, as the consequences for one of the parties are appreciable. A ruling on procedural issues is not binding on the court in the next hearing. The court may proceed on its own motion or upon application by a party.

7. In-Court Settlements

452. In-court settlements are considered a type of ruling, since they have the same effect as a judgment (DA sections 19-11 and 19-12). Parties reaching settlement during court proceedings, through either negotiation, judicial settlement efforts or court-connected mediation, may request that the settlement be entered into the court records as an in-court settlement. Both the parties and the judge or panel of judges hearing the case must sign the settlement. The court must ensure that the settlement states precisely what the parties have agreed upon and that it is not against any public policy considerations. To be enforceable, the settlement must state the precise obligations of the parties and the time limit for the performance of the obligations. The court must inform the parties of the effect of in-court settlements. If the parties do not agree on allocation of legal costs, the court determines the costs at the request of the parties.

453. Once the in-court settlement is entered into the court records, it is binding as a judgment, and the claims included in it have the authority of res judicata. In-court settlements are not subject to general appeal.

II. Small Claims Proceedings

454. Claims of a primarily economic character where the amount in dispute is less than NOK 250,000 (approximately EUR 25,000) are, as a rule, directed to the small claims track. The small claims track provides simpler, faster, less expensive, and more flexible proceedings than the regular track. The small claims track is intended to fit self-represented parties and parties with only limited legal assistance. DA Chapter 10 regulates small claims proceedings. Although the chapter contains rules on small claims proceedings, the regulation is not comprehensive. Provisions in other chapters are applicable *mutatis mutandis* unless they are exempted. The chosen model for regulation results in fragmentation and lack of coherence.

455. Since the Conciliation Boards have mandatory jurisdiction for small claims and dispute resolution boards are ubiquitous, many small claims have already been subject to dispute resolution proceedings. Thus, one could argue that small claims proceedings are in many cases de facto appellate proceedings.

456. The small claims track is mandatory for cases with a primarily economic value of less than NOK 250,000. The disputed value is decisive: the value that the defendant admits is deducted from the amount claimed. Class actions, indispositive cases and cases subject to particular procedural rules (e.g., parental responsibility cases) are never directed to the small claims track. In addition, the court may direct cases with a primarily non-economic value to the proceedings if it deems small claims proceedings to be more appropriate than regular proceedings and if the parties do not object. The court has discretion to direct cases with a value above the threshold value to the small claims track when it finds it appropriate to do so and when the parties consent. Similarly, the court can divert a small claim to the regular track when the case is of material importance to one of the parties, is too complex for simplified proceeding or raises important issues of application of law.

457. The preparatory stage is limited for small claims (DA section 10-2). The court is not permitted to require the parties to file briefs, summaries of facts and closing submissions. As a rule, preparatory hearings are not allowed because they entail additional cost. Thus, there is no division between the preparatory stage and the main hearing. While abolishing the preparatory stage amounts to expedited proceedings, it also has significant disadvantages. During the preparatory stage, the court has the opportunity to clarify issues, to assist the parties in identification of the core disputed issues and – when necessary and appropriate – to provide guidance to the parties. The prevalence of self-represented parties and parties with limited legal assistance is higher in the small claims track than in the regular track; consequently, the need for clarification and judicial guidance is more substantial. It is thus particularly problematic that a preparatory hearing – the ideal forum for providing assistance – is not available. In such cases, clarification and guidance must be provided in writing, although written communication with self-represented parties is not likely to be efficient or to lead to satisfactory results.[66]

458. The parties must provide notice of evidence they wish to present at the main hearing one week before the main hearing. Additionally, the parties are required to submit documentary evidence that they have not previously submitted. This time limit is not formally sanctioned. However, the court has a right to disallow the evidence if the party has clearly acted in a reprehensible way, such as when a party deliberately withheld information on important evidence to hinder the opposite party from preparing for the hearing. The court should also disallow evidence that is irrelevant or results in disproportionate costs. In deciding on disallowing evidence due to lack of proportionality, the court takes into account the value of the claim, the importance of the claim, the type and amount of other evidence presented in the case, and whether evidence is relevant for ruling on the disputed issues. However, the court can only disallow irrelevant and disproportionate evidence when the parties have identified core disputed issues. Since the preparatory stage is virtually non-existent in small claims cases, the scope of the case often remains unclear until the start of the main hearing. Hence, excluding evidence before the main hearing commences entails a risk of excluding relevant and proportionate evidence.

459. The rules on preclusion do not apply in small claims proceedings. The court may disallow new prayers for relief, causes of action and legal grounds for the claims if the amendment would result in significant delay and if the decision to disallow the amendment is not unreasonable.

460. Although the court does not hold a preparatory hearing, it may have limited contact with the parties via telephone. Contact with the parties may be required

66. Christina Jensen, *Small Claims Procedures in the Scandinavian Countries* (Laura Ervo, Pia Letto-Vanamo & Anna Nylund eds, Springer 2021).

in particular to encourage the parties to find an amicable solution. Court-connected mediation should not be used in small claims, as it may delay the proceedings and result in additional costs.

461. The main hearing lasts two to three hours. It should not exceed a full day (five to six hours). One of the parties may participate remotely through telephone or video link. A single judge hears the case, but the parties may request that the court sits with a panel comprising one professional judge and two expert judges. The main hearing follows the same outline as in the general track (DA section 10-3).

462. The court has discretion to waive the main hearing at the joint request of the parties, if it finds that written proceedings are suitable. Written proceedings are not common in practice.

463. To provide expedient proceedings, the court should pronounce its ruling within three months of the case becoming pending. The court may pronounce the judgment immediately after the main hearing or no later than one week after the hearing. The judgment shall be concise and need not contain an extensive description of the case or extensive grounds.

464. The parties may only request compensation for costs relating to travelling costs to the court hearing, court fees, costs arising from legal assistance, the compensation to expert lay judges (if appointed) and costs for presentation of evidence, unless the evidence or costs are unnecessary or disproportionate. The losing party is only liable to compensate the winning party for costs for legal assistance and expert judges amounting up to 20% of the amount in dispute (DA section 10-5). Value added tax is not included in the 20%. The compensation for costs may be smaller or larger if one party has inflicted unnecessary costs on the opposite party by negligent conduct.[67]

III. Provisional Proceedings

465. Norwegian law does not recognize provisional proceedings as such. However, a party may request an interim relief. *See* Part IX Chapter 1 §1 for the rules on interim measures.

§2. Default Proceedings

466. Default proceedings involve a sanction against a defendant who fails to file a statement of defence or a brief required by the court or who fails to enter an appearance at a court hearing (DA sections 16-7 and 16-8). A default judgment is

67. For a more detailed criticism of the small claims proceedings, *see* Anna Nylund, *Norwegian Civil Procedure – How to Make Fast Even Faster*, in *Ways of Implementation of the Right to Civil Proceedings Within a Reasonable Time* (Aurimas Brazdeikis et al. eds, 2016).

only possible when the summons has been successfully served upon the defendant and the court has set a specific time limit for filing the statement of defence, a brief or another procedural step. Only procedural steps that are of 'material importance' for the opposite party or necessary for the proper conduct of the case can be sanctioned with a default judgment.

467. Default judgments can only be granted in dispositive cases – that is, in cases where public policy does not bind the parties' right to dispose of the case. Furthermore, they are only available as a sanction against the defendant. If the claimant fails to take a procedural step in a timely manner, the court dismisses the case.

468. The court must be able to find in favour of the claimant in full or in the main (DA section 16-10). The court may only base the judgment on the cause of action as presented in the statement of claim and only if the facts do not appear to be clearly incorrect.

469. If the court suspects that a party has lawful absence, the court may not issue a default judgment immediately. Rather, it must first give the absent party the opportunity to file for reinstatement.[68]

470. A default judgment is possible only if the court has made the defendant aware of the fact that absence or omission is sanctioned with a default judgment. The claimant must request a default judgment. A decision not to pass a default judgment is subject to appeal.

471. To avoid a default judgment or dismissal and to seek recourse against such a ruling, a party must apply for reinstatement (DA section 16-11). The court grants reinstatement if the party has had lawful absence and cannot be reproached for having failed to apply for extension of the time limit or rescheduling of the hearing. Reinstatement is granted if the default judgment or summary dismissal was wrongful (DA section 16-12).

472. A party must apply for reinstatement either before the court has passed the default judgment or the court order for dismissal or as recourse against such a ruling (DA section 16-13). The time limit for applying for reinstatement is one month from the omission or the service ruling, but courts apply this rule leniently. First, the court may accept an application for reinstatement even if it is filed late. The Supreme Court has accepted an application filed two months after the time limit.[69] Second, a ruling rejecting reinstatement is subject to a new application for reinstatement.

473. The application for reinstatement must be filed at the court where the case was pending, or, in the case of an appeal, where the case would be pending had the appeal been filed on time. The party must explain the reason for the delay and the

68. For the rules setting time limits and rules on unlawful absences, *see* Part III Ch. 3 §2 *supra*.
69. *See* Rt. 2010 p. 49, Rt. 2010 p. 1483, Rt. 2012 p. 1773 and Rt. 2012 p. 1921.

reason why he or she did not apply for extension of the time limit. If possible, the party must also take the omitted procedural step (e.g., submit the necessary brief).

474. The court has discretion to grant reinstatement if it would be unreasonable to deny it. The length of the omission and the nature of the omission are of importance. The longer the party takes to perform the required step, the less likely a reinstatement becomes. Reinstatement will be unlikely to be granted in the case of omission of a simple task, or a task a lawyer would easily recognize as important; conversely, the more complicated and difficult to foresee a task is, the lower will be the threshold for reinstatement. The likelihood that the court will grant reinstatement will also be higher the more important the case and the particular step are for a party. Further, the interests of the opposite party and the role of the procedural step in arriving at a substantively correct solution in a timely manner are also important factors to be considered. The reason for the omission may also influence the outcome.

475. As a rule, the application for reinstatement is decided in written proceedings. Appeal against the ruling on reinstatement is limited to procedural errors and errors related to interpretation and application of law. On appeal, the higher court is not allowed to decide on the merits.

§3. Ex Parte Proceedings

476. Ex parte proceedings, where the proceedings would be conducted without hearing the defendant, are not used in Norway. However, interim relief may be decided without the court hearing the opposite party.[70]

70. *See* Part IX Ch. 1 §1 for the rules on provisional measures.

Chapter 4. Review Proceedings

§1. Appeal

477. Norway has a two-tier appeals system. The first-tier appeal is from the District Court to the Court of Appeal. The second-tier appeal is from the Court of Appeal to the Supreme Court. The recourse against all rulings is called appeal (*anke*), although the rules are different for appeals against judgments on the one hand and appeals against court orders and decisions on the other hand. Before 2008, the recourse against the latter was called interlocutory appeal (*kjæremål*).

478. In small claims cases starting in the Conciliation Board, the first recourse is to initiate regular proceedings in the District Court. The ruling of the District Court is subject to appeal to the Court of Appeal and further to the Supreme Court.

479. In cases of particular importance, a party may appeal the ruling of the District Court directly to the Supreme Court (leapfrog appeal).

I. Appeal to the Court of Appeal

480. The Court of Appeal is the appellate court for all types of rulings of the District Court. The rules for the appeal and the appeals proceeding differ depending on the type of ruling. If the court has labelled its ruling falsely, the type of ruling that the court should have used is decisive, not the type erroneously used.

481. Next, rules for appeals against judgments are discussed first.

A. Appeals Against Judgments

1. The Competence of the Court of Appeal

482. Judgments are subject to appeal based on the grounds of errors in the assessment of facts, errors in the interpretation and application of laws, and errors in the court procedure.

483. The aim of the 2008 reform was to ensure that the appeals process would not be a repetition of the full proceedings but rather a review of (selected) issues and claims. Only erroneous parts of rulings of the District Court should be reviewed. The proceedings in the Court of Appeal are limited to the claims and procedural issues identified in the statement of appeal and derivative appeal (DA section 29-4). However, the reform has been unsuccessful, and proceedings in appellate courts are generally as lengthy as or even longer than those in the District Court.

484. The Court of Appeal may only review the appealed issues and claims. As a rule, the parties are not allowed to add to or modify the claims and relief sought.

The court is further bound by the grounds for appeal. If the parties have only appealed on the merits, the court may not review procedural issues, and vice versa. However, the court must give effect to serious procedural errors that are likely to have had an impact on the outcome of the case. DA section 29-21 lists four such errors. First, a mandatory condition for admissibility was lacking either when the case became pending or when the District Court made its ruling. Second, the composition of the District Court was unlawful. Third, the District Court's ruling is deficient and cannot be rectified, nor can it serve as a basis for appellate proceedings. As a rule, a breach of the adversarial trial (*audiatur et altera pars*) will be considered a serious error. Fourth, the ruling was made against a party who was not present, who was not lawfully summoned or who was lawfully absent.

485. The appeal shall be ruled on by judgment if the court rules on the merits or by court order if the court rules only on procedural issues (DA section 29-23). If the appeal against a procedural error succeeds, or if the court gives effect on its own motion to serious procedural errors, the court must quash the appealed ruling. The court transmits the case to the District Court. The District Court must proceed with the case on its own motion (DA section 29-24).

486. The parties may waive their right to appeal (DA section 29-6). A waiver made before the ruling is pronounced is only binding if it is mutual. A waiver does not preclude the party from appealing on the grounds of procedural errors.

2. The Statement of Appeal

487. The general time limit to make an appeal is one month from the time the ruling was served on the party (DA section 29-5). The District Court has the power to extend the time limit to up to six weeks in time-consuming cases, such as complex litigation and cross-border litigation.

488. The appellant initiates the appeals proceedings by submitting a statement of appeal to the court that made the appealed ruling (i.e., to the District Court). The statement of appeal shall contain the following information:

- the name of the appellate court having jurisdiction;
- the names and addresses of the parties, and when applicable the names and addresses of their representatives and legal counsel;
- the ruling that is appealed;
- whether the appeal applies to the entire ruling or only parts thereof, and if the latter to which parts;
- the claim to which the appeal relates, and the relief sought;
- the errors in the appealed ruling that the appellant alleges and the factual and legal grounds for the errors;
- the evidence the party intends to present; and
- the appellant's views of how the proceedings in the appellate court should be conducted.

489. The statement of appeal must give sufficient information to delimit the ambit of the appeal and to identify the grounds for the appeal. It must give the appellee adequate information to file a reply. The court must have enough information to manage the appeals proceedings. The appellant must pay the court fees, which are twenty-four times the basic fee (one basic fee is NOK 1,223 as of 2022; thus, the appellate fee is NOK 29,352, approximately EUR 2,900). If the statement of appeal is deficient, the appellant shall be given an opportunity to rectify it. If the deficiency cannot be rectified or if the appellant does not rectify it, the District Court must send the statement of appeal to the Court of Appeal, which then dismisses the appeal.

490. After the time limit for appeal has expired, the appellee may file a derivative appeal. If the appellant has appealed on procedural grounds only, a derivative appeal is not available. The time limit for a derivative appeal is three weeks from the service of the statement of appeal (DA section 29-7). A derivative appeal is dependent on the original appeal and lapses if the original appeal is not heard on the merits. If both parties appeal within the regular time limit for appeal, the appeals are independent of each other.

491. There is no preclusion between the District Court and the Court of Appeal (DA section 29-4). Hence, parties are allowed to introduce new grounds for their claims and new evidence supporting their claims. However, they are not allowed to amend the claim or expand the relief sought. There are several exceptions to the rule for claims that are linked to the claims that the District Court has ruled on. These exceptions are situations where:

- the claim cannot be brought in a separate action;
- the new claim amends the claim that the party has made in the District Court, and the reason for the party amending the claim is circumstances that have occurred or become known to the party amending the claim at a late stage of the proceedings in the District Courts, and that hence the party could not make the claim at an earlier stage;
- the opposite party does not object to the party presenting a new claim and the court finds that no important considerations argue otherwise;
- the new claim may be properly heard on appeal, and there are compelling reasons why it should be allowed to be heard; or
- the new claim is a counterclaim that could not have been raised at an earlier stage or the opposite party consents to the party introducing a new counterclaim.

492. Moreover, the relief can be extended if the opposite party consents to it or if the amendment is based on circumstances that have become known to the party after the main hearing in the District Court. Further, the parties can make amendments if they cannot be reproached for not having been aware of the facts before the end of the preparatory stage and the District Court has denied the amendment during the main hearing. The Court of Appeal has discretion to allow new and modified claims and an expansion of the prayer of relief provided if it finds the amendment reasonable. The exceptions give the Court of Appeal ample discretion to allow amendments to the claim and the relief sought. Thus, the restrictions to amendments to the claim and the prohibition to expand the prayer for relief are far from rigid, and amendments are fairly common.

3. Notification and Reply

493. The District Court serves the notification on the appellee urging the appellee to reply within a set time limit, usually three weeks. If both parties file an appeal, then each party is both an appellant and an appellee.

494. The reply shall give an account of the appellee's views on the appeal. It must contain information on the claims the appellee makes, the relief sought, as well as any evidence the appellee wishes to present and the appellee's view on how the appellate proceedings should be conducted (DA section 29-11).

495. Once the appellee has submitted a reply, the District Court transmits the case to the Court of Appeal. The same applies if the appellee does not submit a reply. The appellee is not sanctioned for failure to submit a reply. In the absence of a reply, the court will take into account the submissions of the appellee as they are expressed in the appealed ruling. However, appellees who do not file a reply are in a weaker position than appellees who file a reply, since they do not provide the court with arguments for their case. If a mandatory criterion for admissibility is lacking, the Court of Appeal must summarily dismiss the case.

4. Restrictions to Access to Appellate Proceedings

496. The access to appeals proceedings is restricted in two ways. First, if the claim has a primarily economic character and the value of the subject matter of the appeal is less than NOK 250,000 (approximately EUR 25,000), a leave to appeal is required (DA section 29-13 subsection 1). The value of the subject matter is calculated by taking the value of the prayer for relief made in the statement of appeal and subtracting from it the sum that the District Court awarded the appellant. If both parties have appealed and the value of the subject matter is below the limit for only one of them, only the party with the smaller claim needs a leave to appeal.

497. When the court decides whether to grant a leave to appeal, it must consider the importance of the case for the parties. The importance of the case is assessed based on, *inter alia,* its economic and non-economic importance for the parties, its importance in a larger perspective (e.g., the need to clarify the law) and whether there appear to be significant errors or weaknesses in the appealed ruling or in the procedure at the District Court. The Court of Appeal decides on its own motion whether a leave to appeal is required and, if so, whether it should grant the leave. The statement of appeal and the reply are the basis for the ruling on granting the leave. A panel of three judges rules on the issue. The panel is not required to give reasons for its ruling.

498. Second, the Court of Appeal may refuse to hear a case if it finds that the appeal does not have any reasonable chance for success (DA section 29-13 subsection 2). The refusal may be limited to certain claims or grounds of appeal. The court makes a prima facie assessment of the case based on the ruling of the District Court, the statement of appeal and reply of the appellee. If the court intends to refuse the appeal, it must give notice of this intention to the parties. The parties are given an opportunity to argue why the court may not refuse the appeal or to withdraw the appeal. The court must give notice within one month of receiving the case, but there are no rules on how much time the parties should have to present their views or when the ruling on the refusal should be made. However, if the court has sent a notice, it may not proceed to the preparatory stage before ruling on refusal. A decision to refuse the appeal is made by a panel of three judges in written proceedings. The decision must be unanimous, and the panel must give grounds. The decision to refuse an appeal is subject to appeal on procedural grounds only. A single judge may decide to proceed with the case without making a formal ruling.

499. If the court finds that the appeal cannot succeed, it may summarily dismiss it at any time. It may also at any point bar a party from presenting further arguments and evidence on an issue or claim that cannot succeed.

5. The Preparatory Stage

500. If leave is granted or the case is not refused, the preparatory stage commences. The preparatory stage of the appellate proceedings mimics preparatory proceedings in the first instance. The court contacts the parties to discuss the preparatory stage and the time for the main hearing. During the preparatory stage, the court shall focus on clarifying and concentrating the disputed issues to be reviewed on appeal. The court must also consider:

- whether it shall request written statements;
- whether a preparatory hearing is to be held;
- whether court-connected mediation should be attempted;
- whether the proceedings should be split; and
- the time for the main hearing.

501. If the facts are complicated, the court may request that the parties file a chronological synopsis of the facts.

502. The preparatory stage is tailored to the case. Unless the court deems it unnecessary, the parties shall file written closing submissions at the end of the preparatory stage. The preparatory stage closes two weeks before the main hearing, but the court has discretion to set the time limit for the written closing submission earlier. If the court sets an earlier time limit for closing submissions, the parties make amendments to their closing submissions a few weeks before the main hearing. In these situations, parties will have had the opportunity to make all necessary amendments well in advanced of the main hearing. If the court does not set an earlier time limit, the parties submit their closing submissions two weeks before the main hearing, viz. when the preparatory stage closes. In this case, the parties are allowed to make amendments when the amendments ensue from the closing submissions of the opposite party. The result is that amendments are made a few days before the main hearing or even during the main hearing, resulting in less time for the parties and the court to prepare for the main hearing. Additionally, a party may amend the claim, the prayer for relief, the cause of action and the evidence offered with the permission of the opposite party or the court. Since there is no preclusion between the District Court and the Court of Appeal except for the claim and relief, parties are allowed to amend the cause of action and the evidence supporting the claims, as long as the amendments are made before the preparatory stage is closed or before the end of the time limit set by the court.

503. If the court holds a preparatory hearing, it may decide to give its ruling after the preparatory hearing.

6. The Main Hearing

504. A panel of three judges hears appeals against judgments in oral proceedings (DA section 29-16). The parties may request that two lay judges or two expert judges be included in the panel hearing the case. The proceedings follow the same format as the proceedings in the District Court (DA section 29-18). The court must aim for a hearing concentrated to the main appealed and disputed issues. The main hearing starts with the court giving a brief overview of the case and the disputed issues that the parties have appealed. Next, the appellant gives his or her presentation of the case and main arguments, and then the appellee does the same. The parties present their evidence and expert and witnesses are heard. In the final stage, the parties give their closing arguments. The court has discretion to change the sequence of proceedings and to merge the initial presentation by the parties and the closing arguments.

505. If a party has appealed on procedural issues as well as on the merits, the court may decide to hear the procedural issues in a first hearing and to hear the case on the merits at a later stage. The court will normally decide procedural issues first, but it has discretion to rule on the merits if it finds it appropriate to do so and if the District Court has ruled on the merits (DA section 29-22).

7. Written Proceedings

506. If the appeal is limited to questions of procedure and the interpretation and application of law, the court may choose to use written proceedings. In written proceedings, the court asks both parties to file briefs on specific issues. The parties have a right to file a second set of briefs. The court decides the case based on the information in the briefs. If the parties agree on written proceedings, the court may allow them if it deems it appropriate to do so. The parties may also agree on a mixture of the oral and written formats, in which where some issues are decided based on the written submissions and some are discussed in the main hearing.

B. Appeals Against Court Orders and Decisions

1. Competence of the Court of Appeal

507. Court orders may be appealed on the grounds of errors in the assessment of facts, errors in the interpretation and application of laws, and errors in the court procedure. However, in the case of court orders on procedural issues where the court has ample discretion, appeal is limited to unsound or clearly unreasonable ruling. Examples of court orders where the court has exercised ample discretion are rulings on appointment of an expert, rulings on allocating the case to the small claims track and rulings to disallow evidence that is disproportionate to the importance of the dispute. Central procedural rulings, such as rulings on preclusion, privileges of witnesses and the duty to be a witness, are subject to appeal according to the general rule. Court orders dismissing the case are subject to appeal without limitations (DA sections 29-2 and 29-3).

508. A decision is subject to appeal on only two grounds (DA section 29-3). The first ground is that the decision was based on an incorrect interpretation of the law regarding the power to rule on the issue. This ground includes both the issue of whether the court had the power to make a specific decision and whether the ruling is correct. The appellate court cannot review the outcome as such. For instance, suppose the District Court finds that a procedural rule can only be applied in exceptional cases. The Court of Appeal then has the power to review whether this interpretation is correct but not whether the situation at hand can be characterized as exceptional. The second ground is that the decision is obviously unsound or unreasonable. The threshold to apply the second rule is high.

509. Decisions and some court orders may be appealed both at the time when the court made its ruling and later when the court has given its final ruling on the subject matter of the case. If the court order is the final ruling, it is immediately subject to appeal. If the procedural issues are included in the appeal against the final ruling, a party may appeal both procedural and substantive issues.

2. Time Limit for the Appeal

510. The general time limit for the appeal is one month from the time the ruling was served on the party (DA section 29-5). The court has the power to extend the time limit to up to six weeks. The court may also set a shorter time limit of one week for appeals against rulings related to evidence. After the time limit for appeal has expired, a party may file a derivative appeal if the opposite party has filed an appeal. The appellee has a time limit of one week to file the reply.

3. Appeals Proceedings

511. In appeals against court orders and decisions, the court may forgo the preparatory stage and decide the appeal based on the statement of appeal and the reply. Should further preparation be needed to clarify the issues or for the parties to provide additional arguments or evidence, the court requests that the parties file briefs on the issues in question (DA section 29-14). If necessary, the court may have a preparatory hearing. It may rule on the case after the hearing, if it finds it appropriate to do so.

512. Once the court has sufficient information, it closes the proceedings and rules on the written material. A hearing is required if the fair trial rights of the parties so require; if the case raises complex issues or issues of particular importance for the parties; or if the case raises important questions in need of clarification (DA section 29-15). The court may limit the hearing to specific issues. The proceedings are limited to the appealed issues. The Court of Appeal may rely on the facts as they are described in the District Court's judgment if a party has not contested the description.

II. Appeal to the Supreme Court

A. The Role of the Supreme Court

513. The Supreme Court is a court of precedent: its primary duty is to clarify and develop the law and to ensure equal application of laws. It selects cases raising important questions of law that may be relevant for other cases. Annually, it hears only approximately 100–120 cases, approximately half of which are civil, in a panel of five justices. The grand chamber decides particularly important issues. The court may also hear a case in plenary.

B. Competence of the Appeals Committee

514. To allow the Supreme Court to concentrate on cases raising important issues of precedent, the Appeals Committee (*ankeutvalget*) grants leave to appeal regarding judgments. Furthermore, the Appeals Committee has the power to refuse appeals regarding court orders and decisions. The Appeals Committee sits with a panel of three Supreme Court justices based on a weekly rotation. A ruling to refuse a leave to appeal, to grant a limited leave or to refuse to hear an appeal requires unanimity. Further, the Committee has the following powers (DA section 30-3 subsection 2):

- to reject an appeal when the appeal is not admissible;
- to dismiss a case or part of it, if general courts lack jurisdiction or if the case is res judicata;

- to quash a ruling if the proceedings in the lower court were affected by a serious error according to DA section 29-21 subsection 2;[71] and
- to quash a ruling if the unanimous Committee finds it to be necessary to do so, such as when the lower court made a serious procedural error that violates fair trial rights.

515. The Appeals Committee decides most appeals against court orders and decisions. Cases raising particularly important issues can be referred to a panel of five justices or to the grand chamber (DA section 30-9).

C. Direct (Leapfrog) Appeal to the Supreme Court

516. In cases raising particularly important questions of relevance for other cases calling for expedient clarification, the Supreme Court may grant a leave for direct appeal to the Supreme Court, which means that the parties may appeal the ruling of the District Court directly to the Supreme Court, skipping the Court of Appeal (DA section 30-2). The rules for the proceedings in the Court of Appeal are applicable for the Supreme Court in these cases.

D. Appeals Against Judgments

517. The appeal proceedings are initiated with a statement of appeal. The time limit for the appeal is one month – the same as for the Court of Appeal. The content of the statement of appeal and the reply are also the same as for the Court of Appeal. However, as the Supreme Court is a court of precedent, the parties must ensure that they include arguments regarding why the court should hear the case.

518. A leave to appeal is required for all appeals against judgments when the Supreme Court serves as the third court. A leave to appeal may only be granted if the case raises significant issues of relevance beyond the scope of the current case or if it is important for other reasons to allow the Supreme Court to hear the case (DA 30-4). The court may restrict the leave to specific claims, issues or causes of action. As a rule, the court will not take evidence, as the assessment of the facts in a case does not contribute to clarification or development of the law.

519. The parties are barred from introducing new claims, new or expanded prayers for relief, new causes of action or new evidence after the court has granted a leave to appeal (DA section 30-7). The court may allow changes only on special grounds.

520. A panel of five justices hears appeals against judgments. If the case raises particularly important issues, the grand chamber or the full court in plenary will hear

---

71. *See* s. I, A, 1 *supra*.

it. If necessary, the court may opt for written or oral preparation so as to focus the case even further on the core issues. Otherwise, the court will only have informal interaction with the parties before the main hearing. During the preparatory stage, the court will decide a schedule for the main hearing. The parties prepare a trial bundle consisting of a factual and a legal part. The factual part consists of a description of facts; any written evidence relevant for the case; and court files, briefs and court rulings in the case. The legal part consists of relevant provisions of law, preparatory works (*travaux preparatoires*), case law, legal literature and other relevant sources of law upon which the parties intend to rely in the case. The parties must provide the trial bundle two weeks before the main hearing.

521. The main hearing is normally held within six months of the appeal being filed. The court will normally allocate a time slot of an hour, a half-day or a full day for the legal counsel to present their cases. The legal counsel must present an outline of their presentation, a written statement of the case and their bill indicating the legal costs incurred. Once both parties have made their presentations, both parties are given an opportunity to rebut.

522. The form of ruling is judgment, if the court rules on the merits. If the court finds that there are factual or legal errors in the appealed judgment, the court sets aside the appealed judgment and transmits the case to the Court of Appeal. If the judgment of the District Court is also affected by the same error, the Supreme Court may quash both the ruling of the Court of Appeal and the ruling of the District Court and transmit the case to the District Court. The lower court must proceed with the case on its own motion (DA sections 30-14 and 30-15).

E. Appeals Against Court Orders and Decisions

523. As a rule, second-tier appeals against court orders and decisions are not allowed (DA section 30-6). For instance, a ruling allowing or disallowing expert witnesses in the District Court is subject to appeal to the Court of Appeal, but the court order of the Court of Appeal on the same issue cannot be appealed further to the Supreme Court. If the Court of Appeal made the original ruling on expert evidence, the parties might appeal to the Supreme Court. Exceptions are made in rare cases, especially if the court order raises a general question regarding the interpretation of law. Appeals against court orders and decisions that are not second-tier appeals do not require a leave to appeal (DA section 30-5). However, the Supreme Court may refuse to hear the case if it does not raise issues of significant interest beyond the current case and if no other considerations suggest otherwise.

524. The Appeals Committee decides most appeals against court orders and decisions. It makes its ruling based on the appeal and the reply. If necessary, the Appeals Committee may ask the parties to provide written statements or hold a court hearing (DA section 30-9).

525. If the court finds that the case lacks any reasonable prospect of success, it may dismiss the case without giving any reasons for its ruling. Otherwise, the court will either rule against the appellant, thus upholding the ruling of the Court of Appeal, or rule for the appellant, thus reversing the ruling of the Court of Appeal. Depending on the outcome, either the court transmits the case back to the Court of Appeal where the process will continue or the ruling is final, ending all court proceedings.

§2. Reinstatement

526. Reinstatement is the only recourse available against default judgments and dismissals on the grounds of absence. Reinstatement is not available against rulings of the Conciliation Boards. For more information of reinstatements, *see* Chapter 3 §2 *supra*.

§3. Challenge of In-Court Settlements

527. An in-court settlement is not subject to regular appeal. A party may bring an action to declare the settlement invalid or to amend it pursuant to the rules for invalidity and amendment of contracts. The threshold to declare an in-court settlement invalid is high, and the court cannot take into account incidents or changes that have occurred after the parties entered into the settlement. In practice, courts declare in-court settlements invalid or amend them only in exceptional circumstances. For example, in a dispute on the placement of three piers, the map showing the location of the piers contained several errors. As a result, the placement agreed upon in the in-court settlement violated zoning regulations. The court thus declared the in-court settlement invalid.[72]

528. An action challenging an in-court settlement must be brought at a District Court within six months of the date the party became, or a diligent party would have become, aware of the alleged grounds for invalidity. The action cannot be brought more than ten years after the settlement (DA section 19-12).

§4. Extraordinary Appeals (Reopening)

529. Reopening is the only form of extraordinary appeal available and can be resorted to only when the case is res judicata (DA sections 31-1 and 31-2). Only the final rulings concluding the hearing of the case are subject to reopening. Rulings setting aside the ruling of a lower court are subject to reopening until the lower court makes a new ruling on the merits. Arbitration awards and in-court settlements are not subject to reopening.

---

72. Ruling of Borgarting Court of Appeal LB-2009-59288.

530. A petition to reopen a ruling of a Conciliation Board shall be sent to the District Court. A petition to reopen a ruling of a District Court or a Court of Appeal shall be sent to a District Court or Court of Appeal in a neighbouring district. The Appeals Committee hears petitions to reopen rulings of the Supreme Court (DA section 31-1). The petition for reopening must be submitted within six months of the date when the petitioner became or a diligent petitioner would have become aware of the grounds for petition. A case cannot be reopened after more than ten years (DA section 31-6).

531. Both procedural and factual errors are grounds for reopening (DA section 31-3). However, not all errors qualify for reopening. Five types of procedural errors are accepted as grounds for reopening:

(1) a judge who was not entitled to serve has participated in the proceedings;
(2) there are reasonable grounds to suspect that a judge, an expert or the opposite party has committed a criminal offence in connection with the proceedings;
(3) there are reasonable grounds to suspect that a witness has given false testimony;
(4) an international human rights court or committee has found against Norway in a case on the same subject matter (this exception is limited to human rights treaties incorporated in the Human Rights Act); and
(5) the ruling is against a party who was not lawfully summoned or who was lawfully absent.

532. Reopening due to factual and legal errors may be done on two grounds (DA section 31-4). The first ground is that information on the facts in the case unknown at the time of the ruling suggests that the ruling would probably have been different had this information been known. The unknown information must have existed at the time the ruling was made (DA sections 31-3, 31-4 and 31-5) but must have remained unknown despite the party having taken reasonable steps to investigate all relevant facts in the case. A party who failed to investigate facts and circumstances sufficiently may not rely on the facts and circumstances which a diligent party would have become aware of when petitioning to reopen the case. Facts occurring after the time of the ruling are *facta supervenientes* and are not subject to res judicata. Thus, new facts do not lead to reopening.

533. The second ground is that a binding ruling of an international court or the United Nations Human Rights Committee on the same subject matter suggests that the ruling was based on an incorrect application of international law. Errors related to application of law do not result in reopening unless they involve a binding ruling against Norway.

534. A case may not be reopened if it is likely that a new hearing would not lead to a significant amendment.

535. A petition to reopen a case is heard pursuant to provisions on appeals against court orders and decisions. The court investigates on its own motion whether the conditions to reopen the case are fulfilled. If the petition succeeds, the reopened case shall be heard pursuant to the provisions applicable to the type of case (DA section 31-8). If the court finds it obvious that the petition does not have any reasonable chance of success, it may dismiss the petition without hearing it (DA section 31-9).

Part V. Incidents

Chapter 1. Challenge of Judges

§1. Disqualification of a Judge

536. A professional or lay judge who has a close connection to the issues or parties in a case shall is disqualified from hearing the case. The CJA recognizes three grounds for disqualification.

537. Sections 106 and 107 enumerate the situations in which a person shall always be recused. These situations include when the judge:

- is a party in the case or in a related case, or co-entitled, co-obliged or liable to recourse in relation to a party;
- is closely related to a party through kinship or current or previous marriage, or is a guardian or relative of a party;
- is a chairperson or member of the board of a party;
- has acted on behalf of a party or is closely related to such a person;
- has previously had dealings with the case as an arbitrator, judge or juror, or is closely related to such a person; or
- is a witness in the case.

538. Section 108 has a general clause on recusal expressing the idea that justice not only must be done but also must be seen to be done. For this reason, a person may not serve as a judge when other special circumstances 'capable of undermining confidence in his (or her) impartiality' exist. This rule is open, giving courts discretion to ponder the specific situation.

539. The Supreme Court has ruled on recusal of its justices several times. In Rt. 2009 p. 1617, where the main question regarded shipping companies, the Supreme Court found that one of the justices had to be recused because her spouse had repeatedly served as a legal counsel for shipping companies. The justice was recused despite the fact that none of the parties in the case had been her spouse's clients, since a mere connection to shipping law could undermine confidence in her impartiality. In Rt. 2007 p. 750, a case on long-term lease of ground, eleven of nineteen justices had to recuse themselves. Most of the recused justices had either their home or their vacation home on leased ground, or their spouse, parents or children had a home or vacation home on leased ground. They were recused despite the fact that there are an estimated 300,000 contracts on long-term lease of ground in Norway. As the latter case also involved judicial review, two justices with connections to the Ministry of Justice and the Attorney General, respectively, had also to recuse themselves. As a result, the full court ruling on the main issue in the case consisted of only six justices.

540. In HR-2016-106-A, members of the Norwegian Parliament challenged their pension plans. The majority of fifteen Supreme Court justices had an almost identical pension plans as the members of the Parliament. All fifteen justices recused themselves because the ruling would have had an impact on their own pension plans. Only the five most-junior Supreme Court justices heard the case, since their pension plans were different from the more senior justices' plan. In the *Climate* case HR-2020-2079-P, the Supreme Court found that a justice was disqualified because she had been an active member of one of the nature conservation organizations that had sued the Norwegian Government for issuing oil and gas licences.

541. In HR-2016-681-A, a judge was recused because the counsel of one party worked in the same law firm as the judge's spouse. The law firm had only three lawyers; therefore, the main rule that partnership or employment in the same law firm is not a reason for recusal did not apply. However, in HR-2016-2311-P, in which the legal counsel of a party was married to the niece of a Supreme Court justice, the majority of nine justices found the justice in question to be qualified.

542. Some judges, particularly Supreme Court justices with a career in academia, have published books or articles on issues that may be raised in cases. If the judge has taken a firm position vis-à-vis the key issues in a case, the judge may need to recuse him- or herself. The same may be true in situations where the court has ruled on the same issue earlier, particularly in cases involving judicial review. In the *Climate* case HR-2020-2079-P, the Supreme Court found that a justice was disqualified because she had been a member of the committee preparing the constitutional reform that had dealt with among other environmental rights and the Norwegian Government was challenging the opinion of the committee regarding the nature and position of section 112 of the Norwegian Constitution, which enshrines environmental human rights. The Supreme Court held that the manner in which the Government challenged the role of section 112 constituted an exceptional circumstance that rendered the justice disqualified.

543. Deputy judges work under the supervision of the chief judge of the court. Additionally, the chief judge may assign a judge to supervise the deputy judge. Therefore, if the chief judge or the judge supervising the deputy judge recuses him- or herself, the deputy judge is automatically recused as well (CJA section 109).

§2. PROCEDURE FOR DISQUALIFICATION

544. Judges have a duty to consider in their own motion whether they are qualified. Judges have an obligation to notify the parties of a circumstance that could result in recusal according to section 108, unless the circumstance is presumed to be common knowledge.

545. A party can make a motion on recusal at any time during the proceedings. The motion should be made as soon as possible after the party has become aware of the circumstances that may result in recusal. A motion on recusal a judge according to section 108 must be made immediately after the party is informed of the relevant circumstances.

546. As a rule, the court where the case is pending rules on the motion on recusal (CJA section 116). When the issue of recusal is raised in a court hearing, the judge(s) concerned may not participate in the ruling, if the court is still quorate. When only one professional judge hears a case, the chief judge rules on the recusal or summons another judge to do so. If a party files a motion on recusal during the main hearing, the judge(s) concerned will not participate in the ruling on recusal. The panel of judges hearing the case have the power to rule on recusal if the court is still quorate. If the panel is no longer quorate, a new judge at the same court is summoned to attend the hearing. When a motion on recusal concerns two or more members of the panel hearing the case, all the concerned panel members must step down regardless of whether the grounds for recusal are similar. If a new judge or a sufficient number of new judges cannot be summoned without significant inconvenience or expense, all members of the panel participate in decision-making on the issue of recusals. In small District Courts or when a party asserts that all judges at a specific court should be recused, judges may have to rule on their own recusal.

547. The motion on recusal is often raised in advance of the court hearing. In these cases, the chief judge will rule on the motion (CJA section 117). Should two or three judges on a panel be challenged or should the chief judge be challenged, the court has the option to transfer the case to a higher court or to allow one of the remaining members rule on the issue. The Appeals Committee hears cases challenging judges in the Court of Appeal. A ruling on transferral may only be made on request of the court in which the judges are challenged. However, CJA 116 and 117 do not prohibit judges from ruling on motions on recusal against themselves.

548. The Chief Justice of the Supreme Court appoints a substitute court consisting of five judges to rule on the motion. If a party files a motion on recusal of all Supreme Court justices, the court is still qualified to rule on the motion, as it cannot summon judges or transfer the motion to a higher court. Similarly, if the Supreme Court has diverted the case to the grand chamber, the Chief Justice has the power to recuse justices from participating in the drawing of the ten members of the grand chamber. The Chief Justice is always the eleventh judge serving on the panel, unless he or she has to recuse him- or herself. If fewer than ten justices are qualified, the size of the grand chamber is reduced accordingly (Rt. 2008 p. 1451). The same applies if the Chief Justice recuses him- or herself. However, recusal prior to the drawing of the members of the grand chamber is only preliminary. The grand chamber has the power to overturn recusal.

549. When a judge is challenged before the main hearing takes place, the court has the option to choose between written and oral proceedings when ruling on the challenge. The court may also decide to defer the issue to the main hearing. The Supreme Court must either hold a hearing to decide the issue or defer it to the main hearing (CJA section 117). The court sits in accordance with regular rules on the composition of the court.

550. The ruling on recusal is made individually for each judge. Before making the ruling, the court must hear the person facing recusal. The court must investigate the grounds for recusal on its own motion when necessary. For recusal according to section 108, the court may order the party challenging the judge to provide more information.

551. A ruling on recusal made by a higher court is not subject to appeal.

Chapter 2. Withdrawal of Actions

552. In Conciliation Boards, the claimant does not face any adverse consequences for withdrawal. In a District Court, the claimant may withdraw the action without any consequences before the summons has been served upon the defendant. After the summons has been served, the claimant is considered to waive the claim or the action, and the court will rule for the defendant (DA section 18-4).

553. Withdrawal is often the result of negotiations between the parties; hence, consensual withdrawal is not sanctioned. The claimant may also withdraw the action without sanctions if the defendant does not submit a statement of defence or if the defendant claims that the action must be summarily dismissed.

554. The appellant may waive the appeal without sanctions until the court hearings begin, or in written proceedings until the court has made a ruling. After the court hearing commences, the appellant may waive the appeal with the consent of the respondent. Withdrawal results in dismissal of the appeal, in which case the ruling of the lower court is upheld.

555. A party may bring a new action or reintroduce the withdrawn claim only if the court did not make a final ruling on the claim. Before bringing a new action, the party must first pay the legal costs awarded to the opposite party.

Chapter 3. Rescheduling, Adjourning and Staying Proceedings

556. A party who has a lawful excuse for absence has the right to demand that the hearing be rescheduled or adjourned. Usually, the court will honour the request or make arrangements to enable the party to attend remotely via telephone or other means. The court can adjourn a hearing on its own motion when it believes that an absent party has a lawful excuse (DA section 16-2).

557. The court has discretion to reschedule a hearing if it is necessary to obtain fair proceedings or a sufficient basis to decide the case, or if weighty reasons suggest it is necessary to do so (DA section 16-3). If a party introduces new evidence or arguments or wishes to amend the claim, the prayer for relief, the cause of action or the core legal argumentation, the court has the option to reschedule the hearing to give the opposite party sufficient time to prepare his or her case. Examples of weighty reasons include a self-represented party deciding to appoint a legal counsel (who will need time to prepare for the hearing) and a judge falling ill. The court may reschedule a hearing only if the right to expedient proceedings will not be violated; thus, hearings should not be rescheduled repeatedly in the same case or postponed for a long time.

558. Once the main hearing has commenced, the court may adjourn the main hearing if necessary (DA section 16-4). However, the court shall ensure that the proceedings are delayed as little as possible. Adjournment may be necessary due to illness or due to a party wishing to present new evidence or to amend the claims or cause of action. When the main hearing is resumed, the proceedings must be repeated to the extent necessary. If the main hearing is adjourned for a few days or a week, repeating proceedings is not necessary. Long adjournments may require that the main hearing essentially start over from the beginning.

559. The court may stay the proceedings if a party or a party representative dies or if the estate of the claimant is declared bankrupt and the subject matter of the dispute is part of the bankrupt estate (DA section 16-16). If the defendant is declared bankrupt, the proceedings will continue, alternatively, the claimant may lose legal standing in the case. In Rt. 2010 p. 430, an employee sued the employer for unlawful dismissal. During the court proceedings, the employer was declared bankrupt. The Supreme Court found that claims for damages for unlawful dismissal could be upheld against the bankrupt estate. However, the claim on declaring the dismissal unlawful could only be filed against the employer, not the bankrupt estate. Due to the bankruptcy, the employer (a limited liability company) had ceased to exist and thus, the claimant had lost legal standing. The court proceedings will resume on application from a party, unless one of the parties has lost legal standing.

560. The parties can agree to stay the proceedings once for a minimum of six months (DA section 16-17). The court stays the proceedings after it has received notice of the agreement. After the passing of the agreed period for staying the proceedings, the court resumes the proceedings on application from a party. The court has discretion to resume the proceedings at an earlier time at a unanimous request from the parties. The parties have the power to agree to stay the proceedings only once.

561. On application from a party, the court may stay the proceedings if the outcome of the current case is fully or partly dependent on the outcome of another court case (DA section 16-18 subsection 1). The other case may be pending in a Norwegian court or administrative organ, or it may be pending at an arbitral tribunal or in a court in another country. The cases must be closely connected, often involving at least partially the same parties or the same cause of action. A similar case involving different parties does not fulfil the prerequisite of a sufficiently strong connection. The court has discretion to reject the application if staying the proceedings would result in undue delay or if the connection between the cases is too weak.

562. The court has discretion to stay proceedings for other weighty reasons on the application of a party or on its own motion (DA section 16-18 subsection 2). In doing so, the court must ensure that the proceedings are expedient, cost-efficient and fair. If another case will serve as precedent for the current case and the court considers the precedent to be essential for the outcome in the current case, the court may stay the proceedings. Typically, proceedings are stayed to await a ruling from the Supreme Court.

563. Time limits cease to run when the case is stayed. The parties need the permission of the court to take procedural steps. The court may allow a party to take steps to preserve and record evidence, but it will usually disallow other procedural steps and measures.

564. The court has discretion to limit the stay of proceedings to a single claim. The court may rule on claims on which the proceedings have been conducted before the proceedings were stayed. The consequences of the stay of proceedings cease when the court rules to resume the proceedings (DA section 16-15). Time limits will continue when the proceedings are resumed.

Chapter 4. Third-Party Intervention and Amicus Curiae

565. A third party who has a claim that is closely connected to one of the claims in a pending action against one of the parties in the said action has the right to join the action (DA section 15-3). For example, if A sues X for damages arising from circumstances where X caused damages to B and C as well, B and C may opt to join the action. Third-party joinder results in the third party becoming a party to the case.[73]

566. The court may permit a third party to intervene in the proceedings (*part-shjelp*) if the third party is in a position that makes the outcome of the case particularly important for him or her (DA section 15-7). HR-2021-1415-U serves as an example: several companies had filed a law suit against Bank Norwegian ASA alleging that the bank deliberately bought internet domain names to hinder competition. Google LLC could intervene because the ruling could impact the services that Google is allowed to provide to its customers and its duties to its customers and other companies..

567. Associations, foundations and public bodies that are charged with a duty to promote specific interests may intervene in cases that fall within their purpose and scope. Labour organizations and employers' organizations regularly intervene in cases on labour law if the case at hand raises a question regarding the interpretation of labour law. Organizations may only intervene if they have a full or partial capacity to sue.

568. The third party shall declare intervention in writing or orally at a hearing. Intervention must take place before the court has ruled on the merits. The declaration must include the grounds for the intervention. The parties to the proceedings shall be notified of the intervention and given a time limit for contesting the intervention. The court has discretion to allow or deny intervention. The ruling is not subject to appeal. Intervention is only valid at one court; thus, the intervener must renew the declaration to intervene when the substantive outcome is heard on appeal.

569. The intervener joins the case as it is at the time of the intervention and has only limited rights to take procedural steps. The intervener may take procedural steps on behalf of the main party, such as providing new evidence. However, he or she may not take steps contrary to the party's interests and wishes. If the intervener takes steps causing additional legal costs, he or she is liable to compensate the costs. Associations and foundations may only take procedural steps that are directly necessary to safeguard the interests the organizations represent. The intervener may not appeal rulings. The court does not rule for the intervener, and the outcome does not have any direct effect on the legal rights and obligations of the intervener.

73. *See* Part III Ch. 2 §3 *supra* on joinder of claims.

570. The 2008 reform of civil proceedings introduced a new form of inclusion of third-party interests in civil proceedings, the amicus curiae (DA section 15-8). The amicus curiae must be an association, an organization or a public body, and it may only file a written submission on an issue falling within its purpose and scope. The submission must shed light on a matter of public interest and must be in writing. The court may reject the written submission if its form and content are not appropriate to achieve the purpose of shedding light on a specific issue. If the court does not reject the submission, it becomes a part of the court records and it must form part of the final judgment. The court must send the submission to the parties and give them an opportunity to comment on it. The written submission does not give the amicus curiae any other procedural rights or duties.

571. If a case may have a significant effect on the legal position or rights of a third party, the court must give the party notice of the action (DA section 15-9). Such notice shall contain the necessary details about the action and the reason for notice. Notification of third parties serves the purpose of achieving cost efficiency, promoting substantively correct outcomes and avoiding contradictory outcomes. When notifying third parties, the court gives them an opportunity to consider joining the action or intervening in the proceedings and thus promotes timely joinder and timely inclusion of new evidence and arguments.

Chapter 5. Splitting the Case

572. The court has wide discretion to split the case, either by hearing some issues or some claims separately. The court may also rule separately on one or more claims or issues (DA section 16-1). For instance, the court may hear procedural issues before hearing the case on its merits. If the claimant has claimed damages based on negligence, breach of contract and strict liability, the court may hear and rule on one of the bases for negligence separately. The court may also first hear issues related to liability and then later hear issues related to the amount of damages. Splitting the hearing and splitting the ruling are independent of each other. For claims on damages, the right to split the case is extended; the court may decide to hear the issue related to the liability for damages in a first main hearing, then subsequently rule on liability separately. Only if the court rules for the claimant is the question of the amount of damages heard in a second main hearing.

573. A unanimous court may decide to rule separately on a single cause of action or on the choice of law. The court must obtain the consent of the parties, as the ruling may influence the outcome of the case. When a single judge hears a case, splitting does not influence the outcome. For instance, if the court rules separately on the question of negligence, one judge may find for the defendant and two judges may find for the claimant. The judge finding for the defendant must participate in hearing the rest of the issues. At the second stage, a different judge may find that the claimant has demonstrated negligence contributing to the damages and thus find for the defendant, while the two other judges may find for the claimant. The result of splitting the case is that the court rules for the claimant, although two of the three judges believe a condition for damages based on negligence is absent. Had the case not been split, the court would have ruled for the defendant.

574. Although the court has wide discretion to split the proceedings and the ruling of a case, it must avoid unnecessary splitting resulting in increased costs and delay.

Part VI. Legal Aid and Legal Costs

Chapter 1. Legal Aid

§1. The Public Legal Aid Scheme

575. Legal aid is regulated by the Legal Aid Act.[74] Legal aid is available for citizens who cannot afford to pay for the services of lawyers in cases that are of great importance to the legal aid recipient. As a rule, only natural persons may receive legal aid. However, non-profit organizations may be eligible for legal aid in special circumstances, such as when it is natural that the organization represents important public interests. In cases involving fundamental questions of EEA law, legal persons may also be eligible for legal aid, according to the case law of the CJEU.[75] Legal aid is normally only granted for cases pending in Norwegian courts and administrative tribunals.

576. Eligibility for legal aid depends on the income, economic assets, and family relations of the applicant. The hourly charge is limited to a maximum set by the Ministry of Justice. The Ministry of Justice has set fixed compensation for many types of cases, such as legal advice in family cases. Costs are covered according to the client's financial ability. Since the threshold for full aid is lower than most social benefits, most clients are considered to have sufficient means to pay part of the legal costs.

577. Lawyers have a duty to advise clients on the availability of legal aid and assists clients in filing applications for legal aid if it is needed and the client could qualify for it. Legal aid is subsidiary: it is awarded only when the citizen does not have insurance covering legal aid or access to legal aid through membership in an organization and when advice available through public entities does not suffice.

578. Legal aid consists of free legal advice, free legal representation, waiver of court fees or any combination of these. Legal advice applies when a case is not pending at a court or an administrative body. Legal representation is used when the

74. *Rettshjelpsloven* 1980 no. 35.
75. DC-279/09 DEB *Deutsche Energiehandels- und Beratungsgesellschaft mbH v. Bundesrepublik Deutschland*, ECLI:EU:C:2010:811.

case is already pending at a court or an administrative tribunal. The County Governor grants applications for legal advice, and the administrative tribunal or court where a case is pending grant applications for legal representation.

579. Legal advice is limited primarily to family and inheritance law, landlord-tenant disputes, personal injury and employment disputes. Lawyers have the power to grant legal advice to the client in these cases. The lawyer is compensated according to a pre-set schedule, where the compensation the government pays to the lawyer is low, NOK 1,121 (approximately EUR 110) per hour in 2022.[76] The County Governor has discretion to grant legal advice in other types of cases similar to those mentioned in the law and to persons who do not fulfil the financial conditions, if the costs of legal assistance are substantial relative to the applicant's financial situation and the dispute is of notable interest to the applicant. Legal advice covers the costs arising from necessary legal assistance and advice to solve the issue at hand. In practice, it is usually limited to a pre-set sum.

580. Legal representation is granted for court proceedings when the case is particularly important for the applicant and the applicant has a low income and few or no other assets. In proceedings involving child custody and contact, legal aid is awarded automatically as long as the applicant fulfils the financial conditions. Legal representation covers the lawyer's fees in part or in full, as well as subsidiary costs, such as court fees and costs for evidence, arising from the court procedure. Legal representation does not cover costs arising from the client choosing a legal counsel not based near the court. Exceptions are made for weighty reasons, such as when a lawyer with particular knowledge and experience is required.

581. The third form of legal aid is waiver of court fees (*fritak fra rettsgebyr*), which includes, in addition to court fees, remuneration of witnesses and experts and fees for extracts. The court may grant the waiver in conjunction with granting legal representation, or on application to persons fulfilling the financial conditions.

§2. Private Legal Aid

582. Most citizens rely on private legal aid regimes, particularly legal aid insurance. Many organizations provide limited legal aid for their members. These organizations include the Norwegian Automobile Association (*Norges Automobil Forbund*) and the Norwegian Association of House Owners (*Huseiernes Landsforbund*).

---

76. The Norwegian Bar Association has argued for a 40% increase in the rate to reflect the true costs of the case and align the hourly payment with cases where the client pays the legal counsel. The Government has refused to adjust the rate, despite the fact that it was very low, because doing so would be very costly Advokatforeningen, Salærrapport, October 2017, https://www.advokatforeningen.no/globalassets/advokatforeningen_salaerrapporten2017_web.pdf. Instead, the government has increased the income threshold for legal aid, https://www.regjeringen.no/no/aktuelt/regjeringen-vil-oke-rettshjelpssatsen/id2884583/.

583. Several organizations offer free legal aid. The three faculties of law at Norwegian universities have student-driven legal aid clinics funded by the government. The Church City Mission (*Kirkens bymission*) offers legal services, so-called street lawyers, for people with serious substance abuse problems, as well as children and youth. The Norwegian Bar Associations offers pro bono clinics.

Chapter 2. Legal Costs

§1. Types of Legal Costs

584. Legal costs consist of court fees, fees paid to the legal counsel, compensation paid to witnesses and experts, other costs arising from evidence and travel costs. Economic compensation for indirect losses of the parties, such as compensation for time used in preparation and discussions with the legal counsel, is generally not subject to compensation. However, if the party has expertise to perform tasks that the legal counsel or an expert would perform, the party may claim reasonable compensation.

585. The opposite party is only liable for necessary costs. The importance of the issues at stake, the factual and legal complexity of the case and the monetary value of the case are central to determining the necessity of costs. The court has wide discretion in ruling on costs. Courts often find that some costs have not been necessary and therefore reduce the compensation to be paid. Costs considered unnecessary are costs relating to evidence the court rejects as irrelevant or disproportional. The hourly fee paid to the lawyer may also be unnecessarily high, particularly when the case does not require particular expertise. In simple cases, fees paid to the legal counsel may be at least partly unnecessary.

§2. Compensation of Legal Costs

586. Norwegian civil proceedings are based on the 'loser pays' principle (DA section 20-2): the party who loses the case must compensate the prevailing party for the costs resulting from the proceedings. The action is successful if the court finds for one party, either for all claims or in the main. To determine whether the court has found for one party in the main, the difference between the amount claimed and the amount in the ruling is the central factor. If the parties have several claims, the totality of claims determines the outcome. Central claims are weighted more than peripheral claims, larger claims more than smaller claims and main claims more than ancillary claims. Final rulings on procedural matters ending the proceedings are treated as rulings on the merits.

587. If the court finds in part for one party and in part for the other party, the parties must bear their own costs. However, if the court finds significantly more in favour of one party, the court may award costs to that party, either in full or in part (DA section 20-3). For instance, in an action consisting of two claims. If the court finds for the claimant on one of the claims and for the defendant on the other, then the court has discretion to order the parties to bear their own costs or to order the defendant to compensate all or some of the claimant's costs.

588. There are several exceptions to the main rule of the loser compensating the winner, which allow the court to use division of legal costs as a sanction. A party may be sanctioned for inducing legal costs on the opposite party by delaying the proceedings, introducing costly steps, introducing excessive or costly evidence or increasing costs and prolonging the proceedings in other ways. As civil litigation should be a last resort, inducing the opposite party to initiate court proceedings or upholding claims without any prospect of success is sanctioned. When the court uses legal costs as a sanction, it has a discretion to reduce the liability for costs for the losing party, or it may rule that the parties are liable for their own costs.

589. In addition to using costs as a sanction, the court may make other exceptions from the main rule of cost division. The court can exempt the losing party from liability for legal costs if weighty grounds justify doing so. The DA mentions four examples of weighty grounds. The first is when the case raised legal issues about which the law is unclear. The second is when the evidence was clarified only after the action was brought and the parties could not reasonably have obtained the evidence earlier. In both the first and the second cases, instigating the action was necessary to determine the facts or the law. In the third example, a successful party must bear all or part of his or her costs if he or she can be reproached for bringing the action or has rejected a reasonable offer of settlement. A party can be reproached for bringing the action if the party could have obtained the same outcome in simplified proceedings or using ADR, or if the opposite party was willing to engage in negotiation or in an ADR process to which the winning party did not consent. The fourth example is when the case is of particular importance to the welfare of the losing party and the relative strength of the parties justifies an exemption. For example, in cases where the court rules for a professional landlord, the tenant may be exempted from bearing the costs of the landlord; similarly, the insured party can be exempted from paying the costs of an insurance company provided the case is of particular importance.

590. Furthermore, a losing party that has succeeded to a significant degree may be awarded partial legal costs. In particular, the court must consider what portion of the litigation costs relates to the claims on which court ruled for the losing party (DA section 20-3). For example, suppose the claimant has made ancillary claims amounting to a significant value, and the court finds for the claimant on the main claim but not on the ancillary claims. If a major part of the legal costs ensues from the ancillary claims, the court may order the parties to bear their own costs or may even order the claimant to compensate some of the defendant's costs.

591. The party who has lost in full or in part may be awarded legal costs in whole or part, if the action has been brought without good reason and the party accepts the claim at the earliest opportunity. In this situation, the same result could have been obtained outside the court. The same is true for cost arising from the opposite party's omission to act in a timely and diligent manner (e.g., to make amendments early) (DA section 20-4).

592. Finally, several other rules may result in the winning party bearing some of the costs. For instance, the rule on preclusion in DA section 9-16 gives the court discretion to allow late amendment and addition of claims and evidence. When allowing the amendment or addition, the court may order the party requesting the amendment or addition to pay for the costs arising from it.

§3. Liability for Costs

593. Liability for legal costs is primarily limited to the parties. In joinder of parties when two or more parties are on one side, the court rules separately for liability of costs and awarding of costs for each party. Thus, if the court rules for two parties on the same side, it may award costs in full to one of them while awarding no or only partial costs to the other party on the same side. The court may also make parties on one side jointly liable for costs (DA section 20-6).

594. A third-party intervener is liable for costs in the same way as a party. The intervener has the right to claim compensation for costs arising from the intervention and may become liable for costs of the opposite party (DA section 20-1).

595. A representative of a party is liable for costs only when the entity bringing the action lacked the ability to sue. When dismissing the action on grounds that the claimant lacks the ability to sue, the person stated as the representative of the claimant becomes liable for legal costs (DA section 20-7). A person initiating court proceedings on behalf of an entity declared bankrupt becomes liable for costs arising from the action. In LA-2008-173522, the Agder Court of Appeal found a person who was the true decision-maker in a letterbox company registered in Panama liable for legal costs arising in an action against the letterbox company.

596. Legal counsels are not liable for legal costs under the rules of the DA. However, liability can be established based on CJA section 200, which sanctions negligent and otherwise inappropriate acts during court proceedings, enforcement and provisional measures and applies to court officials, enforcement officers and legal counsel. The sanction includes both damages and fines. In Rt. 1986 p. 930, a legal counsel who gave wrongful information to the court was sanctioned. In Rt. 2008 p. 610, a counsel who leaked to the press evidence the court had struck out as inadmissible was sanctioned with fines. The legal counsel must act clearly negligently in order to be found liable to pay damages.

597. The state can become liable for costs incurred by serious procedural errors, particularly errors and irregularities denying the party fundamental rights of defence, the right to be heard and equality of arms. Other serious procedural errors, such as a recused judge hearing the case or denying the parties justice within a reasonable time, can also result in state liability (DA section 20-12). A judge can also become liable for negligent and inappropriate acts according to CJA section 200 when the error is grave. A claim for compensation must be filed within three months of the action becoming res judicata. Courts of Appeal hear claims on compensation against District Courts, and the Supreme Court or the Appeals Committee hears claims on compensation against Courts of Appeal.

§4. Claim for Compensation for Legal Costs

598. Parties must explicitly claim compensation for legal costs; the court does not award costs on its own motion. The claim must be made at each stage of the proceedings, including appellate proceedings. Appellate courts may rule on legal cost for proceedings in lower courts only if the party has claimed costs in the lower court and renewed the claim in the upper court. The fees paid to the legal counsel must be specified, indicating the hourly fee and the number of hours used in each step.

599. At the end of each court hearing, the parties must submit statements of costs indicating specific items of expenditure up to and including that stage of proceedings. A failure to provide a detailed statement of costs at the end of the main or other hearings results in denial of costs. During the written stages of proceedings, the parties only have to claim costs; they are not required to provide a detailed statement of costs.

600. If the court has not held a hearing when it pronounces its final ruling, then as a rule compensation for legal costs is limited to NOK 15,000 (approximately EUR 1,500). If a party has provided a detailed statement of costs, the court may award higher costs (DA section 20-5 subsection 4).

601. The court reviews the claim for compensation for costs, particularly the statement of costs. Even if the opposite party has accepted or not commented on the statement of costs, the court may reject some of the costs. This rule is an exception to the principle of party disposition. The rationale for the rule giving the court the right to review the statement of costs on its own motion is to reduce legal costs so as to increase access to courts.

Part VII. Evidence

Chapter 1. Burden of Proof

§1. General Principles of Evidence

602. The aim of Norwegian civil proceedings is, *inter alia*, to establish the substantive truth (DA section 1-1). Nevertheless, the party-driven, adversarial nature of civil proceedings modifies this aim significantly. The parties must prove only disputed facts. The parties' agreement on relevant facts is normally binding for the court. When a party admits facts during the court proceedings, the court becomes bound by these facts. If a party admits facts outside the court proceedings, the opposite party must provide evidence of the admittance unless the party iterates the admission in court. However, an admittance of a clearly erroneous fact does not bind the court.

603. The parties are liable for producing evidence to establish the disputed facts (DA sections 11-2 and 21-4). The court may base its rulings only on factual circumstances with a sufficient basis in the evidence provided (DA sections 11-1 and 21-2). The court can induce the parties to present evidence by resorting to clarification and judicial guidance in asking whether a party intends to present evidence related to a disputed fact and inform a party of the consequences of not presenting (sufficient) evidence. Particularly in cases with self-represented parties, the court, as a last resort, can encourage a party to present evidence of major importance (DA section 11-5 subsection 5). In theory, the court has the right to provide evidence on its own motion unless the parties oppose it (DA sections 11-2 and 21-3), but in practice courts refrain from exercising this right.

604. The principle of the parties providing evidence is limited in indispositive cases, such as child custody and contact cases and cases involving mandatory competition law. The court must ensure that the basis for ruling on the factual issues is sufficient primarily by actively encouraging the parties to provide evidence. If the parties do not provide sufficient evidence, the court must ultimately produce evidence on its own motion. In indispositive cases, an admittance does not bind the court.

605. The right of the parties to dispose of the claims and evidence being limited to disputed facts hinders finding the substantive truth. Failure to appear or to file a written statement may result in the court ruling for a party on procedural grounds, through either dismissal or a default judgment.[77]

606. In determining facts, the court may rely on established facts and on its general and specialist knowledge and experience. Established facts comprise generally known information, such as that Paris is the capital of France and that dogs are mammals. The court's general knowledge and experience comprise information that is available to a large number of people. Examples of such information are the location of the public library in the local town or the fact that it takes a longer distance to bring a car to a full stop when the road is covered with snow or ice than when it is dry. The exact distance needed to stop a car in a specific situation is not considered part of the court's general knowledge. The court's specialist knowledge or experience generally refers to the knowledge and experience of an expert judge related to the judge's specific field of evidence. Specialist knowledge must be subject to comments from the parties, and the parties must be given to right to rebut it. Additionally, appellate courts may rely on the facts as they were established by the lower court(s).

607. The content of law is not subject to evidence, as the court knows the law according to the principle of *iura novit curia* (DA section 11-3). The principle does not cover foreign law or certain types of customary law or customs. Thus, the court may allow evidence on the content of and interpretation of foreign law, Sami customary law or customs in a specific field or geographic area. International law, depending on its status, may fall within the same category as national law or foreign law, or somewhere in between. The parties may only submit statements on national law with the consent of the court and the opposite party and when the statement is occasioned by the case. The parties may use legal doctrine freely, as it is not occasioned by the case.

§2. Free Admission and Free Evaluation of Evidence

608. The principles of free admission of evidence and free evaluation of evidence are the foundational principles of the law of evidence (DA sections 21-2 and 21-3). Both principles are believed to enhance the finding of substantive truth. The finding of substantive truth is one of the main goals of civil procedure.

609. The parties are allowed to provide the evidence they consider relevant and necessary to prove their case. There is no prima facie limitation of the type of admissible evidence, nor does any type of evidence carry more weight than other types of evidence. The parties are considered best equipped to decide which types and pieces of evidence or which witnesses will be the best for their case.

---

77. *See* Part IV, Ch. 3 §2.

610. The free evaluation of evidence means that there are no rules on the evidentiary value of any piece of evidence or how the court should weigh different types of evidence. The evaluation of the evidence is thus left to the discretion of the court.

611. Evidence law is also based on the principle of the best evidence available. According to this principle, the parties must strive to present the best evidence, which is the evidence with the shortest possible link to the circumstance to be proved. Consequently, circumstantial evidence, including hearsay evidence, is allowed only when there are no direct witness observations, when the person who witnessed a circumstance is not able to provide evidence, or when such evidence is relevant to strengthen the basis for the ruling on facts. Similar reasoning applies to documents as evidence, and there are only a few limitations as to what kind of evidence may be presented. The free rules on evidence help the court to divert undue influence of biased evidence, as the parties may provide evidence and arguments that speak against them. The less directly a piece of evidence is tied to the facts to be proven, the less the weight the piece of evidence is given. Although circumstantial evidence has low weight prima facie, several pieces of evidence may cumulate to provide strong evidence. According to the principle of adversarial proceedings, the court may not rely on evidence on which the parties have not been given the opportunity to comment.

§3. Burden of Proof

612. The burden of proof is on the party who addresses a fact that changes a legal position. The claimant must initially provide evidence in support of the facts he or she claims. The burden of proof for counter-facts and counterclaims is on the defendant. Once the claimant has provided sufficient evidence, the burden of proof to rebut the facts is on the defendant. In practice, the processes of providing evidence in support of and against the claim are interlinked.[78]

613. The law has several provisions reversing the burden a proof, such as the Consumer Sales Act section 18,[79] which provides a presumption of a defect existing at the time of transferral of risk if the defect appears within six months. The consumer has the burden of proof of the defect and of its appearance within six months. When the consumer has established the defect and the time of appearance of the defect, the burden of proof is reversed.

614. Some full or partial reversals of the burden of proof are based on case law. The Supreme Court has found that in situations where one party has the ability and incentive to secure evidence, the burden of proof may shift, either fully or partially. In Rt. 1990 p. 688, an insurance company denied full compensation for a car crash

78. For more details, *see* Magne Strandberg, *Standards of Evidence in Scandinavia*, in *Standard of Proof in Europe*, 135–159, at 147–154 (Luboš Tichý ed., Mohr Siebeck 2019).
79. *Forbrukerkjøpsloven* 2002 no. 34.

due to alleged drunk driving. The alleged drunk driver had not provided evidence related to the circumstances of the car crash. The Supreme Court lowered the burden of proof for the insurance company claiming the driver was drunk, because it was clearly more difficult for the insurance company to provide evidence, whereas evidence was easily available to the alleged drunk driver.

615. Legal presumptions, such as that the father of a child born in wedlock is the spouse of the mother in the Children Act section 3, might affect the outcome of a case. A party may rebut a presumption by providing evidence overturning the presumption. Similarly, in some circumstance the court may make rulings based on its appraisal. Typically, appraisal is allowed in rulings on damages for non-economic loss.

§4. Standard of Proof

616. The standard of proof is preponderance of evidence. For the court to find for a party, the fact or event must be 'more probable than not' (i.e., more probable than the alternatives). Thus, a buyer claiming that goods were damaged at the time of transfer of risk must prove that the likelihood that the goods were damaged at that time is greater than 50%.[80]

In some contexts, the law operates with a higher or lower standard of proof to protect a weaker party, to protect a party when a substantively incorrect ruling would have particularly adverse consequences or to protect a party who risks administrative sanctions of a punitive character. For example, the Instrument of Debt Act section 2[81] allows a creditor to recover the share of one of several co-debtors from the other debtors when it is 'certain' that the co-debtor is unable to pay or when the whereabouts of the co-debtor are unknown. Another example is the Sales Act section 62,[82] which gives a party to a contract the right to annul the contract when it is 'clear' that the other party will not fulfil the obligations arising from the contract. Further, the Inheritance Act section 51[83] states that a provision in a will lapses when it is 'undoubtedly' no longer applicable due circumstances that occurred after the will was made. The word 'certain' indicates a particularly high level of proof, whereas 'undoubtedly' indicates a level clearly above 50%. In HR-2015-2265-A, the Supreme Court lowered the standard of proof to prove causality between a vaccine and a serious illness. Establishing whether a statutory provision heightens or lowers the standard of proof requires an analysis of its wording and context.

617. The standard of proof may also be higher based on case law in cases where the Supreme Court refers to a 'clear' or 'qualified' preponderance of evidence (e.g.,

80. For more details, *see* Magne Strandberg, *Standards of Evidence in Scandinavia*, in *Standard of Proof in Europe*, 135–159, at 147–154 (Luboš Tichý ed., Mohr Siebeck 2019).
81. *Gjeldsbrevloven* 1939 no. 1.
82. *Kjøpsloven* 1988 no. 27.
83. *Arveloven* 1972 no. 5.

Rt. 2008 p. 1409, . Higher standards of proof are primarily set in cases where one party must establish that the opposite party has acted in a reprehensible manner. Examples include cases in which an insurance company rejects full payment based on neglect and damages related to criminal cases in which the criminal charge is denied but liability may be established on grounds of private law. To avoid double jeopardy (*ne bis in idem*), the standard of proof must be particularly high in such cases.

§5. Duty to Provide Access to Evidence

618. The parties have a duty to give testimony and access to evidence regardless of whether the evidence is in their favour (DA section 21-4), unless a provision in a law gives them an exemption. Formally, a party must disclose the existence of important evidence even if the evidence is not in the party's possession. Disclosure covers all evidence unless the party has reason to believe the opposite party is aware of it. Unlike in many common law jurisdictions, the law does not require the party to present evidence that adversely affects his or her case. The law does not sanction breaches of the duty to disclose directly, nor do courts enforce the rule in practice. Until the DA entered into force, there was no rule mandating a party to inform the opposite party of evidence other than the evidence the party presented to the court. Despite the introduction of a duty to disclose evidence at one's own initiative, the parties still ignore the duty, and courts seldom enforce it. However, a failure to disclose evidence may impact the division of the burden of proof or have other adverse consequences. The court may hold the withholding of evidence or information on evidence against the party. The duty to make investigations to clarify the facts and evidence of the case serves as a counterbalance to rules on disclosure.

619. Persons who parties call as witnesses have a duty to appear in court and testify (DA section 24-1). Witnesses in breach of their duties may be fined or ordered to be transported to court. The court may order a witness to bring documentary or other types of evidence to court.

620. All persons domiciled or staying in Norway have a duty to make items in their possession available as evidence when a court orders them to do so has (DA section 26-5). This rule also applies to items of which a person can gain possession. The concept of an 'item' is to be interpreted broadly to include digital information such as data files. To enable the parties to gain access to evidence, the court may order the parties and other persons to answer questions about whether they are aware of items of evidence and to make necessary investigations in this respect. They may also be ordered to prepare comparisons, extracts or other reviews of information that may be gathered from items of evidence (DA section 26-5). The duty to provide access to evidence is limited, *inter alia*, by the protection of private life and costs for producing the evidence. In Rt. 2012 p. 1819, a party was not obliged to let an expert witness enter his home. However, the party would have had a duty to allow a court-appointed expert to enter his home. In HR-2020-2469-A, the

Supreme Court found that courts can order a party to allow the opposite party to investigate an object that can serve as evidence, in the said case fertilizer that had been transported on a ship.

621. The duty to produce documents that do not already exist as such, such as extracts, reviews and comparisons, depends on the level of difficulty in obtaining the said information. For instance, the court can order a party to provide information on bank accounts, as the information can be easily obtained. However, a party is not obliged to make a list of transactions of a certain type when doing so would be very time-consuming.

622. To gain access to evidence, a party must file a petition for disclosure clearly identifying the item(s) or type(s) of item(s) that he or she wishes to access (DA sections 26-6 and 26-7). Disclosure gives the petitioner the right to ask the opposite party and third parties questions related to the existence of a specific object and, when appropriate, to access to the object. The party must specify the object concerned. The rationale of the rule on specification is to delineate the obligation to disclose to an easily identifiable object and to prevent 'fishing expeditions' for evidence. For instance, a request for information on a bank account must specify the bank and preferably indicate the account number, and a request to access to correspondence must specify the recipient, the topic and time period. A general request covering many banks with unspecified accounts must be rejected. The court has discretion to lower the requirement of specification if it is unreasonably complicated to fulfil the requirements and if the application for disclosure is likely to result in the party gaining access to evidence. In LB-2018-9876, the Borgarting Court of Appeal accepted a request to oblige a party who claimed to be injured to give access to evidence on the specific time of the first claim for compensation. The requesting party did not need to individualize the specific documents that could serve as evidence. Individualizing each document would be virtually impossible.

623. Access to evidence does not imply that the party has the right to present all the items as evidence. For instance, a party may for instance get access to digital or paper files to search for relevant documents and make copies of those documents. The party will then present the copies as evidence or petition that the person who is in possession of the originals present them in court.

624. The right to disclosure is not absolute. First, only objects providing information on disputed facts are subject to disclosure. Second, evidence covered by a duty or privilege of confidentiality is not subject to disclosure. Third, disclosure may be contingent on the party requesting disclosure paying costs arising from providing the evidence. For instance, the party requesting access to evidence may be obliged to pay the other party for providing a report or an overview, review or comparison of specific information. Fourth, should the costs arising from disclosure be disproportionately high, the court may reject disclosure.

Chapter 2. Admissibility of Evidence

625. According to the principle of free admission of evidence, the parties are free to provide evidence unless a specific legal provision prohibits the evidence. The parties are only limited from providing evidence when general conditions for evidence, prohibitions and exemptions apply. The rules on disallowing evidence are common for all types of evidence.

§1. General Conditions for Evidence

626. The DA has four general conditions for allowing evidence: it must be relevant, proportionate, included in the list of evidence and presented in an appropriate manner (DA section 21-7). The general limitations of evidence are closely connected to each other and to the general principles of civil procedure, in particular the principle of proportionality and the principle of the best evidence.

627. The rule on relevance of the evidence is a manifestation of the idea of concentrating civil proceedings to the core disputed elements. Consequently, the court shall disallow evidence unrelated to disputed facts. Irrelevant evidence may be entirely unrelated to the case or related to undisputed or irrelevant circumstances. Relevance depends on the claim, prayer for relief, cause of action and the legal and factual background of these. Likewise, the court may disallow evidence that is not likely to appreciably improve the basis for the ruling, such as circumstantial evidence when direct evidence has already been presented. The boundary between irrelevant evidence and evidence of limited relevance is vague. The consequence for both rules is disallowance of the evidence.

628. The court may also reject evidence it finds should be provided in a different, more appropriate manner. The principle of immediacy requires the parties to present evidence directly to the court; thus, the use of depositions and other witness evidence in writing is limited. For instance, the court will reject hearsay evidence or other circumstantial evidence when the party is able to provide direct evidence. The court may also reject presentation of written evidence when a person can be heard orally or, conversely, may reject all but short questions of clarification to a written report.

629. Evidence must be proportional to the economic value and the importance of the case and the fact to be proven (DA section 21-8). This rule enhances cost efficiency and expediency by providing a tool to limit the extent of evidence. The rule gives the court the power to urge the parties to choose economically sound methods of proof, particularly in cases of lesser value. The value of the case is measured in terms of the economic interest at stake, non-economic interests at stake and the societal interest. The court may allow extensive use of costly evidence in a pilot case although the economic value as such in the particular case is low. A ruling to reject evidence on grounds of proportionality must conform to the requirement of equality of arms. A large amount of evidence on a limited issue may be both disproportional and of little relevance. The court may select the ground for disallowing evidence. The main method is to try to induce a party to limit the evidence to the most relevant pieces giving the best possible information on the disputed facts. The Supreme Court has used the provision on proportionality of evidence to deny costly disclosure. In practice, courts seldom reject evidence as irrelevant or excessive. An important reason for this is that the focus of the preparatory stage is on procedural issues rather than on identifying the core disputed facts and legal issues.

630. The parties must provide a summary of evidence in advance of the main hearing (DA section 21-6). This summary serves many of the same functions as the closing submissions and functions as a supplement to the closing submissions in identifying the core of the case. It specifies the pieces of evidence the party intends to present and states what the evidence purports to establish. The summary of evidence must also specify important information the evidence will provide to the extent that the opposite party is not expected to be aware of it. Based on the summary of evidence, the court may disallow irrelevant or disproportional evidence. The most important function of the summary of evidence is to provide a basis for preclusion. Evidence is precluded under DA section 9-16 at the closing of the preparatory stage. To avoid the threat of preclusion, a party must identify the evidence in the summary of evidence.

631. After the preparatory stage has been closed, a party may submit new evidence only if the opposite party agrees or if the new evidence is a direct consequence of information in the closing submissions of the opposite party. The court has discretion to allow new evidence when the party cannot be reprimanded for providing the evidence earlier, when the opposite party has sufficient opportunities to safeguards his or her interests without the court having to adjourn the main hearing, or when the refusal would be unreasonable. The court may also allow the new evidence if the party introducing the evidence compensates any costs arising from the late presentation of evidence. Additionally, the court has discretion to allow new evidence even after the main hearing has commenced. Courts may not enforce preclusion of evidence in their own motion unless important considerations suggest a need to do so. In practice, courts are reluctant to enforce preclusion: usually the court allows a party to present evidence even if the party has not included it in the summary of evidence.

§2. Prohibited Evidence

632. DA Chapter 22 regulates prohibitions against giving evidences exhaustively. The court must enforce the prohibitions on its own motion to protect sensitive information from being spread. The prohibitions against giving evidence mentioned in DA Chapter 22 are regulated in more detail in other statutes which contain rules on secrecy and confidentiality. The breach of these duties to confidentiality is criminally sanctioned regardless of the manner in which the evidence is presented; hence, a party cannot circumvent the rules by presenting the evidence in another manner (e.g., presenting documents in lieu of calling a witness). Although there are many legal provisions mandating confidentiality, only the situations enumerated in DA Chapter 22 result in a prohibition to give evidence.

633. Confidentiality arising from a need to protect national security or foreign relations is privileged (DA section 22-1). There is also a prohibition to give evidence on discussions in government conferences, such as conferences where the prime minister and the ministers meet (DA section 22-2).

634. Employees at State or municipal authorities, Family Counselling Offices, technical regulatory bodies, postal services, suppliers or installers of telecommunication networks or services and the State airport authority are prohibited from giving evidence when doing so would breach a statutory duty of confidentiality (DA section 22-3). The Ministry in charge of the said type of evidence has discretion to consent to the presentation of such evidence. The court has discretion to overrule the Ministry both by allowing evidence that the Ministry has rejected and by disallowing evidence to which the Ministry has consented.

635. Evidence cannot be presented on court proceedings or testimony that is subject to a duty of confidentiality imposed by a court (DA section 22-4). However, the person whom the duty of confidentiality protects may consent to the presentation of such evidence. Evidence on information from judges or jury members about the basis for a ruling cannot be presented. However, unless the court has imposed a duty of confidentiality on the persons present at the court hearing, evidence on which pieces of evidence, claims and arguments were presented to the court and on the conduct of the court proceedings as they were observable during the proceedings is allowed. Particular rules apply to issues emerging in out-of-court and court-connected mediation.

636. Confidential information entrusted to the clergy, priests and pastors in registered religious communities, advocates, and health care professionals (doctors, psychologists, nurses, etc.) may not be presented as evidence (DA section 22-5). The same applies to the assistants of these persons, such as employees at an attorney's office. The court may grant a privilege to refuse from giving evidence on such issues, as a duty to give such information could undermine the general trust in the rules on confidentiality.

637. Confidentiality is limited to information gained by professionals in their professional role. A member of the bar combining the practice of law with an estate agency has only a duty to confidentiality relating to the practice of law: information obtained as an estate agent is not covered by the rules on confidentiality and hence is not prohibited. The right of an in-house lawyer to invoke confidentiality depends on the tasks of the lawyer. An in-house lawyer performing tasks typical for a legal counsel, such as giving legal advice or preparing legal documents, may invoke the rules for those tasks. The assessment of the attorney-client privilege for in-house counsel is done on a case-by-case basis.

638. The duty to confidentiality is limited in some situations where the dispute relates to the relationship between the client and the professional. In a medical or legal malpractice case, the professional must be able to release some of the privileged information to be able to present evidence on the factual issues in the case. The client may consent to the presentation of confidential information. The consent must be informed (i.e., the client must have information on the grounds and scope of confidentiality and the consequences of consent).

639. Evidence cannot be presented about the character, sexual conduct or general credibility of a party or a witness (DA section 22-6). This limitation relates to the general character, conduct and credibility of a person, not specific conduct relating to the case. For instance, as a rule, evidence on the general drinking habits of a party or a witness is prohibited. However, should a party claim that intoxication is relevant for the case, either because one of the parties was intoxicated at the time in question or because the memory of a witness must be affected by intoxication, evidence relating to the particular incident is allowed. In support of such evidence, the court has discretion to allow circumstantial evidence on the general drinking habits of the individual. The court determines the manner in which such evidence is presented. As a rule, questions on a party's or witness's criminal record or private life shall be put and answered in writing. The court session will be public, but questioning will be written to avoid the public gaining access to the particular information. Written declarations about a party's or a witness's good or bad name and reputation are inadmissible. The prohibition to present evidence applies even when the party or witness the evidence concerns has consented to the evidence being presented. However, when ruling on admissibility, the court takes into account the consent given.

640. Evidence arising from a lie detector using any method of testing physiological reaction is always inadmissible (DA section 22-6 subsection 4). This rule applies to traditional lie detectors measuring pulse and to, among others, magnetic resonance imaging (MRI) of the brain.

641. When hearing evidence despite a prohibition against such evidence, the court shall give an order of confidentiality to all persons present. The court may waive confidentiality or order the part of the hearing where evidence on the prohibited issues is taken to be closed to the public.

§3. Exempted Evidence

642. The DA has several rules giving certain groups of people a privilege to refuse to give evidence and exempting certain types of evidence. Prohibitions to give evidence are absolute, the court must enforce them on its own motion and only the person protected by the prohibition to give evidence may waive the prohibition; however, privileges are relative, and the person who is giving evidence decides whether to invoke the privilege.

643. Close relatives of a party, including current and former spouses or cohabitants, relatives in direct line of ascent (children, parents, etc.) and siblings, may refuse to provide evidence about information that has been given to them by that party (DA section 22-8). The court has the power to extend the privilege to a party's fiancé, foster parents, foster children and foster siblings. The definitions are gender neutral, since Norway recognizes same-sex marriage. The concept of 'fiancé' is seldom used, because cohabitation prior to marriage is the norm and engagements are rarely marked publicly.

644. A party or witness may refuse to provide access to evidence that could result in a penalty for:

- himself or herself;
- his or her relatives in direct line of ascent and descent (children, parents) and siblings; current or former spouses or cohabitants and their relatives in direct line of ascent and descent, and siblings; and
- current spouses and cohabitants of the persons mentioned above (DA section 22-8).

645. The privilege may be extended to cover foster family relations and fiancés. The rule protects against self-incrimination and incrimination of relatives. All sanctions identified in national law as a criminal sanction, as well as sanctions considered as criminal under the ECHR, fall under the privilege. The privilege covers only situations in which giving evidence has a direct causal link to criminal sanctions. Hence, information that law enforcement officials or the prosecution already has and information on criminal actions that are time-barred are not privileged, as these types of information will not contribute to criminal sanctions.

646. In addition to incriminating evidence, the court may give a privilege to evidence resulting in material loss of reputation or welfare (DA section 22-9 subsection 3). The loss of reputation must be determined individually based on the standards in society in general, the particular group to which the person belongs and the particular context. For instance, this rule does not apply in paternity cases (Children Act section 21). The loss of welfare is a wide category but is limited to circumstances having a decisive impact on welfare. In child custody proceedings, the court may give a privilege to a spouse concerning information on where the family lives if the information would put the family at risk of facing violence from the ex-spouse. This privilege is intended only for cases involving severe violence.

647. The court has discretion to order a witness to give evidence or give access to documents despite the privilege if it considers it reasonable to do so considering the nature of the case, the importance of the evidence and the consequences of giving the evidence (DA section 22-9 subsections 2 and 4). The court is more likely to order a person to give evidence in child custody cases than in other cases. Minor criminal offences are protected to a lesser extent than major offences. In the case of relatives, the more distant the relative, the more likely it is that the court will order the evidence to be given. Information resulting in material loss of reputation or welfare has a lower degree of protection than incriminating evidence.

648. Information on trade and business secrets, which is understood as information important for competition, is privileged. The privilege is general and covers all persons with access to such information, but it does not mandate anyone to refrain from giving evidence. The person in possession of trade and business secrets is free to give evidence but may choose not to do so or not to answer certain questions.

649. If necessary and fair, the court may order information on trade and business secrets to be presented (DA section 22-10). The court must balance the interest of arriving at the materially correct solution with the business interests of the entity covered by the privilege. Any alternative methods of gaining necessary information or methods for withholding part of the sensitive data, such as withholding parts of a document or closing the proceedings to the public, must be considered.

650. Editors in mass media have a privilege to refuse to give information on the identity of the author of a published item or the sources on which the publication is based (DA section 22-11). This privilege extends to other persons, such as colleagues, publishers and press agents, who have information on the identity of the author or the sources. The court may order evidence to be given only if important public interests so require and if the information is of considerable importance. The court must balance the value of protection of sources for mass media with the interest at hand in the case. Information on circumstances that it is in the public interest to publish has particular protection, since a free press is essential in a democratic society. Although the provision only refers to mass media, publications on the Internet may also be covered. Films and books are not considered mass media unless the content is of a documentary nature involving criticism of society.

651. When prohibited and exempted evidence is given in court, the court shall impose a duty of confidentiality present at the hearing (DA section 22-12). The court closes access to the hearing to the public. However, the terms of the consent could indicate an open hearing.

§4. Evidence Obtained in an Illegal or Improper Manner

652. The court may disallow evidence that was obtained in an improper or illegal manner (DA section 22-7). The decision to disallow illegally or improperly obtained evidence consists of two steps. First, the court must assess whether the evidence was obtained in an illegal or improper manner. Then, the court must consider whether the evidence should be disallowed.

653. The rule does not distinguish between evidence obtained in an illegal manner and evidence obtained in a manner that is legal as such but ethically reprehensible. Thus, the question is not whether a specific provision forbids the method used to obtain the information but rather whether the act was ethically reprehensible.

Hence, opening a private drawer belonging to one's spouse or co-worker to obtain objects or documents is treated in the same way as acts constituting criminal offences. The assessment shall be limited to the method of obtaining the evidence, not the content of the evidence. In Rt. 2002 p. 1500, an employer was allowed to present e-mails from the employee's work e-mail account in situations where the employer had lawful access to the e-mail account. In Rt. 2014 p. 916, an insurance company could not use video material that its investigator had filmed illegally to prove personal injury insurance fraud, but it could call the investigator as a witness, as hidden observation is not illegal. The lawfulness of evidence obtained abroad depends on the laws of the country in which the evidence was obtained.

654. After the court has found that evidence was obtained in an illegal or improper manner, the court must consider whether to allow it. One factor in this consideration is the importance of the piece of evidence: the more central the evidence is and the more difficult it is to find replacing evidence, the less likely it is that the court will disallow the evidence. Another factor is the blameworthiness of the method used to obtain the evidence: the more blameworthy the method was, the more likely it is that the court will disallow it. In LH-2011-26141, an employer was allowed to present information from GPS data for purposes other than those for which the employer had a permission to obtain data. The drivers of the vehicle equipped with a tracking system knew of the system; thus, the method of obtaining the evidence was not particularly reprehensible. Use of the data was by far the simplest and most inexpensive way for the employer to monitor whether the drivers performed their tasks loyally and properly. Hence, both criteria were fulfilled.

655. Should the presentation of the evidence amount to a new violation or encroachment, the court will be likely to disallow the evidence. Material from CCTV surveillance in a shop does not violate the private life of the clients or the staff, because the shop is a public place, and thus courts tend to allow it. Conversely, material from CCTV surveillance in a locker room would amount to a new violation of private life, and courts would normally disallow it. The latter case is also a more serious violation.

656. If the evidence itself is compromised by the way in which it was obtained, the evidence will generally be disallowed. The more likely it is that the evidence may have been manipulated or otherwise weakened by the method of obtaining it, the less likely the court is to allow it. However, if it is possible to verify that the evidence was not compromised, the evidence should be allowed.

§5. Prohibition Against Written Witness Statements

657. The rules on evidence are based on the principles of orality and immediacy. Therefore, as a rule, all evidence must be presented directly to the judge or panel of judges hearing the case in the main hearing.

658. Witnesses and expert witnesses must appear in court. Written witness statements and other documents made for the purpose of the case are explicitly prohibited, unless the person who wrote the statement or drafted the document gives evidence directly to the court (DA 21-12). For instance, suppose that a month after buying a used car, the buyer discovers some problems with the car and takes the car to a garage. At the garage, the buyer is given a report indicating serious faults, about many of which the seller had a duty to inform the buyer. In subsequent litigation, the buyer may use the report, as it was not produced specifically to be used in litigation. However, if the buyer had requested a detailed report later in order to use the document as evidence, the latter report would be disallowed.

659. The court has discretion to allow written statements if the opposite party agrees or if the person who wrote the statement testifies as a witness. In both cases, the written statement must be a more adequate method of evidence than an oral statement, such as when the content of the report is technical and more easily explained in written form. When an oral report is more adequate, the court shall reject the written report even if the opposite party agrees or the author serves as a witness at court. If a written statement is allowed, the written statement can only be presented once the author is present in the courtroom as a witness. If it is impossible to examine the person who wrote the statement or document, the court has discretion to allow the statement or document without hearing the author as a witness.

660. The rule banning written statements produced for the purpose of litigation does not apply to statements of simple facts. For instance, an overview of the work schedule of an employee may be presented as evidence if the schedule as such is not disputed but is used as evidence to prove that the employee was at the place of employment at a specific time.

661. Court-appointed experts are exempted from appearing before the court when the court does not find their presence necessary. Expert reports are often of a technical nature, where data and documentation are given in the form of pictures, diagrams or tables and in a precise, technical language. Therefore, the most appropriate and adequate way of disseminating such findings is in a written report. The expert may be called to testify in court or remotely via telephone or video link to give the parties an opportunity to ask questions of clarification. However, whether the expert is called to testify depends on the discretion of the court.

Chapter 3. Administration of Evidence

§1. Taking of Evidence

662. The court bases its ruling on the merits on evidence presented to it directly in the oral, concentrated main hearing. To provide for early resolution and clarification of the dispute, the parties must include a tentative list of evidence in the statement of claim and statement of defence. This list of evidence must include a short description of the content of the evidence. As a rule, the evidence itself is presented during the main hearing. The list helps the parties to identify disputed and undisputed issues and to assess which evidence is necessary and whether new evidence is necessary. The parties may add and drop evidence by providing a new list of evidence. Typically, the list of evidence is revised, and at the closing of the preparatory hearing the list of evidence is formalized in a summary of evidence.

663. The list of evidence helps the court to clarify issues and to administer the evidence. The court may assess the relevance and proportionality of the evidence and rule on issues related to the evidence. For instance, the court may require the parties to consider more appropriate or cost-efficient types of evidence. A party that wants the court to appoint an expert or to inspect evidence must do so early on in order for the court to manage the case properly. The summary of evidence is also vital for making a schedule for the main hearing.

664. The evidence is presented to the court during the main hearing (DA sections 21-9 and 9-15). As a rule, parties testify first, then the witnesses, and finally other types of evidence, particularly expert and written evidence, are presented. The court may opt for a different sequence when appropriate. Remote examination (i.e.., examination via telephone or video link) has equal status to examination in the courtroom. There are two exceptions to this rule. First, the evidence may be recorded before the main hearing if it is impossible or cumbersome to take the evidence during the main hearing. Second, evidence may be secured even before the parties have brought an action. Courts are restrictive in allowing the parties to secure evidence.

665. Evidence protected by the rules on prohibition is presented in camera; that is, only the parties, their representatives and their legal counsel are allowed to be present. The court has discretion to rule that a person having a privilege to refuse to give evidence shall testify in camera. When evidence is presented in camera, the court must impose a duty of confidentiality on all persons present at the hearing (DA section 22-12).

666. In purely written proceedings, the court ruling is based on written evidence. However, as witness evidence is to be presented orally, the court may need to examine witnesses or inspect objects in camera or to arrange a court hearing exclusively to receive evidence. If both parties agree, witnesses may provide written testimony (DA section 21-13).

667. Rulings on evidence are generally in the form of a court order. An appeal against a court order on evidence must be filed within one week of service.

§2. Forced Production of Documents

668. All persons domiciled or staying in Norway have a duty to provide access to evidence and to serve as a witness when a court orders them to do so (DA section 26-5). If necessary and appropriate, the court may order a party or a third person to provide a report, overview, review or comparison of specific information. Such a document may only be ordered when it is not disproportionate in the case. Information is increasingly available electronically; hence, providing reports and overviews is often relatively simple. If the request concerns numerous electronic documents, the party making the request must grounds for why the request is proportionate and why all the documents are necessary (HR-2019-997-A). The party requesting a report or overview must pay the costs arising, particularly if providing the information is laborious.

§3. Deposition by Witnesses

I. Duty to Testify as a Witness

669. All persons domiciled or staying in Norway have a duty to testify as a witness in a court when they are called to do so (DA section 24-1). Persons with lawful absence are exempted.[84] Today, lawful absence is normally limited to situations of acute illness or acute problems with traffic or telecommunications, because witnesses can be heard remotely via telephone or video link.

670. Children under the age of 12 are only ordered to witness when the court deems it appropriate (DA section 24-10). Children who are at least 12 but under 16 years of age have a duty to testify, but the court decides whether the child testifies during the main hearing or whether a judge hears the child in his or her chambers or another suitable place. Persons with a serious mental illness and mentally handicapped persons are subject to the same rules as children (DA section 24-11). The court determines whether the person mentally ill or handicapped person shall witness and whether the person shall testify in court or in another place. In parental responsibility cases, children aged 7 and older have a right to be heard during the court proceedings (Children Act sections 31 and 61).

671. A person who is privileged to refuse to give or prohibited from giving evidence shall be summoned to witness unless he or she shall be heard only on prohibited or privileged topics (DA section 24-3). A witness summoned in spite of a privilege or prohibition shall inform the court of the privilege or prohibition and hence gain permission not to appear in court.

---

84. For the definition of lawful absence, *see supra* Part III Ch. 3 §2.

672. Persons domiciled and staying in one of the other Nordic countries (Denmark, Finland, Iceland and Sweden) have a duty to witness in a Norwegian court if the witness statement is likely to be of material importance, under the Nordic Convention on Witnesses, implemented in the Act on Nordic Duty to Testify (*lov om nordisk vitneplikt* 1975 no. 9). Persons domiciled outside the Nordic countries do not have a duty to appear in court to testify. However, the court or a party may encourage the witness to testify in a Norwegian Embassy or Consulate or when bi- or multilateral treaty is put in place, the court may request the authorities of the country were the witness is present for assistance. Some courts use remote examinations (i.e., telephone or video link) to hear witnesses staying abroad, although this method clearly encroaches on the sovereignty of the state where the person is present. Nonetheless, the Ministry of Justice has recommended the method to courts.

II. Summoning Witnesses

673. The legal counsel summons the witnesses the party wishes to call (DA section 13-3). The party may ask the court to summon reluctant witnesses. If the party does not have legal counsel, the court summons or orders the party to summon the witnesses. Witnesses may be summoned informally, via telephone or e-mail, or formally, via letter with a slip of receipt or as via recorded postal delivery. A witness summoned informally does not face sanctions for failure to appear at court. Hence, only benign witnesses can be summoned by using informal methods. Witnesses formally summoned risk being brought to a court hearing as a sanction for non-attendance.

674. The summons to testify shall state the case and the purpose of the court hearing and give the party the necessary details to comply with the duty to attend. When necessary, the court shall inform the witness of prohibitions and privileges to refuse to testify. The summons includes brief details of any provisions on compensation for attendance and the liability for non-attendance.

675. If possible, the witness should be summoned no later than one week before the court hearing. However, the witness can be summoned the day before the hearing, if it is necessary for the case to proceed swiftly or if the hearing of the witness does not cause practical problems for the witness. Remote hearings cause fewer problems for the witness than appearing in court; hence, summonses for remote hearings can be delivered at a later stage. Remote examinations can take place immediately following the summoning, if the witness agrees. Therefore, witnesses can be summoned on the day of the main hearing.

676. Witnesses have an obligation to prepare their testimony when requested to do so in the summons (DA section 24-4). A witness may be asked to review, *inter alia*, notes, minutes from meetings, accounts and other documents or evidence available to the witness. The duty to review material must be sufficiently specified to create an obligation for the witness. The court may also request that the witness bring any relevant documents or objects to the court hearing. The duty to prepare testimony is sanctioned with an obligation to compensate losses resulting from the failure to obey the court order, with a fine or with imprisonment.

III. Witness Examination

677. The court and parties decide together the order in which witnesses are heard. Often the claimant or appellant party examines his or her witnesses first.

678. As a rule, witnesses must wait outside the courtroom and are called in individually to give testimony (DA section 24-6). However, the court has discretion to allow a witness to attend the entire hearing if both parties agree. A witness who assists or has assisted a party in matters related to the dispute may be present at the entire hearing. For instance, a janitor responsible for maintaining premises for a landlord may attend the entire hearing in a tenancy dispute related to those premises, and an executive officer in charge of a disputed file may attend the hearing. As a rule, once a witness is dismissed, he or she may attend the rest of the hearing in the courtroom.

679. The witness must state his or her name, birth date, address, profession, relation to the parties and any other relevant information (DA section 24-8). If there is a concern that a witness or a close relative of the witness will be exposed to a criminal act or another substantive loss as a result of giving the aforementioned information, the witness may give the information in writing to the court. This rule is seldom used, but it is sometimes used in family cases with a history of severe violence. The witness must inform the court of any relationship to one of the parties. When necessary, the court informs the witness of the prohibitions and privileges related to giving information.

680. The witness must affirm to tell the whole truth and conceal nothing (DA section 24-8 subsection 4). A witness refusing to give this affirmation risks fines. Such a witness must still testify regardless of the refusal to give the affirmation.

681. The party who has called the witness questions the witness first (DA section 24-9). When both parties have called the same witness, the parties agree on who questions the witness first. A self-represented party may request that the court examine the witness. The court may examine witnesses it has called, or it may leave the examination to the parties. The testimony starts with the witness having the opportunity to give an account of the relevant events. The witness should be allowed to speak with as little interruption as possible. The party calling the witness will then question the witness. Once the party calling the witness has questioned the witness, the opposite party is given the opportunity to question the witness. The court may also question the witness. Questioning should commence with open questions and gradually move towards closed questions. Questions that in their form or content suggest the desired answer may not be posed unless they are asked to test the reliability of information that the witness has previously given or unless other special reasons justify doing so. The court must reject questions that are not pertinent to the case and questions whose form or content is disrespectful to the witness. However, questions aiming to testify the reliability of the witness or the statement are allowed. Thus, when relevant, the witness must state diseases or conditions that may hamper the quality of the witness's observations or ability to recall memories.

682. The court may structure witness examinations as it finds fit. In complex cases, witnesses may be questioned thematically or chronologically. The court may take over examination of the witness if questioning by the parties is done in an unsatisfactory way. In addition to the court, experts have the right to question witnesses.

683. Witness testimony is oral; hence, the witness may not read a statement. However, the witness may use notes indicating important dates, names, numbers and the like. When using notes, the witness must disclose who made the notes, when the notes were made and the purpose of the notes. For instance, a witness may bring a diary, excerpts from a file or notes made specifically for the testimony. When appropriate, the witness may read directly from the notes.

684. Should other evidence or witnesses contradict what the witness has expressed, the witness is informed of such evidence or statements and questioned specifically on the contradictory accounts. If contradictory testimony is expected, a party or the court may request that the witness stay inside or outside the courtroom until another witness is heard, and the first witnesses may then be re-heard.

685. Witnesses testify in a public hearing. Anonymous witnesses are not allowed. However, the court may order a party or another person to leave the courtroom while the witness is heard. The order is only applicable in special cases when there is a strong fear that the witness will not otherwise give 'an unreserved testimony' (DA section 24-7). In deciding on the matter, the court must in particular consider the fair trial rights of the party ordered to leave the room. The rights of an unrepresented party are more easily violated than those of a party with a legal counsel. The court may instead consider examining the witness remotely via telephone or video link. Once the witness has testified and the party has been allowed to re-enter the courtroom, the court must give an account of the testimony given. Ordering a party or other person to leave the courtroom is different from and should not be confused with ordering part of the hearing to be held in camera.

686. The party calling the witness is responsible for compensating the witness for travel costs and for loss of income. There are no rules for standard compensation for witnesses.

IV. Remote Examination

687. Remote examination via telephone or video link is common in Norway. Remote examination is allowed when direct examination is not practicable or when it is onerous or expensive (DA section 21-10). Reasons for remote examinations include illness, the witness having important obligations that prevent him or her from attending the court hearing and the witness being in a distant location. The court must weigh the cost and burden arising from the witness travelling to and from court with the importance of the witness's statement. The more important the witness's statement and the case are, the more restrictive the court should be in allowing remote examination. Experts are as a rule heard remotely via telephone or video link to save the time of the expert. The process for hearing witnesses remotely via telephone or video link is the same as for hearing witnesses in person. During the coronavirus pandemic, courts have examined all or most witnesses and experts remotely on video link.

§4. Deposition by the Parties Themselves

688. The evidence-taking stage of the main hearing commences with the parties giving evidence. Formal parties, their legal representatives and intervenient give evidence as parties. In a case with joinder of claims and parties, a person is considered a party for evidentiary purposes only for issues related to the claims in which that person is a party or intervenient. The duties of parties are regulated in DA Chapter 23.

689. Parties have a duty to attend hearings if the other party so requests or if the court considers it necessary. The presence of the party is the norm, as the party may actively engage in the proceedings, give evidence and engage in reaching settlement. The party is normally required to attend the entire hearing. The court may grant a party the right to attend the hearing and to give evidence remotely via telephone or video link. In such cases, the party must be available throughout the hearing. When the role of information obtained from the party is minor, when the party is ill, or when other circumstances so require, the court may allow the party to attend only parts of the hearing. Absence is sanctioned with a default judgment or summary dismissal of the case. In indispositive cases, the court may order the police to bring a party to the hearing or issue a fine.

690. At the request of the opposite party or the court, the party has a duty to testify before the court. The court may allow a party to testify remotely via telephone or video link. The party is first questioned by his or her counsel. The court questions self-represented parties. The conduct of the examination of a party follows the same pattern as the examination of witnesses.

§5. Expert Evidence

691. Norwegian law recognizes two types of experts: experts and expert witnesses. Experts are court-appointed, while expert witnesses are appointed by a party. Experts have several privileges beyond those given to expert witnesses. However, expert witnesses are in some respects treated as experts rather than as witnesses.

I. Experts

692. The role of the expert is to provide an expert evaluation of factual information that is not based on direct observation, such as the cause of a bodily injury; the effect of a physical injury on the health and level of functioning of the victim; or the mechanism resulting in damage to machinery or a construction. A medical professional describing the bodily injury to the patient at the time the patient was admitted to care and a car mechanic describing the damage to a vehicle involved in a crash can provide witness statements as long as they are only describing their observations and these descriptions do not require specialist knowledge. To be an expert, a person must provide insight as to the mechanisms resulting in the observed condition or the consequences of the condition. There is a fine line between a witness statement and the statement of an expert, as an expert may testify on pure observations in addition to providing an assessment of the observation, and a witness may testify on the mechanisms causing the condition at hand and the consequences of the condition.

693. An expert may be appointed to discuss legal questions only if the legal question relates to the content of customary or foreign law. Both of these may be unknown to the court and are not covered by the maxim of *iura novit curia.*

694. The court appoints an expert at the request of a party or on its own motion when an expert assessment is required to secure a sufficient factual basis for the ruling. While experts provide valuable expertise to the court, the use of experts is expensive and may amount to a delay in the proceedings. Consequently, the court must weigh and balance the benefits of the expertise provided with the resulting costs. The benefits must be proportional to the cost and delay. An expert may help to balance resources between the parties in a situation where one party can afford to appoint one or several expert witnesses but the other party cannot. Although the court has discretionary powers, it should be cautious in ruling against the unanimous wishes of the parties.

695. As a rule, the court appoints only one expert. In large cases raising complex factual issues in different areas of speciality, the court may appoint more than one expert. One issue may require one type of expertise, while another issue may require another type. For instance, assessment of medical injuries may require expertise in different fields of medicine, and a case on liability for bodily injury resulting from a road accident may require both medical and technical expertise. Similarly, the more complex an issue is and the more experts within the field differ in their opinions, the more likely it is that the court will appoint two experts with similar expertise. Thus, in a matter related to the use of new, experimental technology, the court will often appoint two experts. The choice to appoint more than one expert must be proportional to the interest at stake. The court may also appoint an additional expert to supplement the expert(s) appointed previously.

696. The expert must naturally have both the necessary skills and experience. The term 'skills' refers to education, training, knowledge and practical skills. The court may have a panel of experts for certain types of issues when practicable. Larger courts often have a panel of experts used in child custody cases and other cases related to child welfare. The experts must be impartial and independent. Appellate courts may, however, use the same expert as lower courts.

697. The parties have the right to nominate experts and to comment on the nominated expert(s). An expert who is nominated by both parties and who is willing to serve is appointed unless special reasons suggest otherwise.

698. The court decides on the terms of reference and gives instructions to the expert. The court delimitates the issues the expert shall examine. The parties may be ordered to prepare a draft for the terms of reference. Often, the parties have different opinions as to the exact tasks of the expert and the issues to be investigated; in such cases, the court must try to balance the views of the parties in the terms of reference. The expert has a wide mandate to gain access to documents and premises necessary to fulfil the instructions given. In personal injury cases, standard terms of reference are regularly used.

699. The expert delivers a report on the observations and findings in writing, unless the court decides otherwise. Experts may file a joint report unless the court has ordered them to provide individual reports. The court may require that the expert submit a supplementary report. A supplementary report usually results from the request of a party. The use of written expert reports is a major exception from the principle of oral evidence.

700. The court has discretion to summon the expert to witness in the main hearing. If one of the parties requests that the expert be summoned to testify, the court should summon the expert. Otherwise, the court determines the need to summon the expert based on the report and the issues at hand. The more central the issues of the expert report are, the more important the examination of the expert is. Conflicting expert reports result in the experts being summoned to testify. Often, experts are heard remotely via telephone.

701. In the hearing, experts have privileges greater than those that witnesses have. First, experts may attend the entire hearing. Second, the expert may consult with other experts. Thus, a medical expert may consult with the technical expert and other medical experts in the case. Third, experts may ask the parties, witnesses and other experts' questions. All privileges are contingent on being necessary for fulfilling the assignment that the court has given the expert. The expert does not have to be present at the entire hearing, but the court has a right to mandate the expert to be present when required for the assignment.

702. Experts testify in the same manner as witnesses. However, the expert does not testify under the same oath as witnesses but rather under an affirmation that the expert has performed his or her assignment conscientiously and to the best of the expert's ability.

703. The party who requested the expert covers the cost of the expert. However, if the case has a particularly high interest for one party, the court may order that party to pay the costs. When both parties request an expert, the costs are divided between the parties (Court Fee Act, *lov om rettsgebyr* 1982 no. 86, section 2). The court is liable to pay the experts for their services, and the party that is liable for the costs arising compensates the court.

II. Expert Witnesses

704. Expert witnesses are party-appointed persons with expert knowledge in an area. Parties use expert witnesses *inter alia* when the court believes that an expert is not required, that calling an expert would be too costly or time-consuming, that the person in question does not have the qualifications required to be an expert or that the person in question is not impartial. The parties are free to summon expert witnesses as long as doing so is in accordance with the principle of proportionality and the evidence offered is relevant to the case.

705. Expert witnesses have only part of the privileges of experts. First, expert witnesses may not file written reports unless a written report is considered the most appropriate way to deliver evidence and the expert witness testifies at the court hearing or remotely via telephone or video link. Second, expert witnesses do not have access to premises protected by the right to a private life, such as the home of the other party, unless the person protected so agrees. Third, expert witnesses do not have the right to consult court-appointed experts. Fourth, the court does not pay any compensation to expert witnesses. The party calling the expert witness is liable for paying the expert witness. However, the other party may be liable to compensate the costs, should the party who has called the expert witness prevail.

706. Expert witnesses have two privileges that regular witnesses do not have. First, they may attend the entire main hearing. Second, they may question parties, witnesses and experts. Because expert witnesses have these privileges, the status of a witness as an expert witness should be determined before the main hearing commences. As the line between a witness and an expert witness is difficult to determine, the court may need to rule on the issue.

§6. Affidavits and Written Statements

707. Affidavits are not used in Norwegian civil procedure law. Immediacy and orality are central principles, and thus witnesses are mandated to give evidence orally and directly before the court hearing the case. Exceptions are made only in particular cases, such as when it is impossible to hear the person who wrote the statement or when the statement contains simple factual information.[85]

85. *See* Ch. 2 §5 for more detailed information on written statements.

§7. Inspection by the Judge

708. Inspection by the judge takes place in two different ways depending on whether the objects and documents are presented in a court hearing or at the site outside the court.

I. Inspection of Documents, Electronic Evidence and Small Objects

709. The parties may present documents, evidence in electronic format and objects to the court during the main hearing (DA Chapter 26).

710. When presenting a document, one party gives the court and the opposite party a copy of the document during either the preparatory stage or the main hearing and brings the original document to the hearing. In other than simple cases, the court asks the parties to provide a bundle of documentary evidence prior to the main hearing. In the main hearing, the party presents the document by pointing out the important parts. The review may not be more detailed than necessary. For instance, if the dispute relates to the terms of payment, the party indicates the relevant provision(s), often reading it aloud and discussing it in detail. Other terms will be either not mentioned at all or discussed only briefly. When the exact wording of a passage in the document is central, the passage is read aloud in court.

711. Other objects are reviewed in the manner the court finds to be the most suitable.

712. Persons may be the object of inspection when this is possible 'without undue strain and it is not disgraceful'. Often, the expert invites the person to his or her office for inspection and the expert report is presented later in court, rather than the examination taking place in court. Persons cannot be forced to be subject to inspection. However, a claimant claiming compensation for bodily injuries must subject to inspection under the threat of dismissal of the claim. Parties are subject to more extensive and invasive inspections than other persons, because an inspection is in the direct interest of a party but not of third parties.

II. Large Objects and Sites

713. When objects that cannot be brought to the courtroom, or when bringing an object to the courtroom would result in disproportionate costs or practical problems, the court may inspect the object at the place where the object is located (DA section 27-5). Usually, the inspection takes place during the main hearing. The judge or panel of judges hearing the case and the parties travel to the site where the object is located for the inspection. Should the object or site to be inspected be situated far from the court, the court may ask another court to inspect the object (DA section 27-2 and CJA section 44).

714. Alternatively, the court can appoint an expert to inspect the object or site (DA section 27-2). The inspection of the object by an expert and appointment of an expert are closely related. The task of an expert examining an object is often more limited than that of a court-appointed expert, but the difference is one of degree rather than constituting two clearly different mechanisms. The conduct of the inspection depends on the nature of the object and the disputed issues.

§8. Evidence on the Content of Law

715. Norwegian law adheres to the principle of *iura novit curia* (DA section 11-3). Hence, the court is expected to know the law and apply it correctly, and the parties are not allowed to present evidence related to matters of law. The parties can – and, when appropriate, do – provide relevant documents such as court rulings, preparatory works and legal scholarship or excerpts thereof as part of their legal arguments, but these documents are not considered evidence.

716. There are a few exceptions to the rule. First, customs and customary law are situated at the boundary of fact and law and can therefore be considered a fact. For instance, the existence of a specific custom could be subject to evidence. Second, the content of foreign law is also subject to evidence when the court cannot easily establish it (e.g., HR-2012-2165-U and HR-2012-2166-U). Third, statements on the law that have been produced with the current litigation in mind are only permitted with the consent of all parties. The parties or other entities with a clear interest in the outcome of the case (e.g., an organization) sometimes request legal experts to write a statement on the law when the case raises a difficult issue of interpretation. The parties and their legal counsel may use the statement as they wish in their argumentation: permission is limited to situations in which a party wishes to present the statement as such to the court. Parties are allowed to present without restriction statements that have not been produced with the current case in mind, such as opinions in legal scholarship and information materials.

§9. Recording of Evidence

717. Recording of evidence (*bevisopptak*) refers to evidence in a pending case being taken outside the main hearing. It is an exception to the principle of immediacy.

718. The court orders the recording of evidence after a petition from a party or on its own motion (DA section 27-2). Parties shall make the petition as soon as possible during the preparatory stage of proceedings. The court can allow a recording of evidence if recording is more reliable than presenting the evidence at the main hearing, there is an obvious risk that the evidence cannot be presented in the main hearing or presenting the evidence at the main hearing will result in disproportionate expenses or disadvantages to the parties or to the witness (DA sections 21-11 and 21-3). The reliability of evidence is reduced if the evidence consists of items deteriorating over time, such as fruits or vegetables, or if the evidence involves an inspection of property that may be more difficult in the winter than in the summer. A serious illness causing the condition of the witness to deteriorate may also call for recording of evidence. Time is often an issue; the shorter the duration of the court proceedings, the more likely it is that easily perishable goods will remain usable or that a terminally ill patient will still be able to give evidence. Hence, selecting the right option is challenging. For evidence that runs the risk of disappearance, this risk must be obvious, whereas no such criterion exists for evidence that deteriorates but will still be usable. For disappearing evidence, the cost incurred is not a weighty argument for the ruling on recording. Recording of deteriorating evidence may only be conducted if it does not result in disproportionate costs.

719. Recording of evidence may also be conducted when a delay in taking the evidence would result in significant costs. For example, a witness could be travelling to a remote location with poor communication. Inspecting a vessel or vehicle during the main hearing could result in the owner having to take the vessel or vehicle out of traffic, causing significant economic loss.

720. The court hearing the case, another court or an expert records the evidence. The court may appoint an expert to inspect an object or a site prior to the main hearing (DA section 27-2). There is a sliding scale between appointing an expert to record evidence, appointing an expert to inspect an object and appointing an expert as a court-appointed expert. The regular rules on evidence apply as far as the court considers them to be appropriate (DA sections 27-3 and 27-5). Recording of evidence cannot be made ex parte.

721. Recorded evidence may be presented at the main hearing if the parties' right to an adversarial trial is respected. The parties or their representatives must be present at the recording and must be given the opportunity to question the witness or to participate and contribute to the inspection of an object. Giving a party an opportunity to supply written questions or comments may suffice. If the parties were not present at the recording, they might agree to the court using the recording, or they may be given the right to question the witness whose statement was recorded or the person conducting the inspection during the main hearing. If none of these conditions is fulfilled, the court must weigh the right to an adversarial trial with the need of the parties to present the evidence. Higher courts are entitled to accept recorded material presented in lower courts in the same matter.

§10. Securing Evidence for a Future Lawsuit

722. A party may need to secure evidence when a lawsuit is not pending. Securing evidence is similar to recording evidence outside the main hearing and serves essentially the same purpose. However, since a lawsuit is not pending, the evidence may not be needed for judicial purposes. As recording of evidence is time-consuming and costly, securing of evidence shall not be done just in case it may be needed later. The person requesting the court to secure evidence must show that a lawsuit is likely, that the evidence is central in the lawsuit and will be lost or considerably impaired if not secured immediately or that there is another weighty reason to secure the evidence (DA section 28-2). Statements from parties and witnesses and inspection of objects are subject to securing evidence.

723. A petition for securing evidence is submitted to the court that is competent to hear the prospective lawsuit. Alternatively, the petition may be submitted to the court at the place where the evidence will be taken. The petition must identify the person who is subject to the request to provide evidence and the probable opposite party in the lawsuit. The petition must identify the measures the party requests and the dispute for which the evidence is needed. Upon accepting the petition, the court notifies the likely opposite party in the lawsuit. The petitioner must pay the costs arising from securing the evidence.

724. The court may rule to secure evidence in ex parte proceedings, when the evidence must be secured promptly or when there is reason to believe the opposite party could obstruct the evidence. If the court orders that evidence will be secured in an ex parte hearing, neither the opposite party nor the general public shall have access to the evidence before a period of six months has elapsed or the case for which the evidence was taken has been closed. The court may deny the petitioner access to the evidence if the interest of the opposite party so requires. The court orders the enforcement officer to seize the evidence and keep it in a secure place without giving the parties access to it. Once evidence is secured, the court notifies the opposite party of it. The opposite party has the right to request that the court hold a hearing (DA section 28-3).

725. Typically, securing evidence is related to electronic evidence in the control of the opposite party, as it is easy to quickly destroy electronic evidence. The challenge with electronic documents is the amount of information they contain, much of which is often not relevant to the dispute. Thus, after the evidence has been secured, the parties must agree upon how to sort it. If the parties cannot agree, then the court decides on the sorting method and key words used in searches. Technical staff does the sorting.[86]

726. The petitioner in ex parte proceedings may become liable to compensate the opposite party for any loss resulting from securing the evidence. Liability for costs arises only when the petitioner has no right or claim which the evidence secured could protect or when securing the evidence turns out to be unjustified because the petitioner intentionally or negligently gave false or misleading information regarding the need for the evidence. In ex parte proceedings, the court may require the petitioner to provide a sufficient security and may order the petitioner to pay all expenses arising from securing the evidence (DA section 28-3 subsections 5 and 6).

---

86. For a more detailed discussion on electronic evidence in Norwegian law, *see* Maria Astrup Hjort, *Electronic Evidence in Control of and Adversely Affecting the Opposing Party: A Comparative Study of English and Norwegian Law,* 8 Digital Evidence and Electronic Signature L. R. (2011).

727. The sanction for refusing to cooperate in the securing of evidence is liability to pay costs to the opposite party. In addition, in its ruling on the facts, the court may take into account the refusal as an indication that the party has something to hide.

§11. Information on Infringement of Intellectual Property Rights

728. In disputes on a suspected infringement of intellectual property rights, a party who suspects that he or she is the victim of an infringement may petition the court order disclosure of information. The court may order the person who is suspected of having infringed the right (e.g., a provider of a telecommunication network or seller of goods) to provide information relevant to the infringement (DA Chapter 28A). The order to provide information may only be given if the interest of the rights holder outweighs the inconvenience caused to the person providing the information. The petition must identify the information needed and the person who has the required information. The court orders the manner in which the information must be provided. The petition may be filed before an action has been brought or after the case has become pending. Before an action on infringement has been brought, the petition is made to the court that has jurisdiction on the subject matter or to the court at the place of domicile of the person against whom the order is sought. The petitioner must compensate the costs arising from providing the information. DA Chapter 28A implements the EU Directive on the Enforcement of Intellectual Property Rights.[87]

87. Directive 2004/48/EC of 29 Apr. 2004 on the enforcement of intellectual property rights.

Part VIII. Particular Proceedings

Chapter 1. Class Actions

729. Class actions were introduced in the 2008 DA Chapter 35. Annually, approximately ten class actions are brought to Norwegian courts.

§1. Admissibility of Class Actions

730. When several persons have claims based on identical or substantially similar factual and legal bases, they can opt to file a class action instead of filing separate actions. The same procedural rules must apply, and the same court must be competent for the claims. However, since territorial jurisdiction can be established through joinder of cases and rules establishing exclusive jurisdiction are very limited, the territorial competence of the court does not hinder class actions in practice. Claims belonging to the small claims track may be mixed with claims in the regular track for the purpose of class actions.[88]

731. For a class action to be used, it must be the most appropriate way of dealing with the claims. If the number of persons involved is low, joinder of cases or joint proceedings may be more appropriate. Similarly, if the members have different types of claims or raise different objections, individual proceedings may be more adequate. Individual court proceedings can be coordinated, or one of the cases can be used as a 'pilot case', in which the common issues are determined and later applied in the rest of the cases. After a court has approved a class action, it has discretion to reverse or amend its ruling on its own motion and transfer the case to regular proceedings.

732. Organizations may choose either regular proceedings, where the organization is the claimant making claims on its own behalf, or class action proceedings, where the organization makes claims on behalf of its members. The choice between the two alternatives depends on the nature of the claims. When the members hold identical or substantially similar claims, a class action is appropriate, particularly if the individual claims are of a pecuniary nature. Conversely, cases involving collective rights and rights belonging to an indeterminate group of people indicate that

88. *See* also Camilla Bernt, *Norway*, 622 ANNALS of the American Academy of Political and Social Science (2009).

regular proceedings may be more suitable. The boundary between the two approaches is not clear-cut. A class action on behalf of the members does not preclude the organization from advancing claims on its own behalf.

§2. Types of Class Actions

733. Norwegian law recognizes both opt-in and opt-out class actions, as well as class actions brought by an organization on behalf of its members and the general public. However, opt-in class actions are the default type (DA sections 35-6 and 35-7).

734. Opt-out class actions are used when the potential members have claims of a small value and interest. The claims cannot raise significant issues that must be determined individually for each claimant, or for a group of claimants. The court has discretion to select the most appropriate form of class action. Additionally, it has discretion to turn an opt-in class action into an opt-out class action during the proceedings, and vice versa.

735. Many factors influence whether a class action initiated by an organization or a class action initiated by an individual is more suitable. The more overlap exists between the membership of the organization and the potential members of the group the more likely it is for the organization or association to initiate proceedings. A declaratory action forbidding the defendant from doing something or declaring that the defendant is liable to pay damages is better suited to for organizations than enforcement proceedings in which each individual could be entitled to (pecuniary) compensation. However, the wide mandate of some organizations makes them highly suitable initiators of a class action, particularly in cases involving a large number of consumers. For example, the Norwegian Consumer Council has initiated several class actions.

§3. Proceedings in Class Actions

736. A class action starts when an individual, a group of individuals or an organization files a statement of claim with a request for a class action. The statement of claim must describe the scope of the claims and must give the court a sufficient basis for assessing whether class action is a suitable type of proceeding for the claims. Once the court has approved the class action, it shall define the scope of the claims included in the action, choose between the opt-in and opt-out format and nominate a class representative (DA section 35-4).

737. Upon approval of an opt-in class action, the court must give notice of the class action to those who may wish to join it (DA section 35-5). In opt-out class actions, the court notifies the members of the class action. The format of the notice is contingent on the type of claim. Usually it describes the cause of action, the character of the (potential) members of the group and the value of the claims.

738. In opt-in class actions, potential members of the group must register as class members within a time limit set by the court. The court has discretion to approve late registrations. Only persons who have a claim within the scope of the class action and who could sue the defendant in a Norwegian court are accepted as members.

739. Class members in opt-in class actions may withdraw their membership. The court must keep a record of withdrawals. Class members may withdraw until the court has ruled on the merits of the case. A withdrawal from the class action does not result in the member having to waive the substantive claim. The member may initiate regular proceedings on the same issue and claim. A class member initiating regular proceedings on the same claim is automatically considered to have withdrawn from the class action (DA section 35-8).

740. The court must appoint a class representative, the task of which is to safeguard the rights and obligations of the class and to keep the members properly informed of the proceedings. The representative is liable for the legal costs unless the court decides that the members of an opt-in class action are responsible individually. In addition to the representative, the group must have a legal counsel (DA section 35-9).

741. Should the original designation of the class action unfold as 'clearly inappropriate', the court may on its own motion narrow the scope of the class action. If the court finds that a class action is a clearly inappropriate form of procedure in a given case, it may reverse the ruling to admit the class action. Due to the narrowed scope of the class action or the cancellation of the class action proceedings, some or all the members of the class action may be excluded from the class action proceedings. Within one month of the amendment or reversal, the parties concerned must petition the court to continue to hear their claims. The claims will be treated as individual actions. If a party does not petition the court to continue the proceedings, the claim will be considered withdrawn and the proceedings discontinued.

742. The court tailors the proceedings to fit the class action. The court may hold preparatory hearings, *inter alia*, before ruling on accepting or rejecting the class action, to explore the possibility of settlement and in order to plan the main hearing. The class action may also be diverted to court-connected mediation.

743. During the preparatory stage, the court may split the class action either by separating individual issues from the class action or by creating one or more subgroups. Having created subgroups, the court may hear issues specific to each subgroup in separate proceedings. It may also hear individual issues in separate hearings. The court may split the issue of liability, which is common for all members, from the amount of damages or compensation awarded, which can vary. The members can be separated into subgroups based on, for example, the type of damage they have suffered (e.g., those who have only suffered injury to their property versus those who have additionally suffered personal injury). However, when splitting issues in this way, the court should hear issues related to the class action as a whole before hearing the individual issues. The court cannot split individual claims from the hearing. Individual claims are separated into separate actions. The court may rule on the individual claims after having ruled on the issues common to all cases (DA section 35-10).

744. The court may also decide to split the adjudication of one or more claims. Splitting adjudication is required when the factual or legal background of the cases is not identical, for instance, when different members of the class have suffered different damages or when a member of the class has raised objections. The court may choose one of the claims as a 'pilot' and rule on it. The ruling on the 'pilot' claim is binding on the rest of the claims unless there is a special reason for deviating from the ruling (e.g., significant differences in the factual background of the claims or objections related to expiry of limitation periods). The court will rule later on the other claims.

745. The final ruling in the class action is only binding on the members of the action at the time of the ruling. A settlement is subject to the approval of the court in opt-out class actions (DA section 35-11 subsection 3).

§4. Legal Costs in Class Actions

746. The regular rule that the loser is liable to compensate the prevailing party for its legal costs also applies to class actions. The class representative is responsible for paying court fees and other legal costs, including the legal costs of the opposite party. The class representative is entitled to remuneration for his or her work and to a refund for disbursements, including fees paid to the legal counsel. The court fixes the amount of the remuneration and the refunds for disbursements. If the court finds for the member of the class, the opposite party is liable to pay compensation for the legal costs and to pay remuneration to the class representative (DA sections 35-12 and 35-13).

747. In opt-in class actions, the class representative may request that the court fix a maximum liability for the members of the class. The class representative may also request the court obligate the class members to pay an advance upon registration. The members of the class are responsible for legal costs and remunerations to the class representative of the amount the court has set. The class members may agree on a higher threshold for the liability of costs.

Chapter 2. Family Law Proceedings

748. Particular rules apply to proceedings on parental responsibility, including child custody, residence, relocation and contact. The proceedings are regulated in sections 56–63 of the Children Act. The majority of parents settle issues related to child custody, residence, contact and maintenance during or after mandatory mediation.[89]

749. The procedural rules emphasize settlement through mediation. At the beginning of the court proceedings, the court appoints an expert to (co-)mediate the case, to assess the situation of the parents and the child and to give advice to the parents on co-parenting. The key purpose of the preparatory stage is to achieve settlement between the parents through the use of court-conducted family mediation. The judge and the expert co-mediate the case, or one of them has the main responsibility for mediation while the other serves as an assistant. The expert may have joint and separate meetings with the children and parents. The presiding judge may or may not be present at the meetings.

750. If the case does not settle, the court transfers it to the main hearing. The same judge may continue to sit the case, or the judge may choose to step aside to avoid issues related to partiality. The court requests that the expert provide a report that assesses the best interests of the child. The presiding judge, the expert or both hear the child prior to the main hearing, unless the child has already been heard during the preparatory stage and rehearing the child is not considered necessary.[90]

751. If there is reason to believe that the child may face serious neglect or abuse, the court skips mediation and requests that the expert make an evaluation of the best interests of the child. The case proceeds to the main hearing as soon as the expert evaluation report is ready.

752. The Children Act sections 14–29 contain special rules for parentage cases, in practice paternity cases. The mother, the current legal father, any other man who could be the father and the child have legal standing in paternity cases. The court at the domicile of the child has territorial jurisdiction. The mother and the potential fathers are obliged to testify as witnesses and cannot invoke the privilege to refuse to give evidence when doing so would result in material loss of reputation or welfare. The court has the power to order DNA samples from the mother, the child and the potential fathers. Proceedings are not halted as a result of unlawful absence of a party. The court can make use of statements that a party has given at an earlier

89. *See* Anna Nylund, *A Dispute System Design Perspective on Norwegian Child Custody Mediation* and Camilla Bernt, *Custody Mediation in Norwegian Courts: A Conglomeration of Roles and Processes*, in *Nordic Mediation Research* (Anna Nylund, Kaijus Ervasti & Lin Adrian eds, Springer 2018).

90. Anna Nylund, *Norway*, in *International Handbook on Child Participation in Family Law*, 266–269 (Wendy Schrama, Marilyn Freeman, Nicola Taylor & Marielle Bruning eds, Intersentia 2021).

stage of the proceedings in the event that the party is absent from a later hearing. The court can rule on paternity when a DNA test designates or excludes a potential father as the father of the child.

753. The proceedings in international child abduction cases are regulated in the Child Abduction Act[91] and adoption proceedings in the Adoption Act.[92] The rules in these acts are general and tacitly refer to the Children Act. Thus, in court proceedings the rules and practices in child custody, residence, contact and relocation apply *mutatis mutandis*.

754. The Norwegian Government bears the costs of parentage proceedings unless the court decides otherwise. The ruling is res judicata *erga omnes.* Similar rules apply to other actions where the court has to rule on kinship between persons in a direct line of ascent or descent, Children Act sections 29a–29e.

755. Apart from parental responsibility and parentage cases, courts are involved in public administration of estates of deceased persons and assets in divorce cases (Administration of Estates Act). The court appoints a receiver (*bobestyrer*) to administer the practical issues, such as making a list of the assets and liabilities, and suggest a plan for and to administer the division of the assets. The suggestion on division of property is subject to complaint to the court. The procedural rules in the DA apply to court proceedings.

756. Marriage takes place in church or municipal offices. The County Governor is responsible for divorce proceedings. The jurisdiction of the courts is limited to cases in which the marriage is dissolved due to forced marriage or serious abuse or in which the spouses entered into marriage unlawfully, e.g., one spouse was already married or one of the parties was under the age of 18 (Marriage Act sections 27 and 28).[93] Courts also have jurisdiction if one of the spouses is under guardianship. As spousal maintenance is an exception and most spouses settle issues related to children outside court, courts hear few cases related to marriage.

91. Act relating to the recognition and enforcement of foreign decisions concerning custody of children etc. and on the return of children (Child Abduction Act), *Lov om anerkjennelse og fullbyrdelse av utenlandske avgjørelser om foreldreansvar m.v. og om tilbakelevering av barn (barnebortføringsloven)*, 8 Jul. 1988.

92. Act relating to adoption (Adoption Act), *Lov om adopsjon (adopsjonsloven)*, 16 Jun. 2017 No. 48, in force since 1 Jul. 2018. Participation in child protection cases is regulated in the Act relating to child welfare (Child Welfare Act), *Lov om barneverntjenester (barnevernloven)*, 17 Jul. 1992 no. 100, in force since 1 Jan. 1993.

93. *Lov om ekteskap* 1991 no. 47.

Chapter 3. Proceedings in Administrative Matters on Coercive Measures

757. DA Chapter 36 regulates proceedings in administrative matters on coercive measures, particularly compulsory mental health care and compulsory care of children. However, the chapter does not form a comprehensive or exhaustive regulation of the proceedings.

758. Administrative bodies, such as the Mental Health Care Supervisory Commission and the County Social Welfare Boards, make the initial decision on coercive measures. The parties may challenge the decision by bringing an action to a court. The action falls under the rules of DA Chapter 36 only as long as the decision is valid. When the coercive measure has lapsed, the party may bring an action under the regular rules of civil procedure.

759. The private party has several privileges under Chapter 36. Cases on coercive measures have a priority when setting the date for the main hearing. The main hearing must be held shortly after the case has been filed. The court shall review all aspects of the case, which means that the rules of a party-driven adversarial process are replaced by rules that are substantially of a more inquisitorial nature. The court may decide on facts, claims and causes of action that are not mentioned in the statement of claim, in written statements or during the hearing, and it can ask the parties to provide more evidence or a specific piece of evidence.

760. The court hears the cases with a panel of three judges: one professional judge, one regular lay judge and an expert lay judge. All hearings are closed to the public, and the documents of the case are confidential. The court may also deny the private party access to some documents of the case, if the court deems this to be necessary because of his or her young age or mental health. The (legal) representative of the party has access to the full file and is able to inform the party about the main content of the file.

761. The government bears the costs of the proceedings: there are no court fees, the private party is awarded free legal aid and remuneration to witnesses and experts are paid by the State.

Chapter 4. Restraining Orders

762. Restraining orders (e.g., bans on visits) are part of the criminal law system but are considered civil litigation when they are not issued in criminal proceedings. Restraining orders are regulated in the Act on Criminal Procedure Chapter 17A.[94] The public prosecutor can decide on a restraining order, and the person against whom the order is filed can demand the case be taken to court. The court reviews the decision. A restraining order can be part of a criminal investigation, part of a criminal procedure in court or independent thereof. As it may be independent of a criminal case, it is considered civil litigation, although many of the rules considering coercive measures are applicable.

763. For the court to make or uphold a restraining order, the public prosecutor has to prove that there is reason to believe that a person will commit a criminal act against another person, pursue another person or in any other way disturb another person's peace. All kinds of violence or disturbing behaviour, such as repeatedly sending offensive text messages or posting disturbing comments on social media, qualify for a restraining order. The person protected by the order must request it, or public interest must require issuing of the order. The second alternative is used when the victim is dependent on the perpetrator and therefore will not apply for an order. A restraining order can be issued if it is proportional. Proportionality depends on the severity of the crime that might be committed, the likelihood of such a crime and the age of the person protected by the order. The burden of proof is on the prosecutor. There is no requirement of preponderance of proof, but the risk of crime must be more than theoretical. In other words, there must be specific circumstances (e.g., earlier conduct, threats, etc.) indicating the possibility of a future crime.

764. The restraining order protects a single person or a group of persons, such as members of a family or employees in a business or at a local Social Services Office. The order prohibits the person from being present at a specific place or from contacting another person. The order banning presence can be limited. If there is an imminent risk of a criminal offence being committed, the person subject to the order may be banned from staying in his or her home. Preponderance of evidence is required in these cases.

765. The restraining order must be limited to a set period of time not exceeding one year. The period is three months if the home is included. The order must be lifted as soon as it is no longer likely that a crime will be committed. Free legal aid is available to the subject of the order.

94. *Straffeprosessloven* 1981 no. 25.

766. Restraining orders may be put into effect by using an electronic shackle. This can only be done after the subject of the order has been found guilty of a crime against the person(s) protected. Usually the person protected by the order must contact the police if he or she observes a breach of the order. If an electronic shackle is used, the police are notified of the situation.

Chapter 5. Insolvency Proceedings

767. Norwegian law has two types of insolvency proceedings: debt settlement proceedings and bankruptcy proceedings. The proceedings are regulated in the Bankruptcy Act.

§1. Debt Settlement Proceedings

768. The debt settlement proceedings aim at limiting the debt burden through a payment plan and a relief from part of the debt (Bankruptcy Act sections 1–59). The business of the debtor is reorganized or liquidated. If the debtor is a private individual or non-profit organization, the aim is to rehabilitate the economy. The debt settlement may be either voluntary or court-ordered (compulsory debt settlement). Voluntary debt settlement requires a unanimous decision by all creditors to restructure the debts. In compulsory debt settlements, the vote may be divided. The debtor loses the disposal of the property during compulsory debt settlement proceedings.

769. The debtor files an application for debt settlement proceedings at the local District Court. The court appoints a debt settlement committee consisting of two to three members. The chair is a member of the Bar Association, and the rest of the members represent creditors and employees. The committee oversees the economy and business of the debtor and administers the debt settlement proceedings. The role of the court is limited, particularly in proceedings resulting in a voluntary debt settlement. In compulsory debt settlement, the court makes the final decision on the content of the debt settlement. Unsuccessful debt settlement results in bankruptcy.

§2. Bankruptcy Proceedings

770. The debtor or the creditor initiates bankruptcy proceedings by petition when the debtor is insolvent (Bankruptcy Act section 61). A creditor is obliged to send a bankruptcy notice to business entities before filing the petition (Bankruptcy Act section 63). Since insolvency is often difficult to prove, a debtor is presumed to be insolvent when he or she gives a bankruptcy notice; when he or she files a petition for bankruptcy; or when an attachment or arrest proceeding against him or her results in less than full settlement. The debtor avoids bankruptcy by paying the debt or by offering a sufficient surety or security for the debt.

771. The court holds a bankruptcy hearing before declaring the debtor bankrupt. The creditor petitioning for bankruptcy must pay a security for the cost of the bankruptcy proceedings in order for the court to open bankruptcy proceedings. The security is waived for employees of the debtor and public authorities. The court appoints a receiver, who as a rule is a member of the Bar Association, and if necessary, a liquidation committee. The debtor loses the disposal of the property.

772. During the bankruptcy proceedings, the court holds meetings of creditors. However, the receiver administers the practical parts of the proceedings, including making lists of assets and liabilities and suggesting a distribution of the assets. The court may quash decisions made by the receiver or the liquidation committee. Creditors and third parties concerned may contest debts, the priority of a debt, distribution of assets and other steps taken by the receiver by initiating proceedings at the court or by requesting that the court amend the decision.

773. In the majority of cases, the court cancels bankruptcy proceedings at an early stage due to a lack of assets to cover the costs of the proceedings. In other cases, the court terminates the proceedings when the assets have been distributed and the receiver has submitted the final report.

Chapter 6. Direct Enforcement of Pecuniary Claims

774. Pecuniary claims are directly enforceable without the involvement of a court or the Conciliation Boards. Direct enforcement does not require consent from the opposite party, nor does it require that the parties have signed an instrument of debt. The enforcement proceedings are more thorough than ordinary enforcement, but the control of the claim is more limited than in regular court proceedings. Thus, although the enforcement officer makes an initial assessment of the claim, contracts with unfair or even unlawful terms may pass the assessment.

775. Direct enforcement is only possible for uncontested claims. Once the claim is contested, the direct enforcement proceedings are concluded. Direct enforcement offers an efficient, expedient and economic process for debt collection for both the parties and society. The weakness of the system is the very limited control of the claim, including the cause of action and the legal foundations of the claim, particularly when the debtor is a consumer or a weak party.

776. Pecuniary claims are directly enforceable when the creditor sends the debtor a written notice indicating the grounds for the pecuniary claim and the amount claimed (EA section 7-2 subsection 1 letter f). The notice must be given on paper; electronic communication is not sufficient, except for providers of financial services (letter g). An invoice indicating the contract, service or goods charged for and a notice on direct enforcement are sufficient. The notification of the claim serves, in and of itself, as a ground for enforcement of the claim, interests arising out of the claim and costs for debt collection. The notification must indicate the exact amount or measure claimed and, for interest, the interest rate. A debt collection company may send the notice on behalf of the creditor, as registered debt collection companies have a privilege to act as legal counsel in enforcement proceedings.

777. The enforcement petition must be sent to the enforcement officer in the district at the domicile of the debtor. Alternative venues may not be used. The enforcement petition must contain the same information as a statement of case to the Conciliation Board (EA sections 5-2 and 7-5, and DA section 6-3). Specifically, it must state:

- the territorially competent enforcement officer;
- the names and addresses of all parties;
- the birth dates of private parties and the company registry number for companies;
- the name and address of any legal counsel;
- the claim, prayer for relief, including interests and costs;
- the cause of action;
- the type of enforcement requested;
- the ground for the enforcement, which is the written notice; and
- whether the claimant wishes the claim to be decided by the Conciliation Board should the defendant raise an objection.

778. The enforcement petition must be signed, and any relevant documentation must be attached.

779. After an initial assessment, the enforcement officer either dismisses the petition or decides to proceed with enforcement. In the latter case, the enforcement officer issues a notice of enforcement wherein the defendant is urged to comment on the claim, to provide information on any relevant circumstances and to indicate preferences as to which objects will be seized. The time limit for objections and for providing information is two weeks. The defendant is urged to give information regarding whether he or she wishes to negotiate a payment plan or to try to find another solution. If the defendant wishes to find a solution, the enforcement officer requests that the claimant contact the defendant for negotiations. The claimant is not obliged to comply with the request to negotiate. If the parties agree to negotiate, the proceedings will be stayed for a month, unless the claimant requests that the stay be shortened or prolonged.

780. The enforcement officer must also inform the defendant of the consequences of an objection against the claim. These consequences depend on whether the claimant has requested that the Conciliation Board rule on the claim. An objection combined with a request for negotiations results in a stay of the proceedings for one month before the proceedings are continued. The enforcement officer may also inform the defendant of the time and place for the distraint proceedings.

781. When the two-week time limit has lapsed, enforcement continues in the absence of a reply unless there is reason not to proceed. The enforcement officer gives the claimant the necessary information for the claimant to decide whether and how to proceed with enforcement. If the defendant has indicated a wish to negotiate a solution, the enforcement officer notifies the claimant and stays the proceedings. If the defendant has made objections against the claim, the enforcement proceedings are quashed. However, the claimant may request that the Conciliation Board rule on the claim by notifying the enforcement officer. The notification must be sent before the enforcement officer has notified the parties that enforcement is quashed. A timely notification results in the case being transferred to the Conciliation Board.

782. If the defendant has made an objection and the claimant has requested that the Conciliation Board decide the claim, the enforcement officer transfers the case to the Conciliation Board. The enforcement authority is also the secretariat of the local Conciliation Board; hence, transferral is only a formality. Before the parties are summoned to a hearing at the Conciliation Board, the claimant may withdraw the request that the Conciliation Board decide the case. Withdrawal of the request results in the enforcement being quashed. Should the Conciliation Board find for the claimant, or should the parties enter into an in-court settlement, the claimant must request that the enforcement officer continue enforcement within one month after the time limit for payment set in the ruling has lapsed.

783. The next step in enforcement is distraint. The enforcement officer must notify the defendant of the time and place of distraint proceedings. At the distraint proceedings, the defendant may raise an objection against the claim. The objection has the same consequences as an objection at the prior stage. After the distraint proceedings, the enforcement proceedings proceed in the ordinary manner.[95]

95. For further details, *see* Part IX Ch. 2 §1, I.

Part IX. Conservatory Attachment and Enforcement of Judgments

Chapter 1. Conservatory Attachment

§1. PROCEEDINGS

I. General Rules on Provisional Measures

784. The DA has two sets of rules for provisional measures to secure the enforcement of a claim: rules on attachment (*arrest*) in Chapter 33 and rules on interim measures (*midlertidig forføyning*) in Chapter 34. The general procedural rules for provisional measures are found in DA Chapter 32. Attachment of the financial assets of the defendant is applicable for securing pecuniary claims. Interim measures are applicable for securing other types of claims and consist of the court ordering the defendant to perform something, refrain from doing something or tolerate something. The court may order that an asset be taken into custody or administration. In special cases, the court may order an exit permit restriction for the debtor (*utreiseforbud*).

785. The court grants attachment if the debtor's conduct suggests that enforcement of the claim could be evaded or considerably impeded or that enforcement would have to take place abroad (DA section 33-2). The court can grant an interim measure when the defendant's conduct suggests that the action or execution of the claim would otherwise be considerable impeded (DA section 34-1). Exceptionally, the court may grant an interim measure in a disputed case to avert considerable loss or inconvenience. The provisional measures must be proportional; the loss or inconvenience to the defendant or debtor may not be clearly disproportionate to the interest to the claimant.

786. Provisional measures require a preponderance of evidence for the existence of the debt or claim and for the existence of the ground for the provisional measure (DA sections 33-3 and 34-2). The claimant must provide sufficient evidence for both. If delay poses a risk, the court has discretion to grant a provisional measure even when the claimant has not provided a preponderance of evidence.

787. The petition for provisional measures may be made orally during a court hearing, in writing before the action is brought or during court proceedings (DA section 32-5). The petition must state the names and addresses of the parties; the name of the court; the case number if the claim relates to a case pending at court; the provisional measure requested; the circumstances invoked in support of the claim and the provisional measure; and those documents supporting the measure that are in the claimant's possession. A petition for attachment must also state the amount of the claim and a maximum limit for the attachment. The maximum limit is the claim and sum of the foreseen costs related to the proceedings to enforce the claim.

788. The petition for provisional measures is filed at the District Court where the main claim is pending or at the domicile (ordinary venue) of the defendant (DA section 32-4). In addition, a petition for attachment may also be filed where assets or property belonging to the defendant is situated or is expected to arrive in the near future. For interim measures, territorial jurisdiction is limited to the place where property or assets directly related to the interim measure are located or are expected to arrive in the near future. If the main claim is pending at a court, the court hearing the main claim has exclusive jurisdiction on provisional measures. However, the Conciliation Boards do not have jurisdiction on provisional measures. Hence, the petition must be filed at the local District Court even if the main claim is pending at the Conciliation Board. The ArbA section 8 gives Norwegian courts jurisdiction on provisional measures notwithstanding an arbitration clause.

789. Norwegian courts have international jurisdiction on provisional measures if the court has jurisdiction on the main claim and if there is a sufficient connection to Norway. The requirement for a sufficient connection is particularly high for provisional measures in commercial cases. In Rt. 2015 p. 1040, the Supreme Court erroneously found that the Lugano Convention does not apply to provisional measures. It applied Norwegian rules despite a jurisdiction clause giving the District Court in Stavanger sole jurisdiction on the main claim and an arbitration clause establishing arbitration in Stavanger. The court rejected Norwegian jurisdiction because a particularly strong connection to Norway is required to establish Norwegian jurisdiction on provisional measures in commercial cases.

790. The court makes an initial assessment of the petition for interim measures (DA section 32-6). If the petition does not fulfil the requirements of DA section 32-5, the court must immediately summarily dismiss the petition or set a time limit for the claimant to rectify the deficiency. The court may request that the claimant provide additional documentation in support of the existence of the main claim or the need for provisional measures. A court lacking jurisdiction must transfer the petition to a competent court. If the court finds that the petition is without any reasonable prospect of success, it must dismiss it immediately.

791. The court may order provisional measures in written ex parte proceedings, if notifying the defendant could hinder enforcement or immediate enforcement is required for other reasons (DA section 32-7 subsection 2). The parties or any other person affected by the order may require a subsequent hearing on the measure or on the costs arising from the measure (DA section 32-8). After the hearing, the court may uphold, amend or dismiss the first ruling in whole or in part.

792. The court summons the parties to a hearing on the provisional measures (DA section 32-7). The claimant must be present at the hearing; absence is sanctioned with dismissal of the petition. If either party is lawfully absent, the court adjourns the hearing. In complex cases, the court may request that the defendant file a written statement, including relevant documents, within a time limit prior to the hearing. The court may not sanction failure to file a written statement.

793. For simple claims, the claimant can request that the court hear the main claim in the hearing on the provisional measure (DA section 32-9). The situation could be considered as 'fast track' proceedings for the main claim. The prerequisites for the 'fast track' are that:

- the proceedings provide the courts with sufficient factual and legal basis for ruling on the claim;
- ruling on the main claim will not amount to a significant delay in determination of the provisional measure; and
- the claims do not call for further preparatory steps, as further preparation would delay the proceedings.

794. The court has discretion to reverse the ruling to include the main claim in the event that the conditions for ruling on the main claim are not fulfilled. The court may not rule on the main claim if it finds provisional measures are not called for. A liberal application of the 'fast track' could lead to petitions for provisional measures with the primary object of gaining access to expedient proceedings rather than because provisional measures were actually needed to ensure effective enforcement. The court may reverse the ruling to hear the main claim in the same proceedings. After the court has rejected the request to rule on the main claim, the party who requested that the court rule on the main claim can ask the court to hear the main claim in a separate proceeding. In rejecting the request to rule on the main claim, the court must set a time limit for a request for separate actions, unless the action is already pending.

795. The court has jurisdiction to rule on the main claim concurrently with the provisional measure even if its jurisdiction is based solely on the petition on the provisional measure and it lacks jurisdiction on the main claim based the rules in DA Chapter 4. However, it does not establish jurisdiction for cases in which the Lugano Convention is applicable.

796. When ruling on preliminary measures, the court may require that the claimant provide a security to cover the damage the defendant may suffer from the preliminary measure (DA section 32-12). The court must set a time limit for providing the security. The court may extend the time limit on request.

797. Regular rules for compensation of legal costs apply (DA section 32-10). The court may rule on legal costs in ex parte proceedings. In proceedings on attachment, the compensation for legal costs is included in the sum of the attachment, raising the amount of the attachment with the legal costs.

798. The claimant is liable to pay damages if the provisional measure is discharged or lapses and the claimant's claim did not exist when the provisional measure was ordered. The same applies in the event that the petition was unjustified in other respects because false or misleading information was given intentionally or negligently.

II. Attachment

799. The ruling ordering an attachment shall include the name of the parties, the claim, the maximum amount of the attachment and the grounds for the attachment (DA section 33-4). The court may identify the assets to be attached. On application by the defendant, the court must fix a time limit for the claimant to bring a legal action on the claim. The court may extend the time limit on the request of a party. The court must also inform the defendant that execution of the attachment can be avoided by providing a security. Rulings in ex parte proceedings must include information on the defendant's right to require a subsequent hearing.

800. The attachment must be executed immediately. For easily identifiable assets, particularly those included in a public registry, the court may execute the attachment. In most situations, the court will transfer the execution to enforcement authorities (DA section 33-5).

801. If new evidence or circumstances prove that the main claim or the basis for the attachment does not exist, the defendant may request that the court discharge the attachment (DA section 33-10). The defendant may also request the court to discharge the attachment if the claimant maliciously delays proceedings regarding the main claim. This provision functions as a protection against undue use of provisional measures as a weapon to weaken the opposite party. The provision also emphasizes the temporary character of provisional measures.

802. The attachment lapses automatically when:

- execution is levied on the attached asset for the claimant's claim;
- the court has set a time limit for the claimant to provide a security, and the time limit has been exceeded without the claimant having provided the security;
- the court has set a time limit for the claimant to bring an action on the main claim, and the time limit has been exceeded without the claimant having brought an action;
- the court has not set a time limit for the claimant to bring an action on the main claim or to instigate enforcement proceedings and one year has passed after the court granted the attachment order;

- the main claim either has been paid or has lapsed in another way;
- the defendant has been found not to be liable for the main claim;
- the claimant abandons the right in the attachment; or
- the claimant has obtained an enforceable judgment for the main claim but has not claimed execution within one month after the judgment became final and enforceable.

803. The claimant shall abandon the right to the attachment when the attachment has lapsed. The defendant may also require that the court rule on the lapse of the attachment.

III. Interim Measures

804. The rules on interim measures are less specific than the rules on attachment, as the contents of the orders vary. Interim measures are applied to all types of obligations to do something, refrain from doing something or tolerate something.

805. The ruling ordering an interim measure shall include the names of the parties, the main claim, the grounds for the attachment and a sufficiently detailed stipulation of the protective measures ordered. The court must fix how the interim measure shall be executed, when the measure enters into force and the duration of the measure (DA section 34-2). The court may order the interim measure to become effective only once the claimant has provided a security. The court may also set a time limit for the petition to bring an action on the main claim. Rulings in ex parte proceedings must include information on the defendant's right to require a subsequent hearing.

806. Execution of interim measures is contingent on the claimant lodging enforcement proceedings according to the EA (DA section 34-4). The claimant must lodge enforcement proceedings at court or at the enforcement authority executing the enforcement. The court transfers cases requiring measures by an enforcement officer to the appropriate enforcement officer for execution.

807. If new evidence or circumstances prove that the main claim or the basis for the interim measure does not exist, the defendant may request that the court stay or limit the interim measure (DA section 34-5). The defendant may also make such a request if the claimant maliciously delays proceedings regarding the main claim.

808. The attachment lapses automatically when:

- the time limit setting the duration of the interim measure has expired;
- the court has set a time limit for the claimant to provide a security, and the time limit has been exceeded without the claimant having provided a security;
- the court has set a time limit for the claimant to bring an action on the main claim and the time limit has been exceeded without the claimant having brought an action;

- the main claim has been determined by a final and enforceable judgment;
- the main claim either has been paid or has lapsed in another way; or
- the claimant abandons the right to interim measures.

809. The court may extend the duration of the interim measure and the time limit for the claimant to provide a security or to bring an action. The claimant must apply for extension before the time limit has passed.

810. In cases on infringement of intellectual property rights, the holder of the right may petition that the court order customs authorities to withhold specific goods. The court may order the interim measure even if the recipient of the goods is unknown (DA section 34-7) and the proceedings consequently must be held ex parte.

IV. Rules on Exit Permit Restrictions

811. The rules on attachments apply *mutatis mutandis* to exit permit restrictions (DA sections 33-1 and 33-11 to 33-14). An exit permit restriction may be ordered when there is a danger that the defendant will leave Norway in order to avoid enforcement. It can only be granted if it is necessary and if attachment of assets will not provide a sufficient security. The exit permit restriction may not be a disproportionate intervention. In practice, exit permit restrictions are rare. Normally, the exit permit restriction is executed by confiscating the debtor's passport. However, due to the Schengen Treaty, such confiscation remains inefficient and monitoring travel activity is cumbersome. In particularly serious circumstances, the court may order that the debtor shall be held on remand in custody or be subject to other restrictions. However, courts have not imposed such restrictions in practice.

§2. Judicial Review

812. Rulings on provisional measures are subject to appeal. As the form of the ruling is court order, the appeals proceedings are, as a rule, written.

813. Provisional measure orders are enforceable despite an appeal; however, the court may grant a suspension of the enforcement (DA section 19-13). Suspension applies to both situations where the court has granted a provisional measure and cases in which the court has granted a provisional measure in ex parte proceedings and quashed the first ruling in the subsequent hearing. In the first case, enforcement will follow despite the appeal. In the second case, the provisional measure will be upheld in spite of the subsequent ruling. In both situations, the court may require a security for enforcement or suspension of enforcement.

814. The court before which the case is pending grants suspended enforcement. If a party applies for suspended enforcement before the District Court has transmitted the case to the Court of Appeal, the District Court rules on the issue. After transmission, the Court of Appeal rules on the issue. The same applies in relation to the Supreme Court. Upon transmission, the superior court may reverse the ruling.

Chapter 2. Enforcement of Judgments

§1. Enforcement of Domestic Judgments

I. Grounds for Enforcement

815. Norwegian law recognizes a variety of grounds for enforcement (EA section 4-1). The general grounds for enforcement include judgments and court orders from Norwegian courts, as well as other types of rulings that establish enforceable duties for a party, other government decisions having the same status as a judgment, arbitral awards, in-court settlements and judgments of international or foreign courts which an international treaty makes enforceable in Norway. Special grounds for enforcement allow specific types of enforcement when specific prerequisites are met.

816. Judgments are enforceable when they are res judicata and the time limit for compliance has lapsed. Court orders are enforceable after they are pronounced and the time limit for compliance has lapsed. When the court has split the ruling, the first rulings are enforceable unless the opposite party has made a counterclaim on which the court has not yet ruled. In-court settlements (i.e., settlements recorded in the court files and signed by the parties and the judge) are enforceable as judgments (EA sections 4-12 and 4-13).

II. Organization of Enforcement Authorities

817. The organization of enforcement is fragmented and underdeveloped. Most of the tasks, such as civil enforcement and the secretariat of the Conciliation Boards, are the responsibility of the police. The enforcement officer is the person in charge of enforcement, but enforcement officers are not organized in a unified manner. The District Sheriff (*lensmann*) or the Chief Inspector (*politistasjonssjef*) is the enforcement officer in districts where the police have both criminal and civil tasks. In districts where tasks related to civil execution and enforcement form a separate entity within the police, execution and enforcement commissioners (*namsfogde*) are enforcement officers.

818. The State Agency for the Recovery of Fines, Damages and Costs (*Statens innkrevingssentral*) has limited competency in enforcement proceedings related to payments where the state is the creditor.

III. Proceedings

819. Enforcement proceedings consist of three stages: the initial stage, the distraint stage and the execution stage.

820. A party initiates enforcement proceedings by sending an enforcement petition to the territorially competent enforcement officer (EA section 5-2). The petition must state the names and addresses of the claimant and defendant, the names and addresses of their legal counsel, the type of enforcement requested, identification of the main claim and any ancillary claims (e.g., debt collection costs) and the basis for enforcement. Written documents referred to in the petition must be attached. The claimant, the legal counsel of the claimant or a debt collection agency with debt collection permit[96] may file the petition.

821. The claimant must be identified as the obligee in the basis for enforcement, or the claimant must have acquired the claim legally. The defendant must be identified as the obligator on the basis for enforcement. The enforcement officer makes a prima facie evaluation of the petition and ensures that the petition fulfils the formal requirements (EA sections 5-3 and 5-4). The claimant must be given the opportunity to rectify any errors within a time limit, if rectification is possible.

822. Territorial competence is based on the domicile of the defendant (EA section 2-3). In proceedings on distraint, enforcement proceedings may also be initiated in a district where the defendant has assets. For forced sale of assets and eviction, the enforcement officer in the district where the assets are located or registered is competent. The enforcement officer may transfer a petition to the territorially competent enforcement officer on its own motion (EA section 5-5). The originally competent enforcement officer retains competence despite later changes of circumstances.

823. After a prima facie control, the enforcement officer notifies the defendant of the petition, unless the petition is rejected (EA section 5-6). The defendant is given two weeks to comment and provide information on any relevant circumstance and to indicate any preferences as to the object of the distraint (*utlegg*). The defendant is also given information on the enforcement costs that have arisen and the defendant avoids further costs by paying the amount due, including interest and compensation for costs, within the two-week time limit. The defendant may be given notice of the distraint proceeding.

824. When the two-week time limit has lapsed, the enforcement officer decides whether to proceed with enforcement. If the defendant has raised an objection the enforcement officer may decide to discontinue the proceedings. The enforcement officer may also decide to discontinue proceedings on his or her own motion when there is reason to believe that there is a hindrance to enforcement. The parties may be asked to provide additional statements and evidences relevant to the continuation of enforcement. A decision not to proceed with enforcement must be stated in writing.

---

96. Debt collection permits are regulated in the Debt Collection Act, *Lov om inkassovirksomhet og annen inndrivning av forfalte pengekrav*, 1998 no. 26.

825. The next stage of the enforcement proceedings is the distraint proceedings. The distraint takes place at the domicile or place of business of the defendant, at the place where the tangible assets charged by distraint are located, or when the assets are intangible (e.g., bank accounts, assets in a register) at the enforcement officer's office (EA section 7-9). The defendant must be notified of the time and place of distraint. If a notice of the distraint would substantially complicate the distraint, or if it is highly probable that the defendant does not have sufficient assets to pay for the debts, the enforcement officer may waive the notification.

826. At the distraint, the enforcement officer encourages the defendant to pay and gives information on the consequences of non-payment (EA section 7-11). The defendant is given information on rules on assets exempted from distraint. The enforcement officer asks the defendant or a person of age from the household of the defendant to indicate the preferred objects for distraint and objects exempted.

827. Distraint may be directed to any assets in the possession of the defendant or where a register indicates the defendant as the owner. Assets in the possession of a third party may be set under distraint if it is probable that the defendant is the rightful owner of the assets. Enforcement officers have the right to obtain information from third parties to establish the existence, location and ownership of assets. Third parties concerned may file a complaint at the local District Court to quash the decision of the enforcement officer.

828. The distraint is established when the enforcement officer enters the distraint into the enforcement records. The form of the distraint depends on its object. It is often one of the following:

- the distraint is entered into the register establishing ownership;
- a notice is given to the debtor or employer of the defendant indicating a duty to pay the enforcement officer in lieu of the defendant;
- the enforcement officer takes the object into possession; or
- a notice is given to the obligator of the defendant that he or she shall not fulfil the obligation to the debtor. Rather the obligation remains either unfulfilled or is fulfilled to the enforcement officer.

829. If the defendant does not have assets or (future) income to pay the claim, the enforcement officer terminates the distraint and the enforcement proceedings. The unsuccessful distraint is recorded in the enforcement records. The parties are given an abstract of the enforcement records regardless of whether distraint is successful or not.

830. The parties may file a complaint with the District Court within a month of receiving notice of the distraint. The enforcement officer annuls the distraint if the claimed amount is paid, expired, lapsed or found to be void. Distraint may also be limited if it was originally too large. Objections against general bases for enforcement, which include court rulings, are limited to two grounds: the court or government body has exceeded its powers or the content of the basis for enforcement is ambiguous or self-contradictory. Objections against the claims in a court ruling may only be made relying on facts which have come into existence since the end of the court proceedings (EA section 4-2). The defendant may also claim set-off.

831. The distraint is executed in the third stage of enforcement proceedings. The execution may be made through forced sale, returning the property to its (original) owner, transferring the ownership of property by changing the owner marked in registers, transferral of property into the mortgagee's use and possession, transferral or forced sale of the title document, eviction or by other appropriate measures. The creditor must initiate the execution stage by filing a petition to the competent enforcement officer. The enforcement officer notifies the defendant and gives the defendant a two-week time limit to comment on the realization of the distraint and to give relevant additional information, such as information regarding the value of the assets or on the sale of the assets. The enforcement officer may also give notice on the time and place for the execution. Should the notification harm execution, the enforcement officer may shorten the time limit, reduce the information given to the defendant or proceed directly to execution without giving notice. When the time limit has expired, the enforcement officer proceeds with the execution.

832. The enforcement officer must dismiss the enforcement proceedings if the defendant fulfils the obligation; if the obligation ends; if the claimant so requests; or if the basis for enforcement is quashed, lapses, or becomes void.

833. The enforcement officer may decide to delay a step in the proceedings at the request of the claimant (EA sections 5-11 and 5-12). The interests of the defendant may not be contrary to postponement, and the enforcement officer may take any step necessary to ensure the future success of the proceedings before granting postponement. Typically, the claimant requests postponement when the defendant has expressed an intention to fulfil the obligation voluntarily, such as by requesting a payment plan. Postponement is possible either for a set period or indefinitely. However, postponement may not last longer than two years. The defendant may petition for postponement if the reason for the inability to pay is illness, unemployment or a comparable exceptional reason. If postponement is granted, the defendant must pay one-fifth of the total claims of the claimant and adhere to a monthly payment plan set up by the enforcement officer. The plan lapses if the defendant does not adhere to it, in which case the enforcement proceedings will automatically resume.

IV. Judicial Review

834. The enforcement officer may on his or her own motion reverse a decision to proceed with enforcement proceedings, a decision on the method of enforcement, a decision on the choice of assets for distraint, a decision on the method for sale and other relevant decisions (EA section 5-15). Reversal is possible until the enforcement proceedings are concluded. Reversal is not limited to spelling or calculating errors, nor is it contingent on new information or a change of circumstances. Reversal may not infringe on third-party rights. Third-party rights, or conclusion of the proceedings, do not hinder reversal if the original decision contains a clear spelling error or calculation error or if the content of the decision is clearly erroneous.

835. The right to appeal in enforcement proceedings extends to any person affected by the enforcement (EA section 5-16). Third parties may appeal if the enforcement proceedings affect their rights as owner or co-owner of the assets or as the person entitled to use the assets involved. The person wishing to appeal against measures taken by the enforcement officer must lodge the appeal orally or in writing to the enforcement officer. In practice, the enforcement officer requires the appeal to be written by suggesting that the appellant seek legal advice. The appeal is directed to the competent District Court. The subject of the appeal is the conduct of the enforcement officer, including but not limited to the decision to initiate proceedings, the choice of assets for distraint or the use of force. The failure to act is also subject to appeal. Wrongful decisions, new information and changes of circumstances are grounds for appeal.

836. Appeal is possible as long as the enforcement proceedings have not been concluded. Within one month of the conclusion of the proceedings, the claimant may appeal a decision not to proceed with enforcement, a decision to dismiss the proceedings or a decision on the distribution of costs arising from the enforcement proceedings.

837. The enforcement officer ensures that the statement of appeal meets the formal requirements. If the enforcement officer finds that the decision on enforcement is unlawful, he or she should reverse the decision when possible. If the enforcement officer does not reverse the decision, the appeal must be transferred to the competent court. Necessary documentation and information must be attached.

838. The District Court has full competence to hear both questions of fact and questions of law. It may request information from persons concerned. The proceedings may be written, oral or a combination of both. The first stage of proceedings is normally to serve the appeal to the defendant(s) with a time limit to file a written statement. The District Court may quash on its own motion a decision to proceed with enforcement proceedings, a decision regarding the conduct of the proceedings or choice of assets and other similar decisions. The District Court ruling in enforcement proceedings is subject to second appeal according to regular rules on appeal.

839. The appeal does not defer the enforcement proceedings, unless the enforcement officer or the District Court so decide. Thus, the enforcement proceedings may be concluded while the appeal is pending. The court hearing the appeal has discretion to hear the case even when the enforcement proceedings have been concluded.

§2. Recognition and Enforcement of Foreign Judgments

I. Rules Applicable in the Absence of a Treaty

840. The main rule is that foreign judgments are enforceable only if a treaty or Norwegian law has a provision granting recognition and enforceability. The only exception is when the foreign court has jurisdiction based on a jurisdiction clause, which covers a specific dispute or disputes arising from a specific contract or other legal relation (EA section 4-1 subsection 2 letter g, referring to DA section 19-16 second and third subsections). The judgment is not recognized and is not enforceable if it is contrary to mandatory laws or *ordre public* (public policies).

II. International Treaties

841. Foreign rulings and decisions by administrative authorities are recognized and enforceable only if an international treaty or a provision in law grants them that status (EA section 4-1 subsection 2 letter f). In-court settlements are recognized and enforced in the same manner as Norwegian judgments, if they are enforceable as judgments according to *lex fori.*

842. Several international multi- and bilateral treaties govern the recognition and enforcement of international treaties. The Lugano Convention is the most important of these. It is binding as law (DA section 4-8). When the Lugano Convention has a ground for non-recognition, the judgment is not enforceable. Judgments under Article 61 of the Convention on civil claims arising from non-intentionally committed crimes ruled on in proceedings where the defendant failed to appear contrary to a court order are not recognized.

843. The Nordic Convention on Execution and Recognition of Civil Claims from 1978 and the Nordic Convention on Recovery of Maintenance of 23 March 1962 regulate enforceability and recognition among the Nordic countries (Denmark, Finland, Iceland, Norway and Sweden).

844. Norway is a party to the following conventions with rules on enforcement:

- Convention of 1 June 1970 on the Recognition of Divorces and Legal Separations;
- Convention of 2 October 1973 on the Recognition and Enforcement of Decisions Relating to Maintenance Obligations;
- Convention of 25 October 1980 on the Civil Aspects of International Child Abduction;
- European Convention on Recognition and Enforcement of Decisions concerning Custody of Children and on Restoration of Custody of Children of 20 May 1980;
- Convention of 29 May 1993 on Protection of Children and Co-operation in Respect of Intercountry Adoption;

- Convention of 19 October 1996 on Jurisdiction Applicable Law, Recognition, Enforcement and Co-operation in Respect of Parental Responsibility and Measures for the Protection of Children;
- Convention of 23 November 2007 on the International Recovery of Child Support and Other Forms of Family Maintenance; and
- New York Convention on the Recognition and Enforcement of Foreign Arbitral Awards of 1958.

845. Furthermore, Norway has bilateral treaties with some states. Today, most of the bilateral and Nordic treaties have lost many of their functions due to the Lugano Convention.

846. Judgments from international court and decisions by international administrative authorities, including in-court settlements, are enforceable if a treaty that binds Norway gives them such status. Fines set by the ESA and the EFTA Court are enforceable in Norway (EA section 4-1 subsection 2 letter h). Fines set by EU authorities are not enforceable.

III. Proceedings for Enforcement of Foreign Judgments

847. Norway does not have exequatur proceedings. The District Court is competent for the initial stage of enforcement proceedings (EA section 7-3). The petition to initiate enforcement proceedings must be directed to the District Court at the domicile of the defendant or where the property of the defendant is found. The claimant must attach documents stating the enforceability of the judgment in the state of origin, as enforcement is contingent on the judgment being enforceable in the country of origin. Other documents that an international treaty requires the parties to use must also be attached.

848. The District Court makes an initial assessment of the petition. It notifies the defendant of the petition, unless the petition is rejected. The defendant is given two weeks to comment on the claim and to indicate any preferences as to the object of the distraint. The defendant is also given information on the enforcement costs that have accrued, and that the defendant avoids further costs by paying the amount due, including interest and compensation for costs, within the two-week time limit. After the time limit has expired, the court rules on the enforceability of the judgment. If the judgment is enforceable, the court transfers the case to the competent enforcement officer. Enforcement proceeds are similar to national judgments.

Part X. Out-of-Court Dispute Resolution

Chapter 1. Arbitration

§1. Arbitrability

849. The ArbA of 2004 was the first act devoted to the regulation of arbitration.[97] It repealed the rules of arbitration of the Civil Procedure Act of 1915. The Act was drafted in accordance with the principles of the UNCITRAL Model Law on Commercial Arbitration. Norway is also a party to the New York Convention on the Recognition and Enforcement of Foreign Arbitral Awards of 1958.

850. The ArbA primarily regulates arbitration procedures taking place in Norway. However, provisions on the relationship between arbitration procedure and court procedure and on the recognition and enforcement of arbitral awards regulate both national and international arbitration regardless of where the arbitration takes place. Further, courts have jurisdiction to appoint the panel of arbitrators and rule on challenges of arbitrators and claims that the arbitrators have failed to perform their functions, if one of the parties has its place of business or its domicile in Norway.

851. Dispositive civil and commercial legal disputes may be subject to arbitration. The subject matter of the dispute must entail legal rules or provisions, such as interpretation of contracts or determination of facts in connection with a legal question. The mere determination of a fact, such as the assessment of the value of an asset, does not qualify as arbitration under the act, as it lacks a legal component.

852. Since indispositive cases are not subject to arbitration, many administrative law disputes and disputes involving important issues of public policy, such as competition law and environmental law, are not subject or are only partially subject to arbitration. ArbA section 9 subsection 2 explicitly states that the private law effects of competition law may be subject to arbitration. The provision is a direct consequence of the CJEU ruling in Eco Swiss.[98]

97. *See also* Ola Ø. Nisja, *Arbitration and Domestic Courts in Norway: Sibling Rivalry*, 63 Scandinavian Stud. L. (2017).
98. C-126/97 *Eco Swiss China Time Ltd v. Benetton International NV.* ECLI:EU:C:1999:269.

853. Although arbitration as such is not mandatory, some statutes have provisions giving a party the right to demand arbitration for solving a dispute. The Act on Protection Against Pollution and Waste section 33 serves as an example.[99] It grants the right to arbitration for determining the payment for delivery of waste. The Stock Exchange Act section 41[100] enables the Appeals Committee on Stock Exchange to act as an arbitral tribunal in disputes between individuals.

854. An arbitration agreement in consumer relations is not binding on the consumer if entered into prior to the dispute arising (ArbA section 11). An arbitration agreement with a consumer must be made in a separate document; that is, it cannot be part of a consumer sales contract or similar contract, and it must be signed by both parties. The arbitral tribunal must make the consumer aware of the implication of an arbitral award in terms of scope for appeal and the requirements for arbitration agreements with consumers, unless the consumer is already aware of this. Several other laws limit arbitration agreements entered into prior to the dispute arising in order to protect the weaker party from potentially costly arbitration. The Working Environment Act section 15-16[101] regulating individual labour contracts and the Tenancy Act section 12-1[102] serve as examples.

855. The Arbitration and Dispute Resolution Institute at the Oslo Chamber of Commerce is the main provider of institutional arbitration in Norway.[103] Large commercial disputes are often subject to arbitration in foreign countries, with London being a particular favourite.

§2. Arbitration Agreement and Party Autonomy

856. The parties may agree to submit to arbitration disputes that have already arisen, as well as all or certain disputes that may arise from a specific legal relationship. The arbitration agreement is tied to the subject matter that it covers and not the parties, unless the parties agree otherwise. In case of assignment of the legal relationship to a new party, the new party is bound by the arbitration clause.

857. The ArbA does not regulate the form of an arbitration agreement. Thus, an oral agreement suffices to establish an arbitration procedure. The form of the contract may influence the international recognition and enforcement of the arbitral award and may be a hindrance to arbitration in international arbitration. A written arbitration contract may be either a separate contract, an explicit or even implicit clause in a written contract or a clause referring to a separate document on arbitration. It may also be included, *inter alia*, in a will, gift or bill or in the by-laws of an

---

99. *Forurensningsloven* 1981 no. 6.
100. *Børsloven* 2007 no. 74.
101. *Arbeidsmiljøloven* 2005 no. 62.
102. *Husleieloven* 1999 no. 17.
103. The Rules of the Arbitration and Dispute Resolution Institute of the Oslo Chamber of Commerce are available at https://www.chamber.no/wp-content/uploads/2015/07/Rules-2017-Arbitration-English.pdf.

association. Arbitration agreements involving a consumer must be in writing, similar to arbitration agreements concerning legal relationships regulated in the Maritime Act.[104]

858. According to the doctrine of separability, the validity of the arbitration clause is not contingent on the validity of the contract in which it is induced. Even if the contract is deemed invalid, the arbitration clause can still be valid. The arbitrators have the jurisdiction to adjudicate on the validity of the contract itself (competence-competence), ArbA section 18.

859. The parties may agree to derogate from the provisions of the ArbA to the extent specified for each section of the Act (ArbA section 2).

§3. Composition of Arbitral Tribunal

860. The arbitrators must be natural persons with full legal capacity. The parties may agree on the number, qualifications and selection of the arbitrators. Unless the parties have agreed otherwise, the number of arbitrators is three (ArbA 12).

861. The parties shall appoint the arbitrators jointly. If the parties do not agree on the composition of the arbitral tribunal, each party appoints one arbitrator within one month after the party received the request to appoint the arbitrator. The arbitrators appointed by the parties have one month to jointly appoint a third arbitrator. The third arbitrator is the presiding arbitrator.

862. If a party or the arbitrators fail to appoint an arbitrator within the time limit, the other party may request the court to appoint an arbitrator. The court that would have had jurisdiction on the case in the absence of an arbitration agreement has the competence to do so (ArbA section 6). The court must hear the parties before appointing an arbitrator. According to Article 8 of the Rules of the Arbitration and Dispute Resolution Institute of the Oslo Chamber of Commerce, the Arbitration Institute appoints an arbitrator if the parties or the arbitrator fail to do so within the time limit. The parties may agree on a different process for the composition of the tribunal.

863. The arbitrators must be impartial and independent (ArbA section 13). The act does not define the meaning of these terms, nor does it state when an arbitrator is competent. The requirements of impartiality and independence are understood prima facie as stated in international regulation on the subject. The requirement of competence refers to academic and personal qualifications and earlier experience in arbitration or the subject matter. The competence required depends on the specific case at hand.

---

104. *Sjøloven* 1994 no. 39.

864. Prior to appointment, a possible arbitrator must disclose any circumstances that may be likely to give rise to justifiable doubts as to his or her impartiality or independence (ArbA section 14). Throughout the proceedings, an arbitrator must immediately disclose any new circumstance that is likely to give rise to justifiable doubts as to impartiality or independence. The duty of disclosure does not include the qualifications of the arbitrator.

865. A party may challenge an arbitrator only if circumstances exist that give rise to justifiable doubts to the impartiality or independence of the arbitrator (ArbA section 14). The threshold to challenge an arbitrator is higher than the threshold for giving information on circumstances affecting impartiality and independence. The arbitrator must disclose circumstances that as such do not give sufficient doubt as to the impartiality but may do so if combined with other circumstances. The arbitrator may also be challenge if he or she does not possess the qualification agreed to by the parties. The right to challenge the arbitrator the party has appointed him- or herself is limited to information the party received after the appointment.

866. The challenge of the arbitrator must be submitted in writing to the arbitral tribunal within fifteen days of the party becoming aware of the appointment and the circumstance on which the challenge is based. Unless the arbitrator withdraws or the other party agrees to the challenge, the arbitral tribunal decides on the challenge. If the challenge is unsuccessful, the challenging party may bring the issue before the court within one month. The court's ruling is not subject to appeal. While the issue is pending before the court, the arbitral tribunal, including the challenged arbitrator, may continue the arbitral proceedings and make an award.

§4. Provisional Measures and Preliminary Awards

867. The arbitral tribunal has the right to order provisional measures it considers necessary at the request of a party (ArbA section 19). An arbitral tribunal may decide to separate one or more claims or one or more issues into separate proceedings, as well as to determine separately one or more claims or parts of a claim (ArbA section 33).

868. The Arbitration Rules of Oslo Chamber of Commerce Article 19 gives the arbitral tribunal the right to decide a matter in dispute in a separate or interim award at the request of a party. If the other party objects, the separate award may only be made if there are special reasons for making it. Article 11 gives the arbitral tribunal the right to make orders for provisional measures.

869. Courts have the power to rule on provisional measures even if a dispute is subject to arbitration (ArbA section 8). The general rules on provisional measures in DA Chapters 32–34 apply. In Rt. 2015 p. 1040, the Supreme Court rejected jurisdiction for Norwegian courts for a provisional measure, although the parties had agreed on arbitration in Norway. The Supreme Court held that the threshold for establishing jurisdiction for provisional measures is particularly high for commercial cases. The ruling contradicts both the ArbA section 8 and the DA section 4-8, the latter gives the Lugano Convention supremacy over Norwegian law.

§5. Conduct of Arbitral Proceedings

870. The arbitral proceedings and the arbitral award are not subject to confidentiality, unless otherwise agreed upon by the parties (ArbA section 5). However, third parties have access to the arbitral hearings only if and to the extent agreed upon by the parties.

871. The conduct of the arbitration procedure is left to the discretion of the arbitral tribunal and the agreement of the parties. However, the arbitral tribunal must treat the parties equally at all stages of the proceedings, and the parties must be given the opportunity to present their cases in full (ArbA section 20). The proceedings must also be appropriate (ArbA section 21). The arbitration proceedings are formed in cooperation with the parties. After having discussed the matter with the parties, the arbitral tribunal must prepare a plan for the conduct of the case. The plan may be waived or amended by agreement.

872. The parties decide the place of arbitration. If the parties fail to do so, the arbitral tribunal determines the place of arbitration. The most practical place should be chosen to allow for a proper conduct of arbitration, including hearing the parties and taking evidence. Unless the parties agree otherwise, the arbitral tribunal may meet wherever it considers appropriate to deliberate among its members, to assess evidence or to examine witnesses, experts or parties. The language of arbitration is contingent on the agreement of the parties. In the absence of an agreement, the arbitral tribunal decides on the language. The language chosen applies to all written statements, hearings, rulings and other communication. Danish and Swedish are considered the same language as Norwegian for arbitration proceedings, since speakers of these three languages can understand each other without having to resort to the services of a translator or interpreter.

873. The arbitration is initiated on the date on which the respondent receives a demand for the dispute to be referred to arbitration, unless the parties have agreed otherwise.

874. Once the panel of arbitrators has been set, the claimant shall submit a statement of claim within the time limit agreed upon by the parties or set by the arbitral tribunal. The statement of claim shall specify the claim, the relief sought, the cause of action and legal basis for the claim and the evidence that will be presented (ArbA section 25). A failure to provide the statement of claim within the time limit without reasonable cause results in termination of the arbitration (ArbA section 27).

875. The respondent shall submit a statement of defence with a similar content within the time limit agreed upon or set by the arbitral tribunal (ArbA section 25).

The statement of defence must specify whether the claim made is accepted or contested. The respondent must also present any objections to the arbitral tribunal hearing the case and the grounds for the objections. The respondent may also file a counterclaim. A failure to submit a statement of defence is not sanctioned, and the arbitral tribunal may not treat a failure as an admission of the claims.

876. The parties may bring new claims, expand existing claims and submit new grounds and new evidence for their claims, unless they have otherwise agreed. At the request of a party, the arbitral tribunal may refuse an amendment provided that the need for timely proceedings or another weighty concern indicates that this is appropriate.

877. The arbitral tribunal decides whether the proceedings will be oral, written or a mixture of the two. At the request of a party, the arbitral tribunal must hold a hearing. The tribunal determines the timing of the hearing. The parties shall be given reasonable advanced notice of any hearings or other meetings the parties are entitled to attend, such as meetings with the purpose of inspecting goods or documents.

878. The parties must communicate all statements, documents and other information simultaneously to the arbitral tribunal and the other party. The arbitral tribunal must communicate material it receives directly from third parties to the parties of the case.

879. An absence from a hearing or a failure to submit documentary evidence is not sanctioned. The arbitral tribunal may continue the arbitration and render the arbitral award based on the materials submitted.

880. The parties are responsible for clarifying and proving the factual basis for the case and are entitled to present the evidence they wish. The arbitral tribunal may refuse evidence if it is obviously of no relevance to the final ruling. The tribunal may limit the presentation of evidence if the extent of evidence is not proportional to the importance of the dispute or the relevance of the evidence for deciding on the disputed issues (ArbA 28). The rules on evidence reflect the general principles of evidence in the DA.

881. The arbitral tribunal may appoint one or more experts to report on specific issues determined by the arbitral tribunal. The arbitral tribunal may require the parties to give the expert relevant information and to produce or provide access to evidence. Having submitted a report, the expert may be required to testify at a hearing at the request of the arbitral tribunal or a party. The parties have the right to put questions to the expert and to present expert witnesses concerning the same issues. The parties have the right to challenge the expert on the same grounds as they may challenge the arbitrators (ArbA section 29).

882. The arbitral tribunal, or a party by consent of the arbitral tribunal, may request that the courts obtain testimony from parties or witnesses as well as other evidence. The arbitrators are entitled to be present at the hearing of the parties or witnesses and to put questions.

§6. Arbitral Award

883. The arbitral tribunal decides the dispute in accordance with the rules of law chosen by the parties as applicable to the substance of the dispute (ArbA section 31). In the absence of any designation of the parties, the arbitral tribunal applies Norwegian conflict of law rules to determine which rules of law are applicable. The arbitral tribunal may decide based on fairness (*ex aequo et bono*) only if the parties have expressly authorized it to do so.

884. Should the arbitral tribunal be obliged to take a position on the interpretation of the EEA Agreement or statutory law implementing EEA law, it cannot seek an advisory opinion. However, the arbitral tribunal may ask a court to seek an advisory opinion from the EFTA Court (ArbA section 30).

885. The arbitral tribunal may only decide the claims the parties have raised in the case (ArbA section 32). The ruling must fall within the claims for relief made and the cause of action presented. The ruling on facts is based on the principle of free evaluation of the evidence presented. The arbitral tribunal may separately determine one or more claims of the case or a part of a claim.

886. The rulings are made by a majority of votes cast (ArbA section 34). The presiding arbitrator has a casting vote if an absolute majority is not otherwise achievable. If there is no majority for any outcome when a sum of money or other quantity is determined, the principle of *maius includit minus* applies. For example, if the first arbitrator votes for NOK 800,000, the second arbitrator for NOK 600,000 and the third arbitrator for NOK 500,000, the outcome is NOK 600,000: The vote for NOK 800,000 is interpreted to be in favour of any sum below it, and is counted to be in favour of NOK 600,000 as well. Hence, NOK 600,000 has two votes and NOK 500,000 one vote. An arbitrator, who has found for the defendant when the two other arbitrators have found for the claimant when voting on the issue of liability, is obliged to participate in the voting on the outcome in terms of a sum of money or other quantity. Should a minority of the arbitrators refuse to take part in a vote, the remaining arbitrators may rule on the issue. With the authorization of the parties or the full arbitral tribunal, the presiding arbitrator may rule on procedural issues without involving the other arbitrators in the decision-making.

887. The final arbitral award or an order of the arbitral tribunal for the termination of the proceedings determines the arbitral proceedings (ArbA section 37). The arbitral tribunal shall issue an order for the termination of the arbitral proceedings if the claimant withdraws the claim. If the respondent objects to such termination and the arbitral tribunal finds that the respondent has a legitimate interest in obtaining an arbitral award, the arbitration proceedings shall be continued. The arbitral proceedings are also terminated if the parties agree to do so or if the continuation of proceedings has become unnecessary or impossible. The mandate of the arbitral tribunal terminates with the termination of the arbitral proceedings.

888. The arbitral award shall be in writing and signed by all arbitrators (ArbA section 36). The signatures of a majority of the arbitrators suffice, if the reason for an omitted signature is stated in the award. The award must state the reasons upon which it is based. It must specify whether the ruling was unanimous, and if one or more arbitrators has dissented, it must state who was in dissent and to which aspect of the ruling the dissent is related. The award must state the date and place of arbitration. The award is deemed rendered at the place stated in it.

889. If the parties settle during the arbitral proceedings, they may require the arbitral tribunal to confirm the settlement by way of an arbitral award. The confirmation of the settlement has the same status and effect as an award on the merits (ArbA section 35).

890. The arbitral award is sent to the parties, and a signed copy is sent to the District Court at the place of arbitration to be filed in the court archives.

891. After the termination of the arbitral proceedings, the arbitral tribunal may rectify an award (ArbA section 38). The award may be rectified when it is formulated in a way that does not reflect the intention of the arbitral tribunal due to spelling errors, arithmetic errors, typographical errors or similar obvious errors. The arbitral tribunal may make a supplementary award with regard to claims that were presented in the arbitral proceedings and that this should have been decided on but that were omitted from the award. A party must request rectification or passing of a supplementary award within one month of receipt of the award. The arbitral tribunal sends the request to the other party. Rectification must take place within one month of the receipt of the request. The arbitral tribunal makes the supplementary award within two months of the receipt of the request. The arbitral tribunal may rectify the award on its own initiative within one month of the making of the award. The parties shall be notified and allowed to comment prior to the rectification.

892. The arbitral tribunal determines its own compensation and settlement of expenses (ArbA section 39). The ruling on the costs of the arbitral tribunal is included in the final award or other documents terminating the proceedings. The parties are jointly and severally liable for the costs. The decision on the costs becomes enforceable within one month.

893. At the request of a party, the arbitral tribunal may allocate the division of the costs between the parties as it sees fit (ArbA section 40). It may order one party to compensate all or some of the costs incurred to the other party. The ruling is final.

894. The arbitral tribunal may order the parties to provide a security in respect of the costs of the arbitral tribunal, unless otherwise agreed upon between the arbitral tribunal and the parties (ArbA section 41). The arbitral tribunal may terminate the arbitral proceedings in full or in part if such security is not provided.

§7. Recourse Against Arbitral Awards

895. Recourse against arbitral awards is very limited, except for the determination of the compensation for the arbitral tribunal.

896. The parties may bring the ruling on the compensation for the arbitrators and settlement of the expenses to the competent court within one month from the final arbitral award or the document terminating the proceedings. The court has the power to adjust the costs. The court order on costs is binding for all parties to the arbitral proceedings, including parties who did not bring the ruling to the court (ArbA section 39 subsection 3).

897. The grounds for invalidity of an arbitral award are limited (ArbA sections 42 and 43). A court may only set aside an arbitral award if:

- one of the parties lacked legal capacity;
- the arbitration agreement is invalid under the applicable laws as agreed upon by the parties or, failing such agreement, under Norwegian law;
- the party bringing the action for setting aside was not given sufficient notice of the appointment of an arbitrator or of the arbitration;
- the party bringing the action was not given an opportunity to present his or her views on the case;
- the arbitral award falls outside the scope of the jurisdiction of the arbitral tribunal;
- the composition of the arbitral tribunal was incorrect; or
- the arbitral procedure was contrary to law or the agreement of the parties, and it is obvious that this may have impacted the ruling.

898. When the issue of validity of an arbitral award has been brought before the court, the court shall of its own accord set aside the award if:

- the dispute cannot be determined by arbitration under Norwegian law; or
- the arbitral award is contrary to public policy (*ordre public*).

899. If the grounds for invalidity only affect part of the award, only that part shall be invalid. The action for setting aside an arbitral award must be brought within three months of the party receiving the arbitral award, the rectified award, the supplementary award or a document denying rectification or a supplementary award.

900. If the court finds that there are sufficient grounds for setting aside the award, it may at the request of the party stay the action and refer the case to the arbitral tribunal to resume proceedings. The case may only be referred to the arbitral tribunal if this may result in the reversal of the grounds for setting aside the award. Setting aside an arbitral award implies that the arbitration agreement in question again becomes effective, unless otherwise agreed upon by the parties or implied by the judgment for setting aside. Thus, unless the arbitration agreement was invalid, one of the parties lacked legal capacity or the subject matter does not fall under arbitration, the underlying arbitration agreement is valid even when the arbitral award was set aside.

901. Norwegian courts have the power to interpret arbitral awards. In Rt. 1987 p. 1449, the Supreme Court held that Norwegian courts must interpret arbitral awards in a manner that renders them effective.

§8. Recognition and Enforcement of Awards

902. Arbitral awards are recognized and enforced irrespective of the place of arbitration (ArbA section 45). The party requesting recognition or enforcement must attach the original arbitral award or a certified copy thereof to the request. Unless the arbitral award has been made in Norwegian, Swedish, Danish or English, the party shall also make available a certified translation thereof. An arbitral award is a general basis for enforcement on equal terms with court rulings (EA section 4-1).

903. Recognition or enforcement of an arbitral award may only be refused if:

- one of the parties to the arbitration agreement lacks legal capacity;
- the arbitration agreement is invalid under the laws applicable as agreed upon by the parties or, failing such agreement, under the laws of the jurisdiction in which the arbitral award was made;
- the party against whom the arbitral award is invoked was not given sufficient notice of the appointment of an arbitrator or of the arbitration;
- the party against whom the arbitral award is invoked was not given an opportunity to present his or her views on the case;
- the arbitral award falls outside the scope of the jurisdiction of the arbitral tribunal;
- the composition of the arbitral tribunal was incorrect;
- the arbitral procedure was contrary to the law of the place of arbitration or the agreement of the parties, and it is obvious that this may have impacted the ruling; or
- the arbitral award is not yet binding on the parties or has been set aside, permanently or temporarily, by a court at the place of arbitration or by a court in the jurisdiction whose law has been applied in determining the subject matter in dispute.

904. Courts shall on their own motion refuse recognition and enforcement of an arbitral award if:

- the dispute would not have been capable of being determined by arbitration under Norwegian law; or
- recognition or enforcement of the arbitral award would be contrary to public policy (*ordre public*).

905. If the reason for refusing recognition or enforcement only affects part of the award, only that part shall be refused recognition or enforcement. The court may postpone the ruling on recognition and enforcement of the arbitral award if a party has brought an action at another court for setting aside the arbitral award.

Chapter 2. Court-Connected Mediation

§1. Legislation and Definitions

906. The concept of mediation is undefined in Norwegian law. Almost any activity seeking settlement is considered mediation, regardless of the type and extent of third-party involvement. Therefore, the notion of mediation is broad, and the definition is over-inclusive.[105]

907. Court-connected mediation (*rettsmekling*) should not be confused with judicial settlement efforts (*ordinær mekling*). Judicial settlement efforts include any activities in which the judge encourages the parties to consider finding a solution to the case. Judicial settlement efforts comprise activities which the judge undertakes 'in-robe' (i.e., in the role of a judge) and in which the rules of regular civil procedure pose a limit.[106] Both courts and the Conciliation Board have a duty to consider whether and how the settlement should be promoted at every stage of the proceedings.

908. Court-connected mediation was introduced in Norway in the mid-1990s when a group of lawyers suggested a trial period for court-connected mediation in selected District Courts. The trial period was successful, and it was extended to more courts after the initial years. Since 2008, court-connected mediation has been regulated in DA Chapter 8.

909. Court-connected mediation has become popular, with about 20%–35% of all civil cases going to mediation. The mediation rate varies from court to court. Settlement is reached in approximately 70% of mediated cases.[107]

§2. Rights That Can Be Subject to Mediation

910. The DA regulates mediation in civil and commercial legal disputes. Legal disputes are defined as disputes involving an issue regulated by law and in which the dispute itself involves application of the law. A dispute on the value of an object is not a legal dispute, as resolution does not involve application of the law; likewise, a dispute between an employer and employee on the amount of the employee's salary is not a legal dispute, as salary is not determined by law. Should a party invoke questions of law, such as ownership or discrimination based on sex or ethnicity, the dispute is transformed into a legal dispute and thus would fall under the DA.

---

105. *See* Anna Nylund, *The Many Ways of Civil Mediation in Norway*, in *The Future of Civil Litigation: Access to Courts and Court-annexed Mediation in the Nordic Countries* (Laura Ervo & Anna Nylund eds, Springer, 2014) and Camilla Bernt, *Mediation of Legal Disputes in Norway: Institutionalized, Pragmatic and Increasingly Popular*, in *New Developments in Civil and Commercial Mediation* (Carlos Esplugues & Louis Marquis eds, Springer 2015).

106. For an in-depth discussion on judicial settlement efforts, *see supra* Part IV Ch. 3 §1, I, B, 1, f.

107. Numbers are from the Norwegian Courts Administration and are on file with the author.

911. Although the DA does not restrict the types of cases suitable for mediation, administrative law cases and indispositive cases are often not appropriate due to the strong presence of public policy considerations.

912. Court-connected mediation is not considered appropriate for small claims cases, as unsuccessful mediation would lead to prolonged and more expensive court proceedings. Self-represented parties with limited knowledge of their legal right and civil procedure pose a challenge, as the mediator must be neutral, yet the parties need to make informed decisions. To avoid mediation becoming second-class justice for the less well-off, courts should exercise caution in referring cases involving self-represented parties to court-connected mediation.

§3. Mediation Agreement

913. Court-connected mediation is initiated by the court or the parties. The court has a duty to consider whether it is appropriate to promote settlement and to suggest directing the case to court-connected mediation. One of the parties can also suggest court-connected mediation. Although the consent of the parties is not required for transferring a case to court-connected mediation, courts should be cautious about ordering court-connected mediation against the wishes of the parties. Similarly, a court should not automatically order court-connected mediation when both parties agree.

914. In determining whether court-connected mediation should be attempted, the court must take into account the likelihood of settlement, earlier attempts at finding settlement, particularly through mediation, and the power balance between the parties. Generally, court-connected mediation should be attempted only once.

§4. Persons Who Can Act as Mediators

915. In court-connected mediation, a judge at the court where the case is pending usually acts as the mediator. Courts must also keep a list of qualified mediators, and one of the persons on the list may also serve as a mediator. In practice, not all courts have a list of qualified mediators, and even in courts that have a list of mediators, the courts seldom appoint a person from the list to mediate. In complex cases, the court may appoint an aid to the mediator. The aid may have expertise in a particular field, such as construction.

916. There are no strict formal requirements for mediators. A mediator must have a suitable personality and competence, as well as experience with mediation. In practice, mediator training is not required, as long as the person has experience in finding settlement. To qualify for the list of court mediators, a mediator must have experience in fields supplementing the qualifications of the judges employed at the court.

917. The mediator must be impartial and independent, fulfilling the same criteria as a judge. The mediator must disclose any circumstance that could affect his or her impartiality.

§5. Mediation Procedure

918. Court-connected mediation takes place outside court hearings. The mediator determines the mediation process in conjunction with the parties (DA section 8-5). The parties must attend mediation in person: the attendance of the legal counsel does not suffice.

919. Mediation should not delay the regular proceedings in the event that the parties do not reach settlement (DA section 8-7). The rationale of the mentioned provision is noble – to make court-connected mediation attractive by making it time- and cost-efficient. However, the result of efficiency is that court-connected mediation is, in the main, concentrated on a single mediation session, which in turn can result in undue pressure on the parties to settle and that the parties are not given the opportunity to discontinue mediation to obtain new information or to consider their options. The rule is not absolute: in 2020, the District Court in Gjøvik settled a case worth NOK 305,920,000 (approximately EUR 30,000,000) after having held thirty-one mediation sessions.

920. The mediator must act impartially but otherwise has few restrictions with regard to how to conduct mediation. The task of the mediator is to clarify the parties' interest and to advance settlement. Although the preparatory works stress the facilitative model of mediation, where the role of the mediator is to facilitate negotiations on an interest-based solution, the mediator may also act in a highly evaluative manner by suggesting solutions and evaluating the claims of the parties. The mediator may also estimate the outcome in court proceedings, if he or she finds it appropriate to do so. DA section 8-5 gives the mediator the explicit right to evaluate. In practice, many mediators use a narrow evaluative approach to mediation. Nevertheless, the practice of mediation varies significantly.

921. The mediator may have private meetings (caucuses) with the parties. Some mediators use caucuses extensively, splitting the parties into separate rooms after a short introductory session and bringing them together only once they have settled or to settle the final issues. Other mediators shift between joint and private meetings, and some use private meetings sparsely.

922. Parties may present evidence during mediation. However, court-connected mediation should not involve extensive presentation of evidence, as the goal of mediation is to find a pragmatic, interest-based solution, not to arrive at the same outcome as in civil litigation. Both parties and any witnesses must agree to presentation of evidence. The court may not order a person to give evidence. The right to present evidence causes some mediation sessions to transform into early evaluation sessions or even mini-trials. Thus, court-connected mediation may bear little resemblance to the original ideas of facilitative interest-based mediation.

923. The mediator keeps a record of mediation, stating the court; the time and place of mediation; the case number; the names of the mediator, parties and counsel; whether the parties meet in person; and the names of any representatives. The names of any witnesses or experts must also be recorded.

924. A party who has made an offer of settlement may demand that the offer be recorded. The party may later refer to the record to document that the opposite party did not accept a reasonable offer. Recording an offer of settlement is a clear breach of the principle of confidentiality of mediation and is thus highly problematic. The rationale is probably to induce the parties to accept reasonable offers to avoid costly and time-consuming litigation proceedings.

925. Mediation is confidential (DA section 8-6). The parties cannot testify on what happened during mediation or on information gained during mediation. However, the parties may use information on specific evidence that was referred to in order to demand the disclosure of such evidence. The parties may also refer to an offer of settlement recorded in the mediation record in subsequent court proceedings. Mediators and assistant mediators have a duty to maintain confidentiality in all situations, both inside and outside the court. A mediator may testify on whether a settlement agreement is in accordance with what the parties agreed upon during mediation.

926. Mediation ends when the parties reach settlement or when the mediator finds that full settlement is not feasible (DA sections 8-5 and 8-7). As mediation should be voluntary, the mediator should respect a party's wish to conclude mediation. Continuing mediation after a party wishes to end mediation puts undue pressure on the party to enter into settlement, often on terms that are at least partly against the wishes of that party.

927. An unsuccessful or partially unsuccessful court-connected mediation results in the court diverting the case back to regular civil proceedings, to the same stage as when court-connected mediation commenced. If the judge managing the case was the mediator, the case should be transferred to another judge, unless the parties request that the judge-mediator continue to judge the case. The judge-mediator may comply with the request to judge only if the judge considers it appropriate to do so. The judge-mediator may have accessed information in private meetings that is not subject to an adversarial hearing and that was disclosed in a setting emphasizing confidentiality. Consequently, the judge-mediator should be very restrictive with regard to acting as a judge after court-connected mediation has ended.

928. Successful mediation ends the court proceedings. In practice, some parties in unsuccessful court-connected mediation settle their claims before the main hearing. Court-connected mediation may also result in narrowing the scope of the case, either by partial settlement or by clarification of claims, through which some issues are dropped or become undisputed.

929. Although judicial settlement efforts and court-connected mediation provide for swift settlements, the practices and methods used vary greatly between judges. In court-connected mediation, some judges seek interest-based solutions, while others offer the parties an abbreviated trial. The content of court-connected mediation and the mediation process varies considerably, and the mediation can be in the form of passive shuttle mediation; 'muscle' mediation, where the judge-mediator pressures the parties to settle; highly evaluative mediation; or a process where the judge facilitates discussion, empowers the parties and helps the parties find creative, mutually satisfactory solutions. The variation in practices reduces the quality of court-connected mediation, as it reduces foreseeability. Unless one knows who will mediate the case, one does not know what the mediation will be like or what the results will be. The parties may also be pressured to accept unsatisfactory solutions and a process that is not satisfactory to them. They cannot appeal the process or the result, and the Supervisor Committee for Judges does not consider direct pressure unethical, yet the parties are deprived of their right to a trial. If the case is not settled, court-connected mediation often causes costs and delay.[108]

930. Court-connected mediation has become popular because it offers at least some potential for interest-based solutions and constructive dispute resolution.[109] Nonetheless, in many cases, court-connected mediation is not about just settlement; it is just about settlement. Mediation training is very short, and many judges continue in their role as a judge when mediating. The limited use of external mediators may also hamper the quality of mediation. When mediation is court-conducted, the parties may not understand the difference between the role of the judge and the role of the mediator and between the litigation process and the mediation process. External mediators can be helpful in certain types of cases, such as construction disputes, not because they can evaluate the case but because they understand which problems and questions are the most important to solve. Hence, the quality of court-connected mediation could be enhanced in several different ways.

§6. Settlement Agreement

931. In court-connected mediation, the settlement agreement may be either a regular settlement or an in-court settlement. A regular settlement agreement binds

108. *See* Nylund (2014), pp. 113–117.
109. Lin Adrian & Solfrid Mykland, *Unwrapping Court-Connected Mediation Agreements,* in *Nordic Mediation Research* 83–104 (Anna Nylund, Kaijus Ervasti & Lin Adrian eds, Springer 2018). Lin Adrian & Solfrid Mykland, *Creativity in Court-Connected Mediation: Myth or Reality?*, 30(4) Negot. J. (2014).

the parties as a contract on a contractual basis. Moreover, a regular settlement does not have to fulfil particular requirements to be valid.

932. An in-court settlement is binding and enforceable as a judgment. It is entered into the court records. The matter becomes res judicata once the settlement is included in the court records.[110]

933. An internationally mediated settlement agreement is enforceable as a judgment if it is made in proceedings before a court, and it is enforceable under the Lugano Convention or other international treaties (EA section 4-1(2) letter f). The same applies to settlements before international courts and authorities, particularly the EFTA Court, the ECtHR and the ESA. Such settlement agreements have the effect of res judicata (DA section 19-16).

§7. Setting Aside a Settlement Agreement

934. An in-court settlement is not subject to appeal. A party may bring an action to declare the settlement invalid or to amend it, pursuant to the rules for invalidity and amendment of contracts in the Contract Act.[111] The action must be brought within six months from the date the party became aware of the circumstances.

110. *See* Part IV Ch. 3 §1, I, C, 7.
111. *See* Part IV Ch. 4 §3.

Chapter 3. Out-of-Court Mediation

§1. Legislation and Definitions

935. The enactment of the Dispute Act also marked formal recognition and regulation of out-of-court mediation. DA Chapter 7 regulates selected aspects of out-of-court mediation. The rules apply only when the parties agreed on mediation in writing and expressly stated that the rules in DA Chapter 7 apply to the mediation process.

936. The rules on out-of-court mediation in the DA are seldom used. Hence, they have received only limited attention among lawyers, even though the Oslo Chamber of Commerce provides out-of-court commercial mediation services.

§2. Rights That Can Be Subject to Mediation

937. The DA only applies in civil and commercial legal disputes. Hence, the rules on out-of-court mediation are also limited to these disputes, in the same manner as for court-connected mediation.

§3. Mediation Agreement

938. To initiate out-of-court mediation according to the rules of the DA, the parties must sign a written agreement on mediation. The agreement must state that the parties wish to mediate according to the regulation set forth in the act. An agreement entered into before the dispute has arisen is not binding on consumers.

939. Although an agreement on out-of-court mediation is binding, it is not a hindrance to civil proceedings. The sanction for not participating in out-of-court mediation is in the form of legal costs. The court may order the party who refused to mediate to be liable for part of the litigation costs.

The parties agree on the remuneration of the mediator. If the has court appointed the mediator, the parties can request that the court sets the remuneration.

§4. Persons Who Can Act as Mediator

940. In out-of-court mediation, the parties may agree on the mediator, DA Section 7-2. If the parties are not able to agree, they may ask the court to appoint a mediator from the court's list of mediators if the court has such a list or request the court to appoint a named person as the mediator. The request must be filed in writing and must state the substance of the dispute. The mediator must be impartial and independent according to the same criteria as judges. The mediator may appoint an assistant if necessary.

An advanced payment or a security for the claim for remuneration may be requested. The parties are liable to pay half of the advanced payment each.

The mediator must be impartial and independent, fulfilling the same criteria as a judge. The mediator must disclose any circumstance that could affect his or her impartiality.

§5. Mediation Procedure

941. The rules for out-of-court mediation are almost identical to the rules for court-connected mediation, DA section 7-3. Mediation is confidential, and neither the mediator nor the parties can testify on what happened during mediation. The parties determine the mediation process in cooperation with the mediator. Mediation ends when the parties settle, when the mediator considers it unfruitful to continue the process or when one of the parties requests that the mediation be terminated.

§6. Settlement Agreement

942. In out-of-court mediation, the mediated agreement is only binding as a contract.

§7. Setting Aside a Settlement Agreement

943. As an out-of-court settlement agreement only binds as a contract, the parties may bring an action to declare the settlement invalid or to amend it, pursuant to the rules for invalidity and amendment of contracts in the Contract Act.

Chapter 4. Other Forms of Mediation

944. Mediation is an important part of the Norwegian legal culture. The National Mediation Services (*konfliktrådet*) offers mediation by volunteer mediators free of charge. The services are used mainly in small disputes among neighbours where maintaining the relationship is important, and the mediation model used, which focuses on intra- and inter-personal processes, is suitable. The process is not appropriate for addressing legal issues. Mediation has no impact on limitation periods, and the agreement only binds as a contract. The parties are not allowed to bring their lawyers to the mediation session.

945. Mediation is mandatory for all separating couples with children under the age of 16. Mediation is a prerequisite for filing court proceedings in child custody and contact cases. Mediation is also the preferred way to resolve child custody and contact cases in courts as well (Children Act sections 51–55 and 61). The National Mediation Services offer general mediation for all types of disputes regardless of their nature. Mediation is regulated in the National Mediation Services Act.[112] Most lawyers are not aware of the services offered, and mediation does not stop limitation periods, nor is the mediated agreement binding.[113] The primary function of the National Mediation Services is to offer victim-offender mediation and youth conferencing in criminal cases.

946. Mediation is mandatory in child custody cases for all separating couples with children under the age of 16. Pre-filing mediation is mandatory in all cases related to parental responsibility. Almost 90% of separating parents agree on custody, contact and maintenance out of court. Court-conducted expert-assisted mediation is the primary method for solving child custody and contact disputes in courts. Mediation in child custody cases is regulated in the Children Act and is not discussed in this volume.[114]

---

112. *Konfliktrådsloven* 2014 no. 49.
113. *See* Nylund (2014).
114. For more information on mediation in child custody and contact cases, *see* Bernt (2018), Nylund (2018) and Bernt (2015).

Selected Bibliography

In English

Adrian, Lin & Mykland, Solfrid. 'Unwrapping Court-Connected Mediation Agreements'. In *Nordic Mediation Research*, edited by Anna Nylund, Kaijus Ervasti & Lin Adrian. Springer, 2018.

Adrian, Lin & Mykland, Solfrid. 'Creativity in Court-Connected Mediation: Myth or Reality?'. *Negotiation Journal* 30 no. 4 (2014): 421–439.

Backer, Inge Lorange. 'Goals of Civil Justice in Norway: Readiness for a Pragmatic Reform'. In *Goals of Civil Justice and Civil Procedure in Contemporary Judicial Systems,* edited by Alan Uzelac. Springer, 2014.

Backer, Inge Lorange. 'The Reform of Norwegian Civil Procedure'. In *Reforms of Civil Procedure in Germany and Norway,* edited by Volker Lipp & Halvard Haukeland Fredriksen. Mohr Siebeck, 2011.

Backer, Inge Lorange. 'The Norwegian Reform of Civil Procedure'. *Scandinavian Studies in Law* 51 (2007).

Bernt, Camilla. 'Custody Mediation in Norwegian Courts: A Conglomeration of Roles and Processes'. In *Nordic Mediation Research*, edited by Anna Nylund, Kaijus Ervasti & Lin Adrian. Springer, 2018.

Bernt, Camilla. 'Mediation of Legal Disputes in Norway. Institutionalized, Pragmatic and Increasingly Popular'. In *New Developments in Civil and Commercial Mediation*, edited by Carlos Esplugues & Louis Marquis. Springer, 2015.

Bernt, Camilla. 'Norway (Class Actions)'. *ANNALS of the American Academy of Political and Social Science* 622 no. 1 (2009): 220–230.

Franklin, Christian, Fredriksen, Halvard Haukeland & Halvorsen Barlund, Ingrid Margrethe. 'National Report on Private Enforcement of European Competition Law in Norway'. In *Private Enforcement and Collective Redress in European Competition Law – Private Rechtsdurchsetzung und kollektiver Rechtsschutz im europäischen Wettbewerbsrecht – Contentieux indemnitaire et réparation collective en droit européen de la concurrence*, edited by Bandi, Gyula. Wolters Kluwer, 2016.

Fredriksen, Halvard Haukeland. 'The Troubled Relationship Between the Supreme Court of Norway and the EFTA Court – Recent Developments'. In *The Rising Complexity of European Law,* edited by Peter-Christian Müller-Graff & Ola Mestad. BWV - Berliner Wissenschafts-Verlag, 2014.

Fredriksen, Halvard Haukeland. 'The Two EEA Courts – A Norwegian Perspective'. In *Judicial Protection in the European Economic Area,* edited by Carl Baudenbacher. German Law Publishers, 2012.

Fredriksen, Halvard Haukeland. 'Bridging the Widening Gap Between the EU Treaties and the Agreement on the European Economic Area'. *European Law Journal* 18 no. 6 (2012): 868–886.

Fredriksen, Halvard Haukeland. 'German Influence on the Development of Norwegian Civil Procedural Law'. In *Reforms of Civil Procedure in Germany and Norway,* edited by Volker Lipp & Halvard Haukeland Fredriksen, Mohr Siebeck, 2011.

Fredriksen, Halvard Haukeland & Franklin, Christian. 'Of Pragmatism and Principles: The EEA Agreement 20 Years On'. *Common Market Law Review* 52 (2015): 629.

Fredriksen, Halvard Haukeland & Strandberg, Magne. 'Ex Officio Application of EU Consumer Protection Law in Norwegian Courts'. In *Civil Procedure and Harmonisation of Law*, edited by Anna Nylund and Magne Strandberg. Intersentia, 2019.

Fredriksen, Halvard Haukeland & Strandberg, Magne. 'Norwegian Civil Procedure Under the Influence of EU Law'. In *Transformation of Civil Justice*, edited by Alan Uzelac & C.H. van Rhee. Springer, 2018.

Fredriksen, Halvard Haukeland & Strandberg, Magne. 'Is E-justice Reform of Norwegian Civil Procedure Finally Happening?'. *Oslo Law Review* 1 no. 2 (2016): 72–88.

Hjort, Maria Astrup, 'Sources of Inspiration of Nordic Procedural Law: Choices and Objectives of the Legal Reforms.' In *Rethinking Nordic Courts,* edited by Laura Ervo, Pia Letto-Vanamo & Anna Nylund. Springer 2021.

Hjort, Maria Astrup. 'The EU's Influence on Norwegian Civil Procedure through National Substantive Law'. In *Civil Procedure and Harmonisation of Law: the Dynamics of EU and International Treaties*, edited by Anna Nylund & Magne Strandberg. Intersentia, 2019.

Hjort, Maria Astrup. 'Electronic Evidence in Control of and Adversely Affecting the Opposing Party: A Comparative Study of English and Norwegian Law'. *Digital Evidence and Electronic Signature Law Review* 8 (2011): 76.

Jensen, Christina. 'Small Claims Procedures in the Scandinavian Countries.' In *Rethinking Nordic Courts,* edited by Laura Ervo, Pia Letto-Vanamo & Anna Nylund. Springer 2021.Nisja, Ola Ø. *Arbitration and Domestic Courts in Norway: Sibling Rivalry. Scandinavian Studies in Law* 63 (2017): 261–268.

Nylund, Anna. 'Europeanisation of Nordic Civil Procedure: Does the Map Match the Terrain?' In *Rethinking Nordic Courts,* edited by Laura Ervo, Pia Letto-Vanamo & Anna Nylund. Springer 2021.

Nylund, Anna. 'Institutional Aspects of the Nordic Justice Systems: Striving for Consolidation and Settlements.' In *Rethinking Nordic Courts,* edited by Laura Ervo, Pia Letto-Vanamo & Anna Nylund. Springer 2021.

Nylund, Anna. 'Covid-19 and Norwegian Civil Justice'. In *Civil Courts Coping with Covid-19,* edited by Bart Krans & Anna Nylund. Eleven 2021.

Nylund, Anna. 'Norway - Child Participation in Family Law'. In *International Handbook on Child Participation in Family Law*, edited by Wendy Schrama, Marilyn Freeman, Nicola Taylor & Mariëlle Bruning. Intersentia, 2021.

Nylund, Anna. 'Procedural Autonomy, the EEA Agreement and Norwegian Law: Bridging the Gap and Maintaining It Too'. In *Procedural Autonomy across Europe*, edited by Bart Krans & Anna Nylund. Intersentia, 2020.

Nylund, Anna. 'A Dispute System Design Perspective on Norwegian Child Custody Mediation'. In *Nordic Mediation Research*, edited by Anna Nylund, Kaijus Ervasti & Lin Adrian. Springer, 2018.

Nylund, Anna. 'Norway: An Insider Outside – or An Outsider Inside – European Civil Justice'. In *The European Union and National Civil Procedure*, edited by Anna Nylund & Bart Krans. Intersentia, 2016.

Nylund, Anna. 'Norwegian Civil Procedure – How to Make Fast Even Faster'. In *Ways of Implementation of the Right to Civil Proceedings within a Reasonable Time,* edited by Aurimas Brazdeikis, et al. Vilnius University Press, 2016.

Nylund, Anna. 'Preparatory Proceedings in Norway – Efficiency by Flexibility and Case Management'. In *Current Trends in Preparatory Proceedings*, edited by Laura Ervo & Anna Nylund. Springer, 2016.

Nylund, Anna. 'The Many Ways of Civil Mediation in Norway'. In *The Future of Civil Litigation. Access to Courts and Court-Annexed Mediation in the Nordic Countries*, edited by Laura Ervo & Anna Nylund. Springer, 2014.

Strandberg, Magne. 'Standards of Evidence in Scandinavia'. In *Standard of Proof in Europe*, edited by Luboš Tichý. Mohr Siebeck, 2019.

Strandberg, Magne. 'The-More-Probable-Than-Not-Standard: A Critical Approach'. In *Standard of Proof in Europe*, edited by Luboš Tichý. Mohr Siebeck, 2019.

Strandberg, Magne. 'The Presumption of Innocence in Civil Cases'. In *Revisiting Procedural Human Rights. Fundamentals of Civil Procedure and the Changing Face of Civil Justice,* edited by Alan Uzelac & C.H. van Rhee. Intersentia, 2017.

Sunde, Jørn Øyrehagen. 'Der organische Zusammenhang des Rechts': How the Reception of Savigny Came to Influence Legal Reception in Norwegian Law in the 19th Century and the First Part of the 20th Century'. In *Reforms of Civil Procedure in Germany and Norway*, edited by Volker Lipp & Halvard Haukeland Fredriksen. Mohr Siebeck, 2011.

In Norwegian

Aasbrenn, Gjermund, *Sakskostnader i sivile saker: noen snubletråder.* 56 Lov og Rett (2017).

Aasbrenn, Gjermund, *Tvisteloven § 20-8 – tidspunktet for og omfanget av sakskostnadsavgjørelsen.* 58 Lov og Rett (2019).

Backer, Inge Lorange, *Å lovgi om sivil rettergang.* In Gunnar Bergby, Magnus Matningsdal, Jens Edvin A. Skoghøy & Toril M. Øie eds., Rettsavklaring og rettsutvikling – Festskrift til Tore Schei. Universitetsforlaget 2016.

Backer, Inge Lorange, *Samspillet mellom lovgivere og domstoler fra et norsk ståsted.* In Bertil Bengtsson 90 år. Jure 2016.

Backer, Inge Lorange, *Norsk sivilprosess.* Universitetsforlaget, 2015.

Selected Bibliography

Backer, Inge Lorange, *Samspillet mellom lovgiverne og Høyesterett*. In Toril M. Øie & Tore Schei & Jens Edvin Skoghøy (eds.), Lov Sannhet Rett. Norges Høyesterett 200 år. Universitetsforlaget, 2015.

Backer, Inge Lorange, *Hvem kan saksøkes i offentligrettslige trepartsforhold?*. 47 Lov og rett (2008).

Berg, Borgar Høgetveit, *Materiell prosessleiing i voldgift?* 23 Tidsskrift for forretningsjus (2017).

Bernt, Camilla, *Meklerrollen ved mekling i domstolene*. Fagbokforlaget, 2011.

Bernt, Camilla, *Tilknytningskravet for rettslig interesse i privatrettslige forhold*. 50 Lov og Rett (2011).

Bårdsen, Arnfinn, *Noen refleksjoner om Norges Høyesterett og EFTA-domstolen*. 52 Lov og Rett (2013).

Eldjarn, Erik, *Amicus curiae – retten til å inngi prosesskriv uten å være part i saken*. 51 Jussens Venner (2016).

Eldjarn, Erik, *Materiell prosessledelse*. Cappelen Damm Akademisk, 2016.

Endresen, Clement & Aasbrenn, Gjermund, *Sakskostnader på dagsorden i Høyesterett*. 58 Lov og Rett (2019).

Falbech, Matias, *Vitterlige kjensgjerninger som bevis i sivile saker*. 80 Lov og Rett 2020.

Fredriksen, Halvard Haukeland, *Bør Høyesteretts storkammer reformeres?*. 55 Lov og rett (2016).

Fredriksen, Halvard Haukeland, *Høyesterett som EØS-domstol*. In Gunnar Bergby & Magnus Matningsdal & Jens Edvin A. Skoghøy & Toril M. Øie (eds), Rettsavklaring og rettsutvikling - Festskrift til Tore Schei. Universitetsforlaget, 2016.

Fredriksen, Halvard Haukeland, *Om voldgiftsretters mulighet til å innhente rådgivende uttalelser fra EFTA-domstolen*. 12 Tidsskrift for forretningsjus (2006).

Fredriksen, Halvard Haukeland, *Tvisteloven og EØS-avtalen*. 121 Tidsskrift for rettsvitenskap (2008).

Fredriksen, Halvard Haukeland & Strandberg, Magne. 'Utviklingstrekk i norsk sivilprosess - europeisering, konstitusjonalisering og prinsipporientering'. In Per Bergsjø, Knut Kallerud, Berte-Elen Reinertsen Konow, Asbjørn Strandbakken & Ragna Aarli eds., *Med ære og samvittighet : Festskrift til Magnus Matningsdal 70 år*. Gyldendal Akademisk 2021.

Haukaas, Ørjan Salvesen, *Verneting i internasjonale tvister – er tilknytning til Norge nok for å reise søksmål I Norge?*. 51 Lov og Rett (2012).

Hjort, Maria Astrup, *Hvilket ansvar har dommeren for å legge til rette for et godt avgjørelsesgrunnlag i en sivil sak?* 53 Lov og Rett (2018).

Hjort, Maria Astrup, *Behov for reformering av tvistelovens bevissikringsregler*. 56 Lov og Rett (2017).

Hjort, Maria Astrup, *Sorteringsprosessen i bevissikringssaker og ved beslag inneholdende taushetsbelagt informasjon*. 56 Lov og Rett (2017).

Hjort, Maria Astrup, *Tilgang til bevis i sivile saker. Særlig om digitale bevis*. Universitetsforlaget, 2016.

Hjort, Maria Astrup, *Gjennomføring av internasjonale forpliktelser i sivilprosessen. Om lovgivningsteknikk og påvirkningstendenser i Norge, Sverige og Danmark*. In Aslak Syse & Hand Chr. Bugge & Hilde Indreberg & Arnulf Tverberg (eds), Lov, liv og lære. Festskrift til Inge Lorange Backer. Universitetsforlaget, 2016.

Hjort, Maria Astrup, *Grunnloven § 94 og sivilprosessen: reformforslagene på 1800-tallet*. In Hilde Sandvik & Dag Michalsen (eds), Kodifikasjon og konstitusjon. Grunnloven § 94's krav til lovbøker i norsk historie. Pax Forlag, 2013.

Hjort, Maria Astrup, *Prosessreformen i Adler og Falsens grunnlovsutkast*. In Dag Michalsen (ed), Forfatningsteori møter 1814. Akademisk Publisering, 2008.

Jensen, Christina. *Småkravsprosessen. Funksjoner og virkemidler*. Gyldendal Akademisk 2021.

Jerkø, Markus. *Derivativ sivilprosess.* 61 Lov og Rett 2021

Jerkø, Markus, *Den rettslige bevisbyrden.* 54 Jussens venner (2019).

Jerkø, Markus, *Kravet som juridisk fiksjon: Kommentarer til debatten om rettskraft of HR-2018-1130-A.* 58 Lov og Rett (2019).

Kolflaath, Eivind & Strandberg, Magne, *Norsk bevisteori før og etter årtusenskiftet.* In Ørnulf Rasmussen & Karl Harald Søvig & Sigrid Eskeland Schütz (eds), Undring og erkjennelse. Festskrift til Jan Fridthjof Bernt 70 år. Fagbokforlaget, 2013.

Nisja, Ola Ø. & Shetelig, Kåre Andreas, *Rettslig interesse.* 50 Jussens Venner (2015).

Nylund, Anna, *Meklingsmodeller i tvisteloven: terapi, tvekamp eller kreativ problemløsning?.* 49 Lov og rett (2010).

Pedersen, Jussi Erik, *Begrunnelse av rettsavgjørelser.* Universitetsforlaget, 2016.

Pedersen, Jussi Erik & Sørheim, Stian Ørbeck, *Hvem kan representere kollektiver i tvistemål?.* In Tore Henriksen (ed), Juss i nord: hav, fisk og urfolk. Gyldendal Juridisk, 2012.

Robberstad, Anne. *Hvem har bevisbyrden? Tvilsrisikoen i sivile saker.* Universitetsforlaget 2021

Robberstad, Anne, *Sivilprosess* 5th edition. Fagbokforlaget, 2021.

Robberstad, Anne, *Pretensjoner om søksmålsvilkårene og om sakens realitet.* In Aslak Syse & Hand Chr. Bugge & Hilde Indreberg & Arnulf Tverberg (eds), Lov, liv og lære. Festskrift til Inge Lorange Backer. Universitetsforlaget, 2016.

Robberstad, Anne, *Om forståelser av bevisbyrde.* 46 *Jussens venner* (2011).

Robberstad, Anne, *Pretensjon og realitet i sivile saker.* 42 Jussens venner (2007).

Robberstad, Anne, *Rettskraft.* Fagbokforlaget, 2006.

Robberstad, Anne, *Utenlandske sivilprosessforbilder – for Francis Hagerup og Tvistemålsutvalget (NOU 2001:32)*, in Torbjörn Andersson & Bengt Lindell (eds), Festskrift till Per Henrik Lindblom. Iustus förlag, 2004.

Shetelig, Kaare Andreas & Nisja, Ola Ø., *Rettskraft.* 51 Jussens (Venner 2016).

Skoghøy, Jens Edvin A., *Anketillatelse til Norges Høyesterett.* In Jan Kleineman & Peter Westberg & Stephan Carlsson (eds) Festskrift till Lars Heuman. Jure, 2008.

Skoghøy, Jens Edvin A., *Ansvar for saksomkostninger i sivile saker.* 50 Lov og Rett (2011).

Skoghøy, Jens Edvin A., Betydningen av Den europeiske menneskerettighetskonvensjonen på sivilrettens og sivilprosessens område. In Jon Petter Rui (ed), Rettshjelp fra kyst til vidde – Festskrift til Jusshjelpa i Nord-Norge 20 år. Gyldendal Akademisk, 2009.

Skoghøy, Jens Edvin A., *Dommerrollen gjennom de siste 50 år – noen utviklingstrekk.* 50 Lov og Rett (2011).

Skoghøy, Jens Edvin A., *Kravene til søksmålsgjenstand, partstilknytning og søksmålssituasjonen etter tvisteloven – noen grunnleggende spørsmål.* 45 Lov og Rett (2006).
Skoghøy, Jens Edvin A., *Norske domstoler og internasjonale konvensjonsforpliktelser.* In Herre, Johnny, Johansson, Svente O., Edlund, Lars, Lennander, Gertrud & Kleineman, Jan, Festskrift till Stefan Lindskog. Jure, 2018.
Skoghøy, Jens Edvin A., *Praktiseringen av krav til dommerhabilitet i Norges Høyesterett.* 48 Lov og Rett (2009).
Skoghøy, Jens Edvin A., *Tvisteløsning*, 3. utgave. Universitetsforlaget, 2017.
Skoghøy, Jens Edvin A., *Tvunget prosessfellesskap i offentligrettslige trepartsforhold.* 47 Lov og Rett (2008).
Strandberg, Magne, *Beviskrav i sivile saker – en bevisteoretisk studie av den norske beviskravslærens forutsetninger*. Fagbokforlaget, 2012.
Strandberg, Magne, *Beviskravet I vaksineskader etter Rt. 2015 s. 1246.* 13 Tidskrift for erstatningsrett, forsikringsrett og trygderett (2016).
Strandberg, Magne, *Bevisrettens sannhetsmålsetning*. In Simon Andersson & Karin Lainpelto (eds), Festskrift till Christian Diesen. Norstedts Juridik, 2014.
Strandberg, Magne, *Erstatning for uberettiget søksmål – hva er rettstilstanden etter Rt. 2015 s. 385?*. 12 Tidsskrift for erstatningsrett, forsikringsrett og velferdsrett (2015).
Strandberg, Magne, *Sakskostnader og bevissikring*. 56 Lov og rett (2017).
Strandberg, Magne; Nylund, Anna, *Utsikt til innsikt: En komparativ tilnærming til reform av reglene om anke til lagmannsretten over dommer i sivile saker*. Lov og Rett 2020.
Tørum, Amund Bjøranger, *Norsk ad hoc voldgift i en brytningstid.* 23 Tidsskrift for forretningsjus (2017).
Vangsnes, Jørgen Aandal, *Pretensjonenes plass i sivilprosessen.* 54 Jussens Venner (2019).
Vangsnes, Jørgen Aandal, *Tilknytning som vilkår for sivilt søksmål.* 53 Jussens Venner (2018).
Øyen, Ørnulf. *Hva er «nødvendige» sakskostnader etter tvisteloven § 20-5 (1)?*.60 *Lov og Rett* (2020)
Øyen, Ørnulf. *Tvisteloven og bevisretten – en oversikt.* 55 Jussens venner (2020)
Øyen, Ørnulf, *Hva utgjør det prosessuelle «kravet» i kontraktsrettslige tvister? Noen tanker om Høyesteretts avgjørelse i sak HR-2018-1130-A.* 57 Lov og Rett (2018).
Øyen, Ørnulf, *Gir tvisteloven gode løsninger i store og komplekse saker?*. 55 Lov og rett (2016).
Øyen, Ørnulf, *Forholdet mellom partsevne og rettsevne - særlig om forholdet mellom partsevne etter tvisteloven § 2-1 (2) og rettsevne.* 128 Tidsskrift for rettsvitenskap (2015).
Øyen, Ørnulf, *Prosessuell preklusjon i sivilprosessen.* 49 Jussens Venner (2014).
Øyen, Ørnulf, *I hvilken utstrekning kan det i straffesaker og sivile saker fremlegges bevis som er fremskaffet på ulovlig eller utilbørlig måte?* 49 Lov og Rett (2010).
Øyen, Ørnulf, *Prosessuell preklusjon i småkravprosessen.* 49 Lov og Rett (2010).

Index

The numbers here refer to paragraph numbers.

www.ingramcontent.com/pod-product-compliance
Ingram Content Group UK Ltd.
Pitfield, Milton Keynes, MK11 3LW, UK
UKHW020139290926
15471UKWH00003B/581